Praise for The "Me, Me, Me" Epidemic

"Insightful. Timely. Helpful. *The 'Me, Me, Me' Epidemic* is an important (and game-changing) read for anyone raising kids in our 24/7, give-them-whatever-they-want and never let them experience disappointment, culture. Ready to empower your kids without making them entitled? For the sake of the children, read this book."

> —Dr. Jane Nelsen, author and coauthor of
> the Positive Discipline series

"Every time Amy McCready has been a guest on *Today* I have found myself agreeing with absolutely everything she says. She's a no-nonsense, commonsense communicator, and *The 'Me, Me, Me' Epidemic* offers parents great wisdom and practical advice."

> —Kathie Lee Gifford

"I'm all for practical life hacks that make parenting easier, less stressful, and a whole lot more fun—and the strategies Amy McCready shares in *The 'Me, Me, Me' Epidemic* are both easy AND powerful for anyone juggling life and parenthood in today's hyper-connected, instant gratification world. This is a must-read book, no matter the age of your kids."

> —Christine Carter, PhD, author of *Raising Happiness: 10 Simple
> Steps for More Joyful Kids and Happier Parents* and *The Sweet Spot:
> How to Find Your Groove at Home and Work*

"*The 'Me, Me, Me' Epidemic* is probably the most important parenting book of the decade. McCready brilliantly helps us turn from unhealthy parenting to great parenting in a simple, fun and workable manner."

> —Meg Meeker, MD, bestselling author of *Strong Fathers,
> Strong Daughters*; cohost of James Dobson's Family Talk radio show

"Amy McCready never fails to share the strategies parents need to empower their kids, empower themselves, and know that they are giving their children the very best start in a complicated world."

> —Michele Borba, EdD, educational psychologist; author of *UnSelfie:
> Why Empathetic Kids Succeed in Our All-About-Me World*

"This book immediately motivated me to stop doing things for my children that they can do for themselves. My eyes were opened to the many ways my children could contribute to the family and become prepared to thrive in the real world."

—Rachel Macy Stafford, *New York Times* bestselling author of *Hands Free Mama* and *Hands Free Life*

"Thank you, Amy McCready, for writing a comprehensive, entertaining, on-point parenting guide that will become the dog-eared go-to manual for every parent who wants their child to become a happy, successful adult. Amy addresses the timeliest of childrearing challenges head-on, and then gives parents the tools to navigate through almost any situation with their child."

—Loni Coombs, author of *"You're Perfect" and Other Lies Parents Tell: The Ugly Truth about Spoiling Your Kids*

"Amy McCready has long been one of my parenting heroines. She offers parents a clear path for raising kids who see themselves as part of the larger human landscape—not the center of the universe. She makes it possible for any parent to restore balance and order to their parenting."

—Vicki Hoefle, author of *The Straight Talk on Parenting: A No-Nonsense Approach on How to Grow a Grown-Up* and *Duct Tape Parenting*

"With this book, you'll be raising a child who will put down his iPhone and fold the laundry. Amy McCready understands what kids crave: family belonging. Find out just how capable your kids can be."

—Heather Shumaker, author of *It's OK Not to Share* and *It's OK to Go Up the Slide*

"McCready covers a wealth of suggestions for helping kids become unentitled, along with scripts parents can use and ideas for various ages from pre-school to teen. This user-friendly guide is overflowing with practical, creative, and thoughtful strategies."

—*Publishers Weekly*

"McCready sorts out the sensible from the nonsense. Given the competing noise about parenting, this book should be required reading for parents."

—*Kirkus Reviews*

The "Me, Me, Me" Epidemic

A Step-by-Step Guide to
Raising Capable, Grateful Kids
in an Over-Entitled World

Amy McCready

A TarcherPerigee Book

tarcherperigee

An imprint of Penguin Random House LLC
375 Hudson Street
New York, New York 10014

First trade paperback edition 2016

Most TarcherPerigee books are available at special quantity discounts
for bulk purchase for sales promotions, premiums, fund-raising, and educational needs.
Special books or book excerpts also can be created to fit specific needs. For details,
write: SpecialMarkets@penguinrandomhouse.com.

The Library of Congress has cataloged the hardcover edition as follows:

McCready, Amy.
The me, me, me epidemic : a step-by-step guide to raising capable,
grateful kids in an over-entitled world / Amy McCready.
p.   cm.
Includes index.
ISBN 978-0-399-16997-7
1. Parenting.   2. Child rearing.   3. Child psychology.   I. Title.
HQ755.8.M416   2015   2015005073
649'.1—dc23

ISBN 978-0-399-18486-4 (paperback)

Printed in the United States of America
7   9   10   8   6

Book design by Gretchen Achilles

For Dave, Ryan and Brent—my greatest blessings.

I love you dearly.

Contents

Introduction

What do we see when we look at our kids? We see an imagination capable of turning your great-grandmother's delicate candlestick into a lightsaber to vanquish enemies from the living room. An energy that drags us on a wild-goose chase all over the house and yard looking for a minuscule ballet slipper charm. And a determination that pesters us for days to let them attend an out-of-state concert, and pay for it, too. And yet, beyond the chaos, the griping and the power struggles, we see potential. And that's why I wrote this book. I know that inside each of our precious children is the potential for something amazing: a confident adult who has the drive and ability to make her corner of the planet a better place.

You're reading this book—and I wrote it—because there's a force that can rob from our kids not only their imagination, energy and determination, but also their ability to live rich, fulfilling lives. It's the force of *entitlement*, the idea that life *owes* us something, and it's wreaking havoc on our kids' generation. Children of all ages feel entitled to receive the best of what life has to offer without working for it, to have their whims catered to by their parents and a path paved for success. They believe the world revolves around them—who wouldn't, when everywhere you turn you see a selfie? Over-entitled kids become over-entitled adults with the same childish attitudes, only on a greater scale. It's a big problem, because kids who feel entitled to call the shots all the time are unable to handle it when things don't go their way (like in the real world). What's more, they're just plain hard to live with!

But entitlement is not the end of your kids' story. Imagine a home in which kids take responsibility, contribute to the family, work hard, give back, manage their own finances and feel grateful for what they have. These kids are happy and confident and will be well prepared for whatever adulthood has in store. This is the potential you see in your children—and this can be their future.

Whether you're in the trenches of the entitlement epidemic, with kids who will barely lift their feet so you can vacuum under them, or trying to ward it off to begin with, I'm glad you're reading this book. I've waded through the entitlement trenches with my own two sons and I know firsthand the challenges we parents face. And along the way, I've compiled thirty-five proven tools that *really work* to stop the entitlement train in its tracks. Your family can put an end to entitlement, too, no matter how many treats it currently takes for your kids to get through the store without pitching a fit. You can make a very real difference in a matter of days by applying even just a few of the tools and strategies you'll find in these pages.

The Un-Entitler Toolbox strategies throughout this book will give you the confidence, know-how and even the words to say as you rid your home of the entitled behaviors that are not only driving you nuts but also giving you cause for concern about your offspring's future. Misbehaviors and entitled attitudes ("I can have what I want when I want it!") will melt away, as kids of all ages learn to pitch in around the house, solve their disagreements respectfully, take responsibility for their actions and even put down their smartphones once in a while. This dream is within your reach, and your kids will be better off for it.

The tools you use will bring out your kids' very best behavior (no more chore wars, homework battles and sassy attitudes) and help them develop the responsibility, resilience and respectfulness they need for a successful adult life. You'll do it all while you extinguish the entitlement epidemic and make your home a haven of peace in a world of entitled attitudes.

Let's un-entitle our kids. Help them imagine new worlds (without expecting a team of workers to come in and build it for them), take on their own responsibility (without needing their hand held every step of the way) and put that determination to use serving others rather than expecting to be served. Then, and only then, will our kids unlock their potential to become their very best—without feeling entitled to it.

Kids Rule. But Should They?

It's the evening before Natasha's high school graduation—and Natasha couldn't be more miserable. She's in her bedroom, crying tears of raw emotion over the fact that she's out of her favorite hair gel. Her mother is too busy writing Natasha's name in icing on six dozen cupcakes for her graduation party to rush out to the store tonight to get more. Her mom should have decorated them earlier! Still leaking tears, Natasha reenters the kitchen to let her mom know that she just *has* to have that special hair gel or her hair will be a huge frizzy mess and she'll look like a total dork on her big day. After a few lame suggestions, her mom leaves the cupcakes and goes upstairs to try to squeeze out one last palmful of her own drugstore-brand styling gel and then puts away the mess of cosmetics Natasha has left out on the counter.

Natasha wanders off and texts her boyfriend to pick her up, but he's busy with his friends. The jerk. He just saw his friends yesterday. Maybe she'll threaten to dump him again—that'll make him shape up. Sometimes she wonders why she even has a boyfriend. She finds her dad and remembers that she needs to ask him for extra money so she can buy a couple of new swimsuits and sandals for the season. He sees the evidence of her tears and forks over the cash. It's not as much as she wanted, though, so he promises to put the rest on his credit card, which has been busy lately thanks to another recent purchase: a brand-new car as

Natasha's graduation present. It's supposed to be a secret, but Natasha overheard her dad on the phone with the dealer earlier in the day. "It had better be a convertible," she thinks.

Of course, Natasha is proud to be graduating tomorrow. After all, she managed to stay awake in most of her classes, thanks to her smartphone. Her homework took a lot of effort, but the tutor her parents hired for her was able to complete it just fine. Soon Natasha will be out in the real world, and when she wasn't pitching a fit over having to empty the dishwasher *and* watch her little brother in the same afternoon, and for only $20, she was excited. Finally, she'd be an adult—able to party every night, not just Thursday through Saturday. Her parents have talked to her about enrolling in the community college and getting a job, but Natasha thinks a gap year is a good idea and no one is hiring where she wants to work. She actually inquired at both places—a clothing store and a makeup store—but her parents aren't getting off her back. Natasha knows they'll cool it in a week or two; it's just this business about graduation that's getting them all riled up.

Natasha sighs. If she can't have her hair gel tonight, maybe she should work on her mom about letting her spend next weekend at Amber's parents' beach house. *All* her friends are going, and it wouldn't be fair for Natasha not to go, too. Besides, Natasha is eighteen and done with school—it's time for her to call the shots in her own life. And what a life it will be! If she could just get her boyfriend to pay attention to her, her parents to give her what she wants and a convertible, she'll finally be happy. Look out world, here comes Natasha.

Look out world indeed. Natasha, in case you couldn't guess, is a classic example of an entitled child. She lacks the ability to look beyond herself, delay gratification or work hard to achieve a goal. Nobody likes to see this in a child of any age, and it can be heartbreaking for parents when they realize their child is floundering when it's time to leave the nest. And while Natasha probably doesn't live at your house, some of this tale of the over-entitled may ring a little truer than you'd like. If so, you're in good company. Most first-world parents struggle with some kind of entitlement issues among their kids.

While we might feel jealous of the kids who actually do get new cars for graduation—and a free ride in other areas of life, too—we can also feel sorry for them. If the free-car lifestyle pervades their schooling, work, relationships and leisure time, chances are they've rarely felt the thrill of accomplishment after giving it their best effort, the gratitude of a friend who received their much-needed help for nothing in return, the gratification of finally getting something they've been working or waiting for or the contentment that comes from being happy in the moment. Entitlement does more than drive parents crazy. It also robs kids of the ability to realize the best of what life has for them, while they instead chase impossible dreams.

Entitlement is certainly a big problem. In fact, it's epidemic.

The Entitlement Epidemic

You couldn't afford your own makeup this month because thirteen-year-old Johnny's fluorescent orange must-have sneakers cost your entire discretionary budget. You keep a spare McDonald's bag on hand so you can pretend to three-year-old Emma that her peanut-butter sandwich was made under the golden arches. And in order to get eight-year-old Daryl into bed, you have to let him fall asleep in front of the television, and carry him there.

Since when do parents jump through hoops at all costs to keep children happy? Since when do kids get to call the shots? The truth is kids everywhere—from toddlers to teens—are ruling the roost, and they're not about to abandon their posts without a fight.

Entitlement happens in every family—including mine. Every one of us feels entitled to something on some level—whether it's a stuffed animal we've slept with since birth, our smartphone or simply a good night's sleep. These entitlements are all good things, and we might not be able to imagine life without them. If we think about them, we're grateful for them—but there's no question there are some things we take for granted. And our kids do, too.

Entitlement isn't really a disease, but it has hit epidemic levels in our society. And it's certainly not only rich kids who are afflicted. The entitlement problem spans classes and cultures. It's also not only about stuff. Entitled kids believe the world revolves around them. They expect things to be done for them, a path to happiness cleared and smoothed, without putting in much effort themselves. They feel that something is wrong if they're not happy. At any given minute they should be having the time of their lives because after all, you only live once.

How does the entitlement epidemic present in the typical household? Here are a few clues you might have an entitlement problem in your home:

- You find yourself exasperated at your children's demands but caving anyway.
- You're exhausted keeping up with the house, but everyone's too busy watching TV to help.
- You can't make it through the grocery store without buying a treat.
- You're frequently supplementing your kids' allowance.
- You take responsibility for your kids by doing things for them that you know they should be able to do for themselves.
- You resort to bribes or rewards to get cooperation from your kids.
- You frequently rescue your kids by driving forgotten items to school or reminding them about their deadlines.
- Your child frequently takes issue with rules and expectations at school or in activities.
- Your child is quick to blame others for anything that goes wrong.
- Your child tries to manipulate others to get his way.
- Your child commonly sulks or pitches a fit when she doesn't get her way.
- Your child often complains of being bored and wants to be entertained by you.

- Your child finds it really difficult to wait patiently for something he wants.

Sound like a child you know? In truth, there's not a kid alive who doesn't exhibit some of these symptoms from time to time. Whether you've got a big entitlement outbreak at your house or only a minor case, you'll soon be able to move your kids toward greater independence, responsibility and contentment.

So What's the Big Deal?

Leon F. Seltzer, PhD, in an article for *Psychology Today*,[*] had this to say about entitlement: "Those 'afflicted' with a sense of entitlement demonstrate the attitude that whatever they want, they deserve—and automatically at that, simply because they are who they are. So anything they desire, whether material or relational, should be theirs. It's *inherently* justified; there's no need actually to *earn* it." We all want what we want—and we want to have it *now,* please. In our culture of plenty, immediate gratification is very much a reality. We can make our dreams come true on multiple levels. But are we better off for it?

Dr. Seltzer says we're not. Over-entitled people miss out on some of the best that life has to offer. When they're not used to persevering through multiple frustrations, they won't know the pride that comes from achieving hard-won, worthwhile goals. When they expect raises and other rewards simply because they want them and not because they've earned them, they're set up for frequent disappointment. When they attempt to make others bend to their will because they expect to be served, their relationships will wither. And when all of these combine, we have created a person who will have trouble holding down a steady job, cultivating long-term relationships and completing any task worth completing. Because over-entitled people feel as though the world

---

[*] http://www.psychologytoday.com/blog/evolution-the-self/200909/child-entitlement-abuse-part-1-5

owes them the best it has to offer, they will completely miss out on just that.

But entitlement doesn't happen out of the blue. The problem begins when entitlement becomes a way of life for children. In these cases, kids rule the roost. Mom and Dad rush around trying to meet endless demands, whether that means making meat loaf three different ways to cater to discriminating appetites, rushing to the store because the six-year-old is out of her favorite toothpaste or shelling out hundreds of dollars so the fourteen-year-old can look like a minirockstar. While parents attempt to give their kids every advantage in life, kids learn that they shouldn't have to do anything they don't want to, they can have everything that catches their eye and they can quit whenever they want. It ends up that no one's happy—parents are run ragged, while kids constantly find they need *more, more, more*! And benevolent rulers kids are not. They quickly learn to resort to whining, demanding and downright bullying to get what they want.

Entitlement doesn't just plague our homes: it affects kids' schoolwork, activities and friendships, too. Youngsters expect that their C effort will get A grades or that just showing up to practice will get them a starting spot on the basketball team. Friendships are self-centered, as entitled kids lack the ability to empathize and sacrifice. When problems arise, in school and beyond, anything from the weather to an unsuspecting younger sibling is always to blame. Or perhaps the test was too hard, or it was an off day or "the boss doesn't like me." Possibly, in fact, "it's just not *fair!!*" Clearly, entitlement is a far-reaching problem with a lifetime of effects.

Overparented, Over-Entitled Kids

But *why* are we plagued with the entitlement bug—a veritable disease that affected only royalty in the past? It's certainly not genetic—we're not hardwired to need a new car when we turn sixteen or a balloon every time we get through the grocery store without throwing a tantrum. So why has entitlement hit epidemic levels over the past three decades?

Some key influences on our culture have given rise to the feeling that "it's all about *me*" in the millennial (born after 1980) generation. But that's not where it started—or even where it ended. Here's the big picture.

I'M SPECIAL, YOU'RE SPECIAL, WE'RE ALL SPECIAL

In 1969, the self-esteem movement kicked off with a publication by Dr. Nathaniel Branden called *The Psychology of Self-Esteem*. It told parents, caregivers and society as a whole that self-esteem was of paramount importance for each person, and in so doing, created a cultural revolution.

With this movement, as Po Bronson, author of the *New York Magazine* article "How Not to Talk to Your Kids," points out, every child was assured that she was special. Competitions awarded each participant a prize—not just the winners (because aren't we all winners?)—while grading systems rewarded even the faultiest work and the use of criticism in the workplace was, well, criticized. Children grew up with lavish praise for everything they did, becoming praise junkies who learned to demand acknowledgment or rewards for completing mundane or expected tasks—even once they were all grown up.

Today, these young adults want to be praised, reviewed and patted on the back simply for dressing business casual. Employers struggle to motivate this generation of employees who need frequent feedback and constant attention to know they are doing okay.

Certainly, some of the changes to the way children are viewed and treated are positive: we can be certain no teacher will be taking a ruler to our kids' knuckles, for instance, but the fact remains that the everyone-is-special mind-set does more harm than good, and the effects are lasting. In fact, Jean M. Twenge, a psychologist and a professor at San Diego State University, has shown that teens and young adults are more self-absorbed than they used to be. She's found that college students score higher on the Narcissistic Personality Inventory now than in 1979, that more of them consider themselves above average and that they show a weaker work ethic. The effect has even leached into their writing style: first-person singular pronouns (I, me, my) are showing up more often— a clear indicator of the me generation.*

The Overparenting Problem

With self-esteem on everyone's minds, the baby boomer generation gave rise to kid-centered families—and for the first time in history, soccer practice, ballet and playgroup were put on the calendar ahead of garden club or the softball team at work. And isn't it wonderful that parents should be so involved in their kids' lives?

It is—until they overparent their kids. It's natural that parents want the best for their children and try to provide it. The trouble is, when we try to hand our kids the world on a silver platter, we unwittingly create an entitlement problem.

For instance, many involved and concerned moms and dads become lawn-mower parents, overprotecting kids by mowing down all the obstacles youngsters commonly face, from the crabby kindergarten teacher to the drama teacher who has cast their child only in minor roles for the past three plays. Or worse, the boss at the fast-food restaurant who reprimanded their child for showing up late to work three days in a row. Not only do parents center their lives on their kids, they also do their best to make sure the youngsters never face difficulties, mowing a smooth path for them far into their adult lives. Overprotected kids soon learn that life should be a piece of cake—and if it's not, someone else should have to deal with it. It must be nice to live inside that bubble, but it certainly can't last.

We also overindulge kids by never saying never. Wouldn't we all rather say yes to our kids than no, and face happy smiles rather than a

---

* http://www.slate.com/blogs/xx_factor/2013/08/08/jean_m_twenge_and_narcissism_are_millenni als_more_self_absorbed_than_other.html.

screaming fit? Of course. But the truth is parents are often scared of the "n-o" word and don't use it often enough. We give them whatever they want, when they want it, and slip into the trap of becoming their personal servants, because, frankly, it's easier that way. Our kids get used to having all their demands met, throwing even bigger fits if they are confronted with a negative, and the problem spirals out of control.

And then there's the problem of overpraising. Kids get a sucker for standing in line for three minutes at the bank, prizes for sitting quietly at a desk at school, money for good grades and a cookie to make it through the grocery store without a tantrum. We spout "Great job!" "You're so cute!" and "You're so smart!" to make our kids feel good over the most mundane tasks. They grow up hearing us sing their praises for unextraordinary behavior, and soon won't exhibit good behavior, a strong work ethic or a helpful spirit without promise of a reward or accolades.

We certainly overparent with the best of intentions, but that doesn't change the fact that this parenting style paves the way for our kids to catch the entitlement bug. We don't have to play victim to it, however: as you'll see throughout this book, we have the means to cure our kids for good.

Why Social Media Is Antisocial

As the twenty-first century dawned, so did connected communication, and it wasn't long before Facebook, Twitter, Instagram and other social networking sites began to allow kids the unlimited ability to promote themselves. As if teens needed any more impetus to obsess over their own self-images! Posting photos, tweeting and updating the world on everything from what they ate for breakfast to their turbulent feelings toward younger siblings reinforces the mind-set that "it's all about me" and "you only live once." And since all their connected friends agree with them, there's virtually no reason for them to see the world with any different perspective—especially one that places value on hard work and responsibility.

No wonder teens can hardly be convinced to pick up a vacuum cleaner. Not only would this task not look good on Instagram, but it would also go against the kingdom of one they've built for themselves.

And let's face it—we adults don't always set the best example here. When we post photos as readily as our fifteen-year-old and check our smartphones under the dinner table, we model the it's-really-all-about-me attitude we're trying to change in our kids. Our instant messaging sends a message to our kids that the virtual world has the final word in our family.

The result is pervasive damage to the work ethic, relationships and self-image. Not only do kids see the Kardashians and their type everywhere, but they also do their best to measure up with the help of social media. With the Kardashians and the Rich Kids of Instagram as a standard, who wouldn't feel entitled to the best of everything life has to offer?

We'll talk about each of these concepts more later in the book, but for now, I hope to make clear that we're facing an uphill battle when it comes to un-entitling our kids. But it's certainly not impossible, especially when we start in our own homes.

Three Hots and a Cot

All this begs the question: what, exactly, *are* kids entitled to? Parenting educator and emergency room physician Leslie Marshall uses the army phrase "three hots and a cot" to remind us that in addition to a loving family, kids need the basics—food, shelter, clothing, safety, medical care. But talk about wiggle room! For instance, nine-year-old Jack probably doesn't actually need the $50 bike helmet with monster horns on it when one at half the cost is cool enough and will keep his head intact. Four-year-old Abby certainly should be able to get her feet into her everyday shoes without needing your help, but might require a helping hand for snow boots. And seventeen-year-old Dayton really can share a room with his little brother, even if the little brother occasionally talks to himself in the middle of the night.

How can you tell whether you're playing fair or being played? We'll revisit this in chapter 2, but for now it's enough to know that if you feel manipulated, annoyed or that something's not right, you're probably correct. You need to let your kids know to adjust their expectations.

Almost as crucial as access to clean water and a roof over their heads is the satisfaction of two psychological needs that are fundamental to the efficacy of all the tools in this book. Unlike entitlement, these needs are hardwired from birth.

To more fully understand what your child truly needs on a psychological level, let's take a look at what's going on in their minds (other than "How can I sneak some candy when Mom's not looking?").

Over one hundred years ago, kids were to be seen and not heard. Many worked their childhoods away in factories or on farms and were not typically treated with respect. But all that began to change when psychologist and medical doctor Alfred Adler asserted that all people, including children, deserve to be treated with dignity and respect. The notion of respect and the idea that children are social beings who behave according to how others perceive them and react to them became the foundation for much of Adler's work. Three Adlerian principles have informed this book, and they are:

PREMISE 1: A CHILD'S PRIMARY GOAL IS TO ACHIEVE BELONGING AND SIGNIFICANCE

These are the two most basic human psychological needs and they're built-in, present from birth. A sense of belonging is achieved when a child feels emotionally connected to other family members. He knows his place in his family and how he fits in. A sense of significance comes from feeling capable, being able to make meaningful contributions to his family and having a sense of personal power—some level of influence or control over what happens to him. In fact, everyone has a basic need for power, and if we don't get it in positive ways, we will resort to negative actions.

PREMISE 2: ALL BEHAVIOR IS GOAL-ORIENTED

When kids act up, they're doing more than pitching a fit over a candy bar (or permission to go to a party). Without even knowing it, they're on a mission to achieve the belonging and significance they crave. If they don't receive belonging and significance in a positive way, they'll resort to negative means. Misbehavior is always a symptom of a deeper issue, and by addressing the underlying issue, we can cut back on a lot of the bad deeds.

PREMISE 3: A MISBEHAVING CHILD IS A DISCOURAGED CHILD

Your child's misbehavior speaks volumes. On a subconscious level, the whining is a plea for "pay attention to me, I want to belong," and the tantrums mean "I'm lashing out because I feel powerless and need you to help." (They also want the candy bar, but they're a lot more likely to take no for an answer if their psychological needs for belonging and significance are met.) Kids don't actually want to misbehave; they simply see it as the only alternative to achieve their emotional needs—even if the attention and power they get from the behavior are negative.

Understanding your child's need for belonging and significance is so important to curing the entitlement epidemic with your kids. Here's the summary:

1. Your child's need for belonging and significance is built-in. There's nothing you can do to change that: belonging and sig-

nificance are things your kids are actually entitled to—unlike a ride to a rock concert in another state. You can either work with your child's psychological needs to empower them in positive ways or against them. I know which I'd rather do, and thousands of parents worldwide agree when they see the results.

2. A sense of belonging comes from plenty of positive attention from the people who are most important to them. With this, kids will feel emotionally connected to you and confident about how they fit in with the family unit. Without it, they'll resort to whining, acting helpless, nagging and interrupting to get attention and feel included any way they can. A sense of significance for your kids comes from feeling like they have some control over their own lives and the ability to make meaningful contributions. If they don't feel this way, they'll battle you on every decision, throw tantrums when they're not happy, ignore your requests altogether and talk back to try to feel like they have some power over you.

3. You can't just fill your child's attention basket or power basket once—you need to replenish it daily, and more for a younger child. Each of the tools in this book will help you do that.

When your kids feel strong senses of belonging and significance, their need to act out to achieve them in errant ways, like whining or battling, plummets. Remember that your child has no idea that her misbehavior is linked to her need for belonging and significance, or even that these needs exist, so it's up to you to help her achieve them in positive ways, preventing bad behavior from happening in the first place. The tools in this book will help you do just that in addition to un-entitling your kids—and as you use them, you'll start to see a huge decrease in misbehavior.

What else is your child entitled to? A Band-Aid when he scrapes his knee—but it shouldn't have to have Buzz Lightyear on it. A timely drink when she's thirsty—a drinking fountain will do, though, rather than a rainbow slushy with sprinkles from the food court. A story at bedtime as part of your routine—but not half a dozen and three extra songs. A ride to the neighbor's house when the wind chill is below zero—but not when it's seventy degrees and sunny. And while this book isn't about nit-picking what's reasonable or not, we'll help you set the limits that are right for your family—and not get played.

Punishment, Discipline: What Works, What Doesn't

While this book is about helping your kids live lives free of entitlement, it's not a book of punishment or tricks to get your kids to behave. Chances are you've tried those, and they haven't worked. Take a classic example:

It's six thirty on a school night during a busy week. You and your kids have grabbed fast food at a restaurant for dinner before making one more stop and heading home. As you dig into your sandwiches, five-year-old Erica launches into a series of unfortunate events. She interrupts every ten seconds, sings loud enough for *everyone* to hear, comments on how your fish sandwich "stinks like it came from the toilet" and won't stop kicking her brothers under the table. And if that's not enough, she wants an ice-cream cone for dessert—and to cop an attitude at the same time. You don't know where, exactly, she learned to call you the worst parent in the entire history of the planet, but once you said no to the ice cream, she started broadcasting the notion throughout the restaurant, complete with dramatic tears. The girl has a certain flair for drama, but you wish she'd save it for theater class rather than perform a tragedy at a fast-food restaurant.

You're desperate to leave and you give her to the count of three to put on her coat—but you've made it to three and a half and she's no closer to doing as you say. You tell her she's lost TV for a week, but she ignores you. You try to drag her away for a time-out, but she digs in her heels. Now even the guy making fries is watching to see what the "most horrible parent ever" is going to do with the screaming girl—and you realize you are out of patience and options. You just want to finish your errands and go home—so you give in and then slink out of the restaurant, ice cream in hand, feeling lower than the mice you know must gather near the Dumpster in the parking lot every night.

What happened? Why does your little girl choose the worst times to act out? Why won't she listen?

OUT WITH THE OLD, IN WITH THE NEW

The problem isn't totally her, and it's not completely you, either. In fact, it stems from the fact that while parenting standbys like punishment, time-outs and counting 1-2-3 may have worked once, they've lost their impact. What's more, while twenty years ago your parents could give you a look and you'd snap to attention, society has changed so that people—and kids—don't blindly obey anymore. And that's a good thing—I don't think any of us would want a return to the days when husbands would command that dinner be on the table by six o'clock, or principals could apply corporal punishment to kids.

Aside from outdated discipline techniques, there's also the fact that after a long day at school and of running errands, Erica's feelings of belonging and significance are at an all-time low. While on the outside she's telling the table what your fish sandwich smells like, on the inside she's practically screaming "I desperately need positive attention from you, but I haven't had that all day so I'll settle for any kind of attention I can get!" There's no excuse for bad behavior, but we have to admit nobody's at their best after a marathon of checkout lines.

That's not to say we can let our kids run rampant all over us as a lot of entitled kids do. But we do have to change tactics, which is what this book is all about.

In Erica's story, in addition to bad behavior, we also see some truly entitled behaviors. She felt entitled to being the center of attention and to the ice cream—and in fact, she wasn't going to give up without more of a fight than her tired mom could handle. Chances are Erica was used to getting her way and knew just how far she could push her parent. Even though Erica's mom probably had used punishment, time-outs and counting 1-2-3 in the past, the fatal flaw of these techniques is that they did nothing to address the *root* of the misbehavior. Erica had learned nothing from past incidents of having TV taken away, standing in a corner or hearing her mom drag out "two and a haaaaalllfff . . . ," especially since if Erica's mom is like most parents in a similar situation, Erica managed to get her way a good portion of the time.

And when Erica's mom held her ground and resorted to punishment for Erica's misbehavior, she unknowingly contributed to the problem. Punishment actually drives kids to think about how to get back at Mom or Dad instead of correct their behavior. What's more, it forces kids to operate out of fear of punishment rather than out of the desire to do right, and it teaches them nothing, other than to simply try harder not to get caught next time.

If we apply positive strategies and correctly use consequences, however, not only do we build up plenty of misbehavior-preventing belonging and significance, we also partner with our kids to help them learn what to do instead in the future for a happier outcome—the astonishing result is that they actually want to behave better. We'll cover consequences later in the book, as well as plenty of preventive measures. This, by the way, is called "discipline," a word that often gets misused among parents. "Discipline" comes from the Latin "discipulus," which means student, one who is learning or a willing convert. There's no mention whatsoever of grounding your kids for an entire year or spanking them. We do need to train our kids in everything they need to know for a responsible, independent and effective adulthood, but there are plenty of positive ways to do that without any of the negative and ineffective repercussions of punishment, yelling, counting 1-2-3 and all the rest.

I keep mentioning positive, effective tools and strategies. They come from what I call the Un-Entitler Toolbox—my collection of parenting tools based on the fundamentals of Adlerian psychology, the work of Rudolf Dreikurs, MD, who further developed Adlerian child-rearing principles and of Positive Discipline, based on the groundbreaking training and books from Jane Nelsen, EdD. H. Stephen Glenn, creator of the *Developing Capable Young People* curriculum, also inspired some of the tools in this book.

Remember the Adlerian principles of needing to belong and feel significant? The Un-Entitler Toolbox strategies are what you'll use to make sure your child gets plenty of each every day, thus preventing lots of errant actions and entitlement-based misbehaviors. Each tool provides a helping of belonging or significance (or both), and each helps address and ward off entitlement outbreaks, as well as a wide variety of downright bad behavior. I'll outline thirty-five tools throughout this book, with the words to say and helpful tips so that you put them to work right away.

The first un-entitling tool, Mind, Body and Soul Time, is my personal favorite, and the most effective. The tool gives your child a hefty dose of both belonging and significance and builds your relationship, too. Once you start to put it into use—and stick to it—you'll begin to see your kids' behavior problems melt away.

Un-Entitler: Mind, Body and Soul Time (MBST)

Mind, Body and Soul Time is the single most important tool in the Un-Entitler Toolbox, and it will serve Erica's mom well down the road as she addresses her daughter's negative attention-seeking misbehavior. This tool entitles children to their primary emotional needs—belonging and significance. It also prevents attention- and power-seeking behaviors like whining, acting helpless, throwing tantrums, fighting with siblings, staging bedtime battles and more.

You may have noticed that your child feels entitled to your mind share during all of your waking hours—and if she's not getting your attention, she'll find a way to turn all eyes on her. In fact, parents often tell me that no matter how much attention they give their child, it's never enough. Your young one continually feels entitled to attention for her every whim, even if the parent is on the phone, mowing the lawn, taking a relaxing bath or simply trying to get a good night of sleep. Mind, Body and Soul Time effectively un-entitles the child from this mistaken belief by providing her with plenty of positive attention in advance, so you can expect your child to be able to wait for your attention at other times. With this tool, you'll be regularly filling your child's attention and power baskets, so she has no reason to act out to get what she needs. You're preventing bad behavior from happening in the first place. What's more, with this tool in daily use, you can feel confident and guilt-free using the other tools to put an end to all those annoying misbehaviors.

PUT IT TO USE

To use Mind, Body and Soul Time, each parent sets aside ten minutes, once or twice a day, to spend with each child. During that ten minutes, you'll ignore other distractions, be fully present in mind, body and soul and do whatever your child loves to do. Will you be painting toenails with your twelve-year-old, or pretending to be an airplane with your preschooler? Either way, your child calls the shots, within reason, for ten minutes.

This tool offers a big boost not only to your child's sense of belonging as you fill her attention basket but also to her significance and personal power, since the child makes the decisions on what activity you'll do or what you'll play with. When you take the time each day to emotionally connect with your child and get into his world, communication improves. Even your teens are more likely to open up if you're willing to listen to their music once in a while or play their favorite game—and doing so builds a relationship that will last a lifetime.

Most important, by giving kids what they *are* entitled to—your unconditional love and some undivided time and attention each day—you'll feel confident not giving in to demands for things they are *not* entitled to.

As good as that sounds, many parents wonder "How can I possibly find ten or twenty minutes in my already-too-busy day to spend with each child?" In truth, this tool is going to save you time. As you consistently implement Mind, Body and Soul Time, you'll spend less time fussing about negative attention- and power-seeking behaviors and your kids will be more cooperative when you ask them to help out with family tasks. You'll have more time on your hands and enjoy parenting a lot more.

SUSPEND DISBELIEF

Mind, Body and Soul Time isn't magic—but it sure works miracles for families across the globe. If you haven't read my previous book, *If I Have to Tell You One More Time . . .* , you may be skeptical that this tool will pack much of a punch in improving behavior. This is one time I'm going to ask you to suspend disbelief and trust me. Parents who consistently use this tool describe it as the magic bullet or game changer. It really works—but only if you give it a try. Read on for tips that will ensure you enjoy great success from this tool.

Tips and Scripts

- Identify ten to fifteen minutes during your daily routine when you can realistically and consistently spend one-on-one time with each of your kids.
- For young children, you'll see even better results if you can do MBST two times per day, as they need their attention basket filled regularly.
- Turn off all distractions: no phones, TVs, computer, etc.
- Give your MBST a name. Call it what you want as a family—Jason and Daddy Time, Together Time—just make sure you're 110 percent present in mind, body and soul during your special time.

- Be creative. There's no reason MBST has to happen only at home or only in your family room. Turn travel time in the car into MBST by simply switching off the radio and letting your child tell you about her day (or the supercool underwater rocket she's inventing). Jog along with her as she's training for the cross-country meet. Or play with your child as she takes her bath, wake her up a few minutes early every day for an impromptu pillow fight or find a little extra time for reading together at bedtime.

- When you begin, be sure the activity can be completed, or reach a good stopping point, within ten minutes. If you have more time, great! But it becomes a form of entitlement for your child to insist on playing an entire game of Clue, or building all of Saint Basil's Cathedral out of Legos before he will let you be done.

- If you find your child has trouble settling on an activity, work with her to make a list of activities you can do or ways to play in ten minutes and hang the list on the refrigerator.

- Make sure you get credit for the MBST you spend with each child. End your time together by labeling it and saying "I really enjoyed our special time together! I can't wait to paint more dinosaurs with you tomorrow!" That reminds your child that you filled her attention and power buckets and that you enjoyed spending time with her!

- For young kids, set a timer to let them know when MBST is over. If it's a tough transition, have an activity in mind for them to pick up afterward.

In the midst of our busy, media-saturated,
overscheduled lives, taking time to really know
someone is the ultimate act of love.

—Rachel Macy Stafford, author of *Hands Free Mama: A Guide to
Putting Down the Phone, Burning the To-Do List, and Letting Go
of Perfection to Grasp What Really Matters!*

YES, BUT . . .

I still can't find the time.

It can be tough at first to carve out the time, but you'll soon find it's well worth your effort. Cut back on things that don't matter as much—leave the laundry or e-mails for later or spend a little less time on Pinterest. Build your MBST with each child into your routine so you're not as likely to put it off. Better yet, if you put your family MBST schedule on the refrigerator, it will hold you all accountable. View MBST like a nonnegotiable business meeting. If you have to miss it, let your kids know in advance and reschedule with them at that time.

If it helps to ease into MBST, try starting with ten minutes once a day and work up to twice a day if that's doable for your family. Be sure to fully engage during that ten minutes, and chances are you'll see so much improvement in your child's behavior that the time will open up for you.

And remember that it's okay to do MBST in a variety of situations and at different times—the important thing is to connect on your child's level and have fun!

I have a large family.

If it's impossible to spend MBST with each child every day, schedule it several times during the week on a calendar everyone can see. In large families especially, it's easy for kids to feel like they aren't getting sufficient one-on-one time with Mom and/or Dad, so it's extra important to make time for each of them.

The siblings always want to join in or my kids interrupt each other's time for emergencies.

Whether your kids genuinely enjoy spending time together or are simply trying to get extra attention, it's paramount that MBST is spent one-on-one. Kids need time when they don't have to compete for their parents' notice and when they can be themselves.

Although screen time should be limited, this is one time you might want to consider letting younger siblings watch approved programming while they wait for their turn for MBST. Also, scheduling MBST as part of the routine will help—once your kids get used to the rules, they're more likely to stick to them.

To minimize interruptions, work with your kids to establish MBST ground rules. For example, it's not okay to interrupt your sibling's MBST except for true emergencies. (A nosebleed may be an emergency, but not being able to find the sock puppet you made in art class last week is not.) And if you interrupt your siblings' MBST, you'll lose a few minutes of your time. Schedule your primary interrupter last so he's less likely to butt in on his siblings and therefore lose out on a few minutes of playing superheroes with Dad. Keep in mind, however, that if a child frequently interrupts, there's likely something else at play and you'll need to use a different tool to address the issue. Losing out on too much MBST will only make the problem worse. One possible solution to ward off interruptions in the first place is to place a pad of paper in the kitchen or family room so kids can write or draw what they want to tell you so they don't forget.

I travel for work and am only home on weekends.

In addition to touching base with each child long-distance every day, if possible, you'll want to schedule extra time for them when you are home—a bike ride or a game of Monopoly, for instance. Make sure the time is spent one-on-one, as kids really thrive from the personal attention without siblings around.

How do I handle discipline problems during or before MBST?

It's unlikely you'll experience too many discipline problems during MBST, especially once you get going. If you do, simply use the positive strategies found in the rest of this book to correct misbehavior and keep going with MBST. And if seven-year-old Clayton commonly has problems not jumping on the sofa while blasting off his space rockets, suggest a list of alternate activities he can choose from.

Can I take MBST away as a punishment?

Please don't! Kids need daily attention from each parent. If you take it away, your child will be lacking in belonging and significance, and attention- and power-seeking behaviors will likely escalate. The one exception to this rule is that you may deduct time from MBST for a child who is disrupting a sibling's MBST. This usually corrects the problem quickly, but if the behavior continues, you'll want to try a different technique or switch up your MBST routine so that no child is deprived of MBST for more than a day. You'll find plenty of other proven methods to address discipline issues throughout this book.

My teen thinks MBST is stupid.

Chances are, your teenager needs time to get used to the idea—and to learn to trust you not to simply use it as an excuse to pry into her life (although certainly you'd be open to hearing about what *really* happened at the homecoming dance if she'd like to share). Stick with it even if it feels strange at first for both of you and be creative about the activities you might suggest. Maybe cooking a new recipe together, helping her practice her backhand or letting her teach you how to edit photos online will help her start to relax and have fun. Just be sure to not interrogate her about her new boyfriend, what Krista's parents let her do during spring break or anything else during your time together. No matter how tempted you are.

And if it's the only way to get started, it's okay to tune in to technology with your teens. Just aim to do something active like play a video game or listen to music rather than staring blankly at the tube. Even if you're not particularly adept at shooting down aliens, your child will be thrilled that you took the time to (try to) learn.

My child uses all her MBST trying to decide what to do.

Sit down with your child and make a list of fun ten-minute activities. Pull it out and refer to it when you need to. If you know your child usually has trouble deciding, you can also plan an activity in advance by noticing what your child's playing with or working on during the day. Say "You're building quite the train track—is that something you'd like to do during our Mind, Body and Soul Time later today?" Let her change her mind if she wants to, but at least you'll have a place to start.

Should both parents do Mind, Body and Soul Time?

Yes, your kids need one-on-one attention from both parents. If there are two parents in the home, both should find time every day to fill each child's attention basket. If your spouse isn't totally on board yet, don't worry. As your partner starts noticing the great results you get with Mind, Body and Soul Time, he or she will likely want to join in.

2

The Great Give-In

The story is so familiar; I probably don't have to recount it. The scene is the grocery store. You've got your kids, a grocery list a mile long and dozens of other people who are just as desperate as you are to get home for dinner. Then the tantrum happens (you're not going to buy the overpriced plastic dinosaur cup for three-year-old John that the store has so conveniently placed in the breakfast cereal aisle) and all of a sudden your challenge has gone from difficult to unbearable. Three looooonnnnggg minutes of intense negotiation later, John is still yelling, people are staring, you're desperate—and before you know it, the dinosaur cup ends up in the cart (plus another one for his five-year-old sister) and your child is smiling happily (triumphantly even?) through his tears.

It happens in the car, at home, in stores, at the park—you name it. It's the great give-in, and it's one of the biggest contributors to the entitlement epidemic. Desperate parents everywhere cave when their kids push them hard enough, teaching them all kinds of unhelpful lessons: for instance, that rules can be broken and that it's perfectly acceptable to use bad behavior to accomplish a goal.

The trouble is kids generally know exactly how hard they have to push—and which buttons—to get exactly what they want. They're smart—don't think for a minute that the wheedling, negotiating, pointed words and tears are pure emotion. They're calculated, because when they tried these tactics the first time and we gave in, they learned that this type of behavior works, and they are more than happy to use, wheedle, negotiate and whine again in the future. In fact, since John was rewarded for his bad behavior with a new dinosaur cup, you can bet he'll set his sights on the *Cars* cereal bowl or something else next time.

This isn't a problem that's limited to toddlers throwing tantrums in the grocery store aisles, either. Older kids (and even adults) often expect to get their way if they simply whine enough. For instance, take sixteen-year-old Cadence, who is apparently the only girl in her group of friends without a designer handbag. You know that's not true, but she nevertheless reminds you of this statistic every day. She whines ("All my friends think we're poor!"), she complains ("I hate this old purse!") and she negotiates ("But I got all As and Bs this semester!") until finally, you wonder if you really are depriving your child. So you take her to the mall—just to look, of course. After all, maybe you can find a cheaper lookalike that will fit the bill. Cadence is all energy and enthusiasm—she knows just what stores she wants to visit, she can rattle off which of her friends got which bag where (or bangle or whatnot) and, of course, she has her hopes up. Soon her heart is set on a bag that costs more than your family's monthly cell phone bill and the look in her eyes tells you she's in it for the long haul. You are weary and annoyed but you also want Cadence to be happy. And to put an end to her wheedling. So you say the unthinkable: "I suppose . . . you did get good grades this semester." Cadence squeals, delighted. And you? You're just trying to enjoy her good mood and wondering when the next major crisis will hit.

Yes, the great give-in is a problem that endures through all the ages and stages of childhood. But it is a problem that can be solved. And you're certainly not the only one who gives in—the vast majority of parents report that when they just can't take the whining anymore or when they just really need to get the groceries and get home, they hand over the forbidden fruit to their child. Read on to learn why you're not alone if you've caved, and some tools you can use to put an end to the battles—and your own propensity to give in.

Why We Cave

Think back to your child's baby days. The sweet little outfits, the milestone-a-minute growth, the purple-faced crying fits (it can't all be cute, can it?). Whatever your parenting style, no doubt a good part of your day was spent trying to meet all of baby's needs and most of her wants, in an effort to avoid those purple-faced crying fits. That's what we're programmed to do—no one wants to listen to a poor, innocent, helpless baby cry for long.

Fast-forward a few years, and if you haven't changed tactics, your child continues to expect to receive everything she wants—but she's no longer poor, innocent and helpless. She might be a bit less likely to turn on the tears, but she'll have other ways of accomplishing her goals. And why wouldn't she? Consider that for the majority of American children:

- Every time their favorite cartoon isn't on TV, we can change the channel, pop in a DVD or pull it up on our computer (or mobile device, if we're out and about). And because of this easy availability, there's no longer any tolerance for boredom or waiting patiently at the dentist.
- Big-box and discount stores, as well as a wide variety of cost-cutting Internet sites, can provide the playroom of their dreams, delivered to their doorstep.
- The variety of food available just for snack time rivals that of princes and princesses centuries ago.
- We often can zap away any minor pain or illness within minutes of digging into our well-stocked medicine cabinet.
- Their closets and dressers contain enough clothing to outfit a neighborhood one hundred years ago. And they can attire themselves as their favorite characters or look like their beloved junior celebrity.

Ever since our child's earliest years, we've had an aversion to letting our kids experience disappointment, but we've also had an ability to provide whatever they want that's unparalleled in history. With nothing to stop us, we do provide. After all, our kids' requests aren't always unreasonable. Whether they're asking for pretzels instead of raisins at snack time or dying for the new rock-star action figure for Christmas, we can respond to them like never before. In the past, on the other hand, this simply wouldn't have been possible due to financial, time or availability constraints. Today's kids are accustomed to getting what they want, often right when they want it. And is that so terrible? If they need a new lunch box, for instance, why shouldn't they be able to decide whether they want My Little Pony or Barbie? Or a lunch bag, if they prefer it?

In fact, it's gone so far that if we can't provide exactly what they want, we often feel compelled to provide a consolation prize. With the younger set, this sounds like "You may not climb over the back of the sofa, but here's a cookie!" As kids get older, it might be "Those jeans are too expensive but I'll buy you this designer shirt instead." Kids learn not to accept the hard facts of life (You may not climb over the sofa or the jeans are too expensive) because they're continually hearing "You can't handle being told no, so I'll give you something to help soften the blow."

This doesn't mean we need to say no more often just so our kids hear it. We can say yes, as long as we reinforce a positive behavior. "If you'd like to climb, let's save it for next time we're at the park!" Or "Those jeans are expensive, and I can only cover half the cost. Would you like to use your allowance to cover the rest?" By doing so, we're retraining our kids to accept limits and find positive, creative ways to achieve reasonable results. They'll also learn valuable life lessons in the process (If you spend your allowance on jeans, you won't be able to go to the movies with your friends). What's more, they find that the best things in life (climbing, designer jeans), aren't off-limits entirely, they're simply conditional—which is something that will help guide them in their adult years.

Efficiency and convenience are also major players in the great give-in. How many times do we cave in to our kids' demands simply because we're running late for the soccer game, we're on our third errand, the school bus is coming or we're in public? Or we rescue our kids by rushing the forgotten permission slip, gym shoes, science project, etc., to school simply because we don't want to be that parent or we don't want our child to experience the disappointment of being left out. These pressures—which are all very real—often get in the way of successful child rearing. We're all busy parents who want the best for our kids, and it's often easier to find the forgotten gear for the child, tie the shoes, allow the treat and so on, so that they don't actually have to feel disappointment, and we can accomplish everything in our jam-packed schedule.

Sometimes, too, we feel we need to make up for things we think are parental failures on our part. In other words, we feel guilty that we've been working overtime and arrived home after bedtime every day last week or that we lost our job and our Christmas tree felt empty and we overdo it by giving in to their requests to stay up late or bring home a new toy. Or maybe we yelled at the kids when we were in a bad mood or just had a new baby or had family vacation plans fall through—the list goes on. In truth, however, giving in is just a temporary fix for our own insecurities. Yes, the kids will survive a smaller Christmas, a parent's long working hours, or a staycation instead of a week at Disneyland. What won't serve them well is the attitude that because things didn't go their way, they're owed compensation. You can spend extra time with the kids on the weekend and make the staycation special on your terms, without giving in to kids' extra—and often unrelated—demands.

Of course, the most obvious reason we give in to our kids' whims is because tantrums—wherever they are and at any age—can quite quickly ruin our day. For us, for our kids, and for anyone within earshot. We want to avoid them like the plague.

A Tale of Two Tantrums

We've all been there: on the brink of a child's tantrum, ready to do anything to stop it before it starts. But there's help even for the most tantrum-prone child. First, it's important to recognize that there are two different kinds of tantrums—meltdown tantrums and entitled tantrums—and they need to be handled differently. Consider these scenarios:

THE MELTDOWN TANTRUM

You have so much to do this afternoon. You and three-year-old Bryant start by returning books at the library (and of course picking out a few more). Then you run to the bank and the post office—where, unfortunately, there's a long line. After that, you head into the hardware store, which you have to circle twice to find replacement light switches. By now, Bryant is beyond ready to be at home playing with his trains. He starts whining, but you fend off the worst of it with a bag of fruit snacks you dig up. Finally you make it to your big errand of the day—the once-a-month trek to the local warehouse store. Inside, Bryant fixates on a humongous canister of cheese puffs and decides he must have them. At all costs. Even if it takes flailing on the floor and making you look (and feel) like the worst parent in the world.

Bryant can't tell you "No, really, I'm waayyy past my limit here and I'm too inexperienced to know how to cope." Yes, Bryant's behavior is unnerving, ill-timed and even embarrassing as other shoppers wonder which alien creature has inhabited your child's body—but he has been running on empty for a while now. His basic needs (A nap? A filling snack? A sense of belonging and significance?) aren't being met, and he's at his limit, so he loses it in a big way.

THE ENTITLED TANTRUM

Twelve-year-old Megan wants to stay overnight at her friend's house. Normally you'd agree, but Megan has only known this friend for a couple of weeks, and you haven't met the parents. What's more, you have a dinner to get to, which means the babysitter would have to drop Megan off, so there would be no chance to get acquainted with the parents beforehand. It just won't work out this time. You tell Megan as much, and after some push back ("Everyone else is going!!! Serena is really nice, I've met her mom and she's great! I'll be fine! This is so unfair! You never let me do anything!!!"), she ramps up her reaction, slams doors and starts telling the world that you're the worst dad in the world.

Clearly, Megan feels entitled to having things go her way, and can't handle it when they don't. She's pitching a fit because she mistakenly feels she should get what she wants, when she wants it.

Just like in three-year-old Bryant's case, meltdowns happen when we've run one too many errands and the child is subsisting on snacks salvaged from the bottom of your purse and a fifteen-minute car nap caught between stops. Similarly, they happen when a child doesn't have the verbal skills to express herself and feels frustrated at being misunderstood. Even older kids are prone to meltdown tantrums—if our Saturday morning soccer star is still in his uniform at 3:00 p.m. and lunch was soda and a tiny hamburger, we know exactly why he rolled his eyes and grumbled under his breath when we asked him to unpack the soccer bag. Not that there's any excuse for bad behavior, but kids can only take so much. Think of it this way: how do you feel after a long day of work when someone narrowly beats you to the short checkout line or cuts you off in traffic? Or how about when you've been on the phone for an hour trying to convince the person on the other end that there's a problem with your Internet service, and that yes, it is plugged in? When your patience is shot, you just might have a minimeltdown of your own. You're not proud of it, but it happens.

Your best bet in curbing a meltdown tantrum is to offer comfort in any way you can (without giving in) and then prioritize the rest of your to-do list. So when your hungry, tired three-year-old is crying tears of desperation over a giant canister of cheese puffs, offer to buy him a banana instead. At least he'll no longer be hungry, and you can finish up anything you *have* to do and hightail it for home. And for a teen who is rampaging through the house at the injustice of having to vacuum the living room, recognize that his foul mood might be due to the all-night bowling party he attended for youth group last night matched with the stress of basketball tryouts and a huge essay exam in his government class to look forward to on Monday. You can sympathetically suggest he lie down for a power nap before completing his work, and offer to quiz him on the Constitution later—but avoid letting him off the hook entirely. Essentially, provide what the child needs, while holding him to the good behavior. Then chalk it up to a learning experience for you and make any necessary adjustments in the future. If meltdown tantrums happen a couple of times a week, you might want to make some bigger changes in your life, like earlier bedtimes, so your kids are getting their needs met and learning appropriate behavior.

Once you've addressed the problem of meltdown tantrums, there's still help for the entitled kind. Just as with Megan, who felt entitled to spend the night at her friend's house, an entitled tantrum happens when a child feels *owed* something. She's throwing a fit simply because she feels like she should be able to go to the sleepover even though you said no for good reason or she wants to go to the swimming pool instead of her piano lesson or because you didn't buy the right kind of breakfast cereal. Her wants are paramount and she shows no regard for the feelings of others or the needs of the situation (like the inconvenience it would create for her parents). At the heart of this kind of tantrum is that the child wants special treatment—to receive some object or privilege merely because she wants it, and not because she's worked for it or waited. This is the behavior we'll spend the rest of the book discussing and addressing. Soon, you'll be armed with the tools you need to make entitled tantrums history.

How They Get What They Want

Now that we know why our kids often feel entitled to the very best that life has to offer, how does this relate to their bad behavior?

First, we need to look into the minds of our children (and, in truth, many adults). If, since birth, you've had your every need met and your slightest whim catered to—if you've been the center of a loving parent's world for longer than you can remember, you would find it hard to take no for an answer, too. Instead of accepting a no, you would focus your energy on doing whatever it takes to get a yes. And if you haven't developed *positive* ways to achieve what you're hoping for (saving up allowance to buy a new toy, practicing free throws to improve skills and get more playing time), you'll resort to *negative* ways.

In fact, here's a page from the Entitled Kids Manual.

ENTITLE ME! TOOL: WHINING

When your parent says no to something you want or something you want to do, simply turn on your whining voice. This particular type of voice has been known to shatter glass and parents' eardrums—in fact, your parents will actually tell you, "You're hurting my ears with that voice!" But keep it up and eventually you will wear them down.

How to Use It

Start whining as soon as your parent says no. Raise your voice to a very high pitch (the higher the better), talk slightly through your nose and say "But Mooooommm . . ." Complete this sentence with a few good reasons why you should get what you want, and rephrase them over and over if you get pushback from your parent. If you need help thinking of ideas, pick from these categories:

- Your brother/sister is allowed to have it/do it.
- You were allowed to have it/do it before (either by this same parent or another adult).
- You really, really *need* it because (you're starving, everyone else has it, you're bored, etc.).
- You haven't been allowed to have anything/do anything fun all day, or perhaps all week.

If your parent hasn't given in after a few rounds of argument, go for the guilt trip. Keep up the whiny voice, and try:

- You don't really love me.
- You're the worst mom/dad in the world.
- I hate you.
- You love [sibling's name] more than me.

If your parent still doesn't give in, launch into a full-blown tantrum (this is the next tactic). And finally, if you still haven't gotten what you want, try whining again later on. Sometimes this tool can take multiple attempts over a period of several days to finally wear down your parent—but it's highly effective, so don't give up.

Most kids are very aware of this tactic and many others: tantrums, negotiating, power struggles and more. They develop and use strategies that work for them—in fact, we wouldn't have whining, tantrums and all the rest if they *didn't* work. So that becomes our job: to make sure these tools have no place in our home by rendering them useless.

Unfortunately, it's not enough to stand firm half of the time, or even most of the time. That's because every instance we give in when our kids whine, cry or battle us to get what they want, we tell them "You earned it!" We reward the hard work of petitioning, send the message "You're right!" and let them know that they're entitled to the candy at the grocery store or unlimited text messages on the cell phone plan. We *guarantee* they will use this same tactic again.

On a psychological level, these types of misbehaviors are also ways for them to achieve their emotional needs—belonging and significance—every bit as much as the cookie before dinner. Think about it: when your child is throwing a tantrum or building up to one, he's secured 100 percent of your attention and energy. And if he wins? What a power trip! He's bent you completely out of shape, and controlled you with his actions. He's achieved the attention and power he was (subconsciously) looking for. No wonder tantrums are such a powerful tactic.

That's why it's important to use Mind, Body and Soul Time and other tools you'll learn later on to fill your kids' attention and power baskets in a positive way, so they won't seek them out in negative ways. In fact, once your kids' baskets are filled, you'll find they accept no for an answer much more readily. If, however, your child is on a mission for attention and power, she'll turn the cookie into a good excuse to capture a large part of your mind share, even though it's negative, and gain a sense of power by distracting you from the bell peppers you were sautéing.

We see, then, that if kids can't have what they want, they at least want our attention and to feel some sense of control over us. For these reasons, all the tactics they use meet some of their needs, albeit in a negative way, and contribute to their effectiveness. Perhaps you recognize some of these other tactics from the Entitled Kids Manual:

The Limit Pusher
Selective Hearing
Backtalk and Battles
Special Treatment
Personal Servant
The Negotiator
Everyone Can Tantrum!

Fortunately for parents everywhere, we have our own Un-Entitler Toolbox—and there are tools to address each of these annoying, entitled misbehaviors. The four at the end of this chapter will help you cut back on the payoff (negative attention and negative power) your kids receive from the likes of whining, battling and negotiating. Put them to use, and your kids will quickly learn that their negative tactics have lost their efficacy entirely, and they'll lie forgotten and dusty on the garage floor of their memory—soon to be replaced by the types of tools (hard work, patience, cooperation, etc.) that will serve them well for years to come.

Now that we know how our kids get us to give in, let's take a look at some ways to put an end to the great give-in—for good.

> Childhood happiness has become the scorecard by
> which adults measure their success or failure as parents . . .
> Constantly striving to please your kids turns them into
> your boss. Their happiness becomes your
> performance review.
> —Lisa Earle McLeod, author of *The Triangle of Truth*

Give Up Giving In

It doesn't take a twelve-year-old to tell us that if kids' demands are constantly met, they will keep asking. Who wouldn't? The more we give in, the more we foster the entitlement attitude in our kids. And remember—adults often feel just as entitled as children. When we accidentally forgot to pay a bill last month and the friendly person on the phone wouldn't waive the late fee, we got mad—he waived it last time! Or when we aren't allowed to use an expired coupon, we feel upset—it expired only yesterday, after all! It's hard when we don't get what we want.

Which begs the question, how do we make it stop? You'll learn more about cutting down on bad behaviors like whining, negotiating and all the rest at the end of this chapter. But how, exactly, do you stop giving in? Here are a few action items for cutting back on caving in.

Start Small

Identify one common give-in that's causing you stress. For instance, does your child dominate your iPad? Does your four-year-old still expect to ride in a stroller through the mall? Does back-to-school clothes shopping dip into your holiday budget? Can you get through the grocery store without handing over a cookie? Pick one thing to start with.

Reveal the Rule

Let your child know about your new expectation. Say "You can use my iPad for fifteen minutes per day." Or "You're old enough now to make it through the store without a cookie. Cookies will be special treats at other times at home, but I'll no longer give you one every time we go to the store."

Stick Your Ground

Once you've put a rule in place, keep it firm. Loosen up only if the circumstances really are special—for instance, you might allow your child extra TV time if she's sick, but not simply because she's whining extra loud or you have a to-do list a mile long.

Once you've successfully quelled one entitlement issue, pick another. But don't feel like you need to solve every problem all at once or you'll frustrate yourself and your kids. Once you've un-entitled them in a few areas of life, the rest will start to fall into place as they get used to the new system.

Keep in mind that your kids aren't going to be happy with the changes. There will be tears. Probably loud, desperate tears. Entitled kids *love* the kingdom they've built for themselves and would rather eat broccoli every day for a week than step down from it. But they'll actually be more content and happier down the road if you derail the entitlement train they've been riding—and the sooner the better.

Once you've stopped routinely giving in, you'll want to be on high alert for entitlement episodes in the future. It can be hard, especially at first, to determine whether something is a reasonable request or an entitlement issue, so use this litmus test to tell: if you start to feel annoyed at what your child is asking you to do, if you need to bend over backward to do it or if you feel put out, it's very likely entitlement. For instance, it's perfectly reasonable for you to pack a lunch every day for your six-year-old. But for your sixteen-year-old? If you're tired of the burden, you should certainly be able to hand it off without a big fuss.

Expect Pushback

Anticipate that your kids will continue to nudge any limits you set up until they leave the house (and even then), so you'll need to stay on top of the game. (In fact, Pushing Limits is one of the tactics in the Entitled Kids Manual.) For example, the nightly bedtime battle: kids work every angle to put off going to bed so they can pretend to be a kitten for even five minutes more, or catch a few more sharks from the living room couch. Same thing with curfew—they're happy to negotiate for forty-five minutes to get an extra thirty out with their friends.

Allow Disappointment

Things happen. Life circumstances change. Previous indulgences become impossible. That's okay. Say you've been able to treat the family to a trip to a water park three summers in a row—but funds are short this year. There's no need to dip into savings simply so they don't have to face the disappointment of only getting to visit the neighborhood pool (even if they try to convince you otherwise). Your kids will survive, and even learn from the disappointment, as we'll see in chapter 7.

Be Honest

While you probably shouldn't sit down with your kids and review the excruciating details of the family budget, for instance, it's wise to let your kids know what's going on, and in advance. You can say "Sorry, kids—business hasn't been great this year, so we'll have to skip the water park." Or "I'm feeling so rushed in the mornings that

I can't manage to pack your lunch. You're old enough to take on the job, and I'll really appreciate your help." You'll appeal to your kids' natural sense of empathy, and they'll be less likely to pitch a fit if they have a better understanding of the situation.

Seek Input

Sometimes you can turn setbacks into a problem-solving opportunity that your kids can be a part of. For instance, gather everyone and tell them "We're all disappointed about the water park, but maybe we can all try to find some ways to save up so we can go next summer. Any ideas?" Or "Can anyone think of some ways we can streamline our morning routine so we don't have problems getting out the door on time?" Your kids will probably jump at the chance to share their two cents, and it'll give them something to do rather than push back.

Be the Model

This one should be obvious, but it isn't always. Keep in mind that parents set the tone for the house—and parents can be just as guilty as kiddos when it comes to complaining, whining, negotiating, pitching a fit and generally acting entitled in an attempt to get another person to cave. We don't always know we're doing it, and sometimes a little negotiation is completely justified—even within earshot of your kids if you keep your tone respectful and use logic. But the more you can clean up your own communication, the better you'll enable your kids to clean up theirs.

Giving in really can be a desperate parenting measure of the past at your house. But that's not to say your kids will like it. In fact, they'll continue to whine, needle and protest to get their way. Fortunately, there's help for that, too. While you work to give up giving in, there's no need to listen to (much) whining in the meantime. Use the following tools to put an end to the annoying misbehaviors that used to get you to cave to endless demands.

HEALTHY INDULGENCES: TREATING WITHOUT ENTITLING

Yes, you can sometimes let your child have a cookie when he asks for one (or when he doesn't). After all, life is full of pleasures we want to share with our kids, from trips to the zoo to staying up late to cracking the cover of a brand-new book—and there's absolutely nothing wrong with that. But does the fact that one time we stopped for ice cream on the way home from the dry cleaner's mean our kids must *always* feel entitled to a post-cleaner ice-cream stop? And should we *never* stop for ice cream simply because we don't want to have to say no the next hundred times we pick up our cleaning? Here are some guidelines for treating without spoiling:

- Without being preachy, remind them what a special treat this is.
- Be sure not to link the special treat to good behavior, or the child will come to feel entitled to special treats anytime he behaves.
- If you can, plan it in advance and let your kids look forward to it. They'll learn patience in the meantime.
- If your child nags you for more when the treat is over (or next time you pass the ice-cream store), simply say "We sure enjoyed that ice cream, didn't we? Maybe we can do this again some-time!" Then change the subject. The Asked and Answered tool at the end of this chapter will help you put an end to all the ne-gotiating that might ensue.

DOUBLE TROUBLE

Double standards are your worst enemy when it comes to teaching your kids positive habits. Sure, we provide our kids free room and board, but that doesn't mean we're entitled to hold them to a differ-ent standard than we hold ourselves to. For instance, don't we all at

times leave odds and ends out on the counter but expect kids to pick
up after themselves, yell at our kids for yelling at their siblings or expect kids to do chores after school while we lie on the sofa after a hard
day at work? If your kids haven't called you out on this yet, they will.
Remember that while none of us are perfect parents, kids learn more
from our actions than our words.

Un-Entitler: Ignore Undue Attention

Most of us reading this book are attentive parents. We talk to our kids,
tune in to their needs and do our best to help them learn and feel included. And that's wonderful! At times, though, kids have trouble real-
izing that while they are a *big* part of our lives, they are not the *only* part
of our lives. They commonly feel entitled to our attention all the time,
and show it through whining, acting helpless, interrupting, clinging to
us and more. This happens when we're on the phone, trying to get some
work done, attempting to use the bathroom in private—you name it.
And although we treasure our little angels, we can't help but feel that
sometimes they're simply pests!

What's a parent to do? We want to meet their needs and give them
plenty of attention, but we also have to teach our kids to be independent. And we have to do something—fast!—about all the whining.
That's when Ignore Undue Attention comes into play. It sounds like a
simple tool, but it's an excellent way to teach your kids that they're not
entitled to your attention 24/7, and save your sanity at the same time.

PUT IT TO USE

Your first step is to be sure you're keeping your kids' attention baskets
full with Mind, Body and Soul Time. Not only will you be able to expect
better behavior in general, and fewer attention-seeking misbehaviors,

but you'll also feel more confident using this tool. If you regularly provide your kids plenty of positive attention, it's okay to expect them to do without it when the spotlight's not on them. What's more, if you use this tool *without* also using Mind, Body and Soul Time, you can expect some new bad behaviors to crop up as your child tries to get the attention she's seeking—even if it's negative.

Now, reveal to your kids that "It's not okay to interrupt my conversation while I'm on the phone or if I'm in a conversation with someone else—like your dad or your brother. In the future, if you do try to interrupt while I'm busy speaking with someone else, I'm not going to respond to you. After I put down the phone, I'm all ears." Or "I will no longer pay attention to your whiny voice—when you talk to me in a normal voice, I'll be happy to talk with you."

Be sure to train your kids in the behavior you expect. For instance, make sure they know what constitutes an emergency while Mom is on the phone (someone is bleeding) and what does not (the space cowboy superhero's rocket ship had a crash landing behind the couch and can't be reached by four-year-old arms). And practice the difference between whiny and normal using your best ventriloquism and a couple of stuffed animals.

To help your kids get accustomed to the new approach, develop a nonverbal signal you can use to remind them in the moment but without giving them attention for the negative behavior. Agree on the signal—possibly a talk-to-the-hand gesture or covering your ears—with your kids ahead of time so they'll know what it means when they see it.

Then do what you say. Next time you're catching up with your insurance company over the phone and your child seems to desperately need your attention (there's a really cool bug with a green belly outside), simply use your nonverbal signal and then walk away. If you're faced with a whiny voice—or asked to tie your seven-year-old's shoes or whatever the pesky behavior is—give the signal and then retreat to another room without saying a word. Once your kids have gotten some practice with this tool, you can drop the signal and simply leave the scene.

Your child may get upset—let him. There's no need to get involved, however, as he has been warned, and he gets plenty of positive attention thanks to Mind, Body and Soul Time.

Tips and Scripts

- Even a "Remember what we talked about . . ." is too much to say. Once your child is familiar with the tool, any acknowledgment from you counts as attention, which guarantees your child will use the tactic, whether it's whining or interrupting, in the future.
- The first few times your kids interrupt you or whine, offer a redo. Help your child practice the correct behavior (waiting for you to finish your conversation, talking in a normal voice).
- Especially for young kids, keep in mind that the twenty minutes it takes for you to finish hearing about Aunt Stephanie's trip to Venice is an eternity. If your five-year-old has been itching to talk to you—but still waiting patiently—for a few minutes, it's okay to excuse yourself briefly from the conversation to see what he needs. Teens, however, can usually wait it out.
- Keep a notepad handy that your kids can write or draw on to help them remember what they wanted to talk to you about. That way, they'll be able to take action in the moment without interrupting (plus, you can glance at it and see if they've missed the fact that accidentally tying a string too tight around a sibling's finger really is an emergency). In this case, you can point to the notepad as a nonverbal signal. If they don't get the message, be sure to role-play using the notepad after the fact.
- Teach your kids what kinds of things they can interrupt for (the dog just threw up) and how to do so politely ("Excuse me, but Max just threw up on your new living room pillow"). Role-play so they get the idea. Tell them that conversations aren't the only things that can be interrupted—the same rules apply for reading a book, watching TV, using a computer or anything that captures another person's attention.
- Be respectful of your kids' conversations and activities, too. Don't

interrupt them to fetch a couple of fresh batteries from the basement for your flashlight when they are engrossed in creating a blanket fort in the living room. If the whole house is mindful about undue attention—and how it's no fun to be interrupted—your efforts to quell it will be more successful. By the same token, watch your tone of voice. Parents are as capable of whining as kids—and fully as capable of modeling a respectful tone.

YES, BUT . . .

When I use this tool, my child follows me, crying, whining, or yelling.

First make sure your child's basic needs are met—she's not hungry or tired—and that you've filled her attention basket with Mind, Body and Soul Time. Recognize that your child wouldn't use this behavior if she didn't think it'd work. She's pretty sure that if she keeps it up, louder or longer, you'll cave and give her the attention she wants. To quell it, use the bathroom technique. Retreat to your bathroom, an area of the house usually associated with privacy, and say "I'm just going to go to the bathroom. I'll come out when you calm down and can speak respectfully." Rest assured you'll only have to do this once or twice before your child gets the picture.

My child says rude things, calls me names or causes more bad behavior until I have to pay attention.

Ignore, ignore, ignore. Move to another area of the house. If you respond to your child's declaration that you're a poopy-head or "I hate you," you're almost guaranteed to hear it again next time. You do need to step in, though, if your child engages in destructive behavior. Do so, but say as little as possible so as not to reinforce what she's doing. Remember that the best way to minimize negative attention-seeking behavior is to give the attention proactively and consistently with Mind, Body and Soul

Time. If she's getting the attention she craves in other areas, there's no need for her to act up to get it.

We're in the grocery store.

Your best bet here is to prevent the tantrum from happening in the first place. Provide plenty of opportunities for positive power throughout the day (giving a toddler choices as well as meaningful jobs to do, such as put the forks and spoons away, feed pets using a measuring cup, match socks, etc.), and even at the store. Young kids love checking items off a list, for instance, so try bringing along a clipboard and a crayon for your child to use. Or if you're stocking up for Thanksgiving dinner and you'll be in the store a while, bring along an old mp3 player with audiobooks or kids' songs.

Chances are you'll see a great reduction in tantrums with these strategies, but they might still happen. First be sure to inform your child in advance what you'll do if he pitches a screaming fit in the store (tell him that you won't respond and he won't get what he wants with those antics). Practice good behavior by role-playing. When the tantrum happens (because your child is sure to want to test your resolve), be unaffected and don't react. Remember that she has the right to express her feelings, and you have the right to not participate. Don't even try to talk her down—your child will love the attention and increase the volume. Get to a quiet space—even the car if you need to—and let her finish her tantrum. When she's calm again, return to your shopping, knowing that she'll be less likely to resort to tantrums in the future.

Un-Entitler: Pull Over and Wait

It happens all the time: the kids in the backseat can't agree on whose superpowers are cooler, and you can't concentrate on your driving because of all the bickering. And if it's not that, they're battling you about why they have to go to the bank with you in the first place. Or holding a most-annoying-noise contest. How do you get them to stop and get to where you're going? This tool will bring peace and quiet—or at least pleasant conversation—to your travels, using a tactic that you've probably heard before. It's time to take your dad's old "I'm going to pull this car over!" seriously, because it works—as long as you warn your kids in advance.

PUT IT TO USE

First, when you're not in the car and everything is calm, tell your kids that you have a new plan for in the car. Say "Remember the other day when we were in the car and you were arguing about whether it's better to be able to fly or turn into a werewolf? Well, it's really not safe for me to drive when you are acting up in the backseat. So I'm not going to put our family at risk anymore. When you're fighting or yelling in the car, I'm going to pull over and wait until I hear quiet, and then I'll continue. Now to make sure we're on the same page, what's going to happen the next time you fight or are too loud in the car?"

This tool will work best if you can plan for the next trip—and presumably the next backseat battle—to someplace your kids actually want to go. So try to reveal your plan on a Friday night before you'll be dropping both kids off at friends' houses Saturday morning, for instance.

When your kids start getting unruly, quietly pull over to a safe place (the side of the road, a parking lot, etc.). Turn off the car and pull a book or magazine out of the glove compartment. Don't say a word. When it's quiet, start up the car and pull back onto the road.

Your kids will quickly get the message that drive time is not fight time. However, chances are they'll still slip up on occasion in the future—which means you could be using this tool on the way to swim lessons, Grandma's birthday party, the big football game and all the rest. Yes, you'll probably arrive late every so often, but you need to remain unfazed. They'll soon learn that the faster they quiet down, the less time they'll be spending in a stopped car, and backseat bickering will be a million miles away.

Tips and Scripts

- You'll be able to cut down on backseat battles in the first place if you provide plenty of positive attention and power in the form of Mind, Body and Soul Time to each child every day.
- Be proactive by turning drive time into talk time. If your nine-year-old is giving you the play-by-play of his latest Little League practice, he won't be able to convince his little sister that the ugly fairy is going to turn her favorite doll into an alligator, and incite a minicatastrophe. Likewise, if you're asking your six-year-old what kind of breakfast cereal she'd like this week, she won't spend as much time whining about going to the store in the first place.
- Make sure everyone who drives your kids around is on board. It'll be most effective if even Grandpa doesn't let them get away with acting up in the car.
- If you're really worried about being late somewhere and you expect your kids to act up, use plenty of positive tools ahead of time (like Mind, Body and Soul Time) and then leave early. It's much better to play a game of I Spy in the parking lot than it is to follow the bride into her own wedding.

YES, BUT . . .

We often use highways and interstates to get where we're going, so it's hard to find a place to pull over.

Do the best you can while keeping everyone safe. If your kids are still acting up when you arrive at the next exit, take it. If not, keep going.

Un-Entitler: Sail Out of the Wind

There's nothing that gets under your skin quite like an intense power struggle with your child. What seems like a simple disagreement ("No, you may not get a pet python.") soon escalates ("But Carter has one! You never let me do anything!"). Regardless of who's right and who's wrong—and who wins—no one comes away feeling good about herself or the relationship.

What can you do about it? You can't stop your child's emotions, tantrums and furies (in other words, take the wind out of *her* sails). The wisest thing, then, according to child psychiatrist Rudolf Dreikurs, is to simply take your sail out of her *"wind."* Essentially, when you sense a storm brewing, remove your sail by fleeing to higher ground and leaving the room. Your child wants to get his own way—but he also wants your attention. And by engaging you in a fierce battle over pet snake ownership, for example, he not only secures your undivided attention, he also, sometimes, gets what he wants. When you remove the attention payoff, not to mention the give-in, you're sending the message that you're not interested in a fight and you're not going to change your mind. After several rounds of this, your child will get the picture. Power struggles will quickly lose their force, and you can stop battles in their tracks—before they reach category 5 levels.

PUT IT TO USE

First, in a calm moment (when there's no storm brewing), warn your children "I'm no longer going to argue with you about my decisions, and if you don't speak to me respectfully, I will leave the room. When you're calm and can have a respectful conversation, I will be happy to talk with you." Next time a power struggle begins to escalate (you'll know because you'll feel angry and provoked), simply remove your sail by leaving the room or silently refuse to participate. Any conflict needs at least two people, so you can end it by removing one of the participants (yourself).

Tips and Scripts

- Before you use this tool for the first time, pick a calm moment to warn your child. Tell him "Just like I'm working on using my calm and respectful voice with you, I expect you to talk through your disagreements with me respectfully and calmly. When you talk back to me or use a disrespectful tone, I will choose not to participate and I will leave the room."
- This tool will only work if you become truly unresponsive. Ignore, ignore, ignore—no matter what your child unleashes, unless it's dangerous for the child or others. Resist the urge to try to get the final say. (Remember, ignoring is for manipulative tantrums, not the meltdowns described earlier.)
- Be willing and available to discuss the disagreement on respectful terms when the initial storm is over. Remember, you're walking out on the bad behavior—not your child.

YES, BUT . . .

When I leave, my child follows me, crying, whining or yelling.

Use the bathroom technique, from page 44.

We're in the grocery store and people are staring as my child raises her voice.

As in the Ignore Undue Attention tool (page 44), don't get sucked in and don't react. Head to a quiet corner of the store or to the car if your child becomes too disruptive. Prevent power struggles in the first place by giving your kids plenty of opportunities to build significance.

Isn't it important for kids to learn to negotiate?

Learning to respectfully disagree is important, but it's very different from whining and badgering. When kids whine and badger, they're simply trying to wear you down. On the other hand, kids should feel free to maturely present facts that would bring about a different conclusion—in other words, respectfully disagree. And if, in fact, they tell you something you didn't know that changes your mind, great—just let them know it's the new information, presented respectfully, that made the change. Whatever you do, don't alter your ruling unless your kids present their facts and opinions in a calm and respectful way. Even if their point is sound, it's a no-go unless they use their big-kid manners.

Un-Entitler: Control What You Can (Control the Environment)

One fundamental truth we have to accept as parents is that we can't control our kids. We like to think we can, but in reality, it's impossible to control another person by any reasonable means. What we can control is the environment around them—our house.

Controlling the environment works in two ways: by arranging the physical space so kids can successfully do things for themselves and by limiting access to things that are off-limits.

The benefits of this tool abound. It cuts back on entitlement by empowering kids to take on more responsibility rather than expecting to be waited on hand and foot. It fosters capability and independence and frees up your time. And there's more good news: it cuts back on the whining you hear on a daily basis.

PUT IT TO USE

To get your kids making their own breakfast, doing their own laundry and more, you'll need to Control What You Can—your household environment—to fully enable them to take on the tasks. That might mean spending this weekend reorganizing your closets, laundry room, kitchen cabinets and refrigerator so that everything they need is simple to find, ready to use and within reach.

To begin, imagine there are no adults living in the house with your kiddos—how would you have to rearrange the physical environment to set them up for success? Then make any necessary adjustments. Things like labeling toy bins for easy cleanup, investing in kid-sized lawn tools and putting healthy snacks at eye level in the pantry can help your kids take care of themselves and their domain independently.

For instance, if you'd like your five-year-old to be able to fix her own cereal and milk for breakfast, keep the bowls, spoons, napkins and cereal at her level. Buy a child-sized pitcher and fill it with milk so that she doesn't have to struggle with a full gallon. For a teen who's old enough to do his own laundry, not only should you train him in the task (see chapter 3 for more details), you should also make sure he can always find the detergent, stain treatment, a laundry basket and anything else he might need. Even a two-year-old can choose her own outfit if closet rods are installed at the right height—and what a huge boost of personal power! Your whole family will benefit from a revamped kid-friendly environment.

On your side is the fact that kids are really tuned in to their environment and often love to help out and do grown-up jobs. In fact, parents are often the ones who stop kids from helping, worrying about their doing it wrong or making a mess. When kids are told "You'll make a mess if you pour your own juice" a few too many times, they'll eventually stop trying—and expect us to do for them what they're completely able to do by themselves. (After all, doesn't everyone spill a little juice from time to time?) By empowering them toward greater responsibility by making a few adjustments to the environment, you'll give them a huge boost of confidence, and opportunities to work on important skills.

To use this tool to cut back on your kids' whining and nagging for things that are off-limits, either permanently or at specified times (think about sweets, off-season clothing, video games, computer access past 9:00 p.m., etc.), take another critical look at your house and control the environment with some simple adjustments. Remember: *to see it is to whine for it.* Put the no-nos behind closed doors, password protect them or simply don't bring them into the house, and you won't find yourself having to say no all the time.

"Out of sight, out of mind" applies quite well to the distractible younger set. If you tuck away the video games and lay out puzzles on the coffee table instead, smashing zombies will no longer be the first thing on their minds when they get home from school or the first thing they whine for when they roll out of bed.

Try buying (or making your own) single-serving bags of snack crackers, temporarily putting away board games that commonly incite miniriots, replacing all the ice cream in the fridge with frozen yogurt and storing all off-season clothes in the attic instead of in reachable corners of your kids' closets.

With this tool, you'll soon find that you're able to let down your guard around the house—and even better, your kids will feel more in control of their own world in a positive way.

Tips and Scripts

- Talk to your kids openly about the new setup. Say "You're really growing up—and I'm confident you can take over packing your own lunch every morning all by yourself." Take them on a tour of your arrangement, so they know they can easily access everything they need. If you've decided to rid the house of junk food, however, there's no need to make a giant announcement. Simply wean them off it slowly. Yes, they'll probably miss it, but the answer is easy: "We're all out of cookies. You'll find apples and grapes in the fridge."

- If you've bought kid-sized tools, bins and organizers, expect them to be used. Train your kids in the proper behavior (see chapter 3) and use consequences to follow through. (Consequences are discussed in chapter 5.)

- You might be tempted to toss all the video games, since eight-year-old Harry has a history of pitching a huge fit when his gaming time is over. But you'd be better served starting with something less drastic. Put them all in a cardboard box until homework is done—and if Harry continues to battle you when his thirty-minutes-per-day limit is up, keep them in the box permanently for a few months as he gains the maturity he needs to put them away when it's time. The same goes for other situations, too—start with something less drastic, and work your way up if you need to.

- Remember that younger children, especially, develop new skills at a rapid pace. If last month three-year-old Norah had trouble pouring her own milk even with a kid-friendly pitcher, next month she might be ready to master the skill.

YES, BUT . . .

My kids still nag me for sweets and other things that are off-limits.

This tool is meant to reduce the nagging and no-ing that goes on in your home, but it won't quell it completely. Remember, just because your child nags or complains about something doesn't mean you have to respond to it. Use the other tools in this chapter to put an end to the whining and nonstop demands.

My kids don't want to take on new responsibilities.

That's all part of the entitlement problem. Your first step is to make sure they *can* manage the tasks, physically, with all the correct-sized tools they need. Many kids will naturally want to fend for themselves once they see it's possible. But for the trickier cases, read on. Throughout the book you'll find strategies for training your kids and holding them accountable.

Un-Entitler: Asked and Answered

This tool is for all the times your child thinks your answer is up for negotiation or pesters you repeatedly with the same request. Whether your eight-year-old is asking to go to the neighborhood pool alone or your fourteen-year-old thinks last night's chocolate cupcakes are a breakfast of champions, they'll likely believe that your resolute no is up for negotiation. After all, best friend Krista can go to the pool by herself, and cupcakes aren't really that different from pancakes, are they? A feeling of entitlement convinces your kids that if they ask you enough, you'll change your mind, especially if they've had success with this in the past.

PUT IT TO USE

The next time your child initiates negotiations over swimming alone, cupcakes or anything else, use Asked and Answered, a tool created by Lynn Lott, MA, MFT, author of *Chores Without Wars* and coauthor of the Positive Discipline series of books. After you've answered her question ("No, it's not safe to go swimming alone") and she comes back five minutes later to ask again, go through these five steps:

> **Step One:** Ask "Have you ever heard of Asked and Answered?" She'll give you a funny look and likely respond no.
>
> **Step Two:** Ask "Did you ask me whether you can go swimming alone?" She'll say yes.
>
> **Step Three:** Ask "Did I answer your question?" This is where you'll get a "Yes, but. . . ." Go straight to the next step without responding.
>
> **Step Four:** Ask "Do I look like the kind of parent [or grandparent or teacher or babysitter] who will change her mind when you ask me the same thing over and over?" Your child will grunt, give you a

dirty look, protest or do any combination of these. She also might
walk away and stop badgering you.

Step Five: If your child asks the same question again, simply respond
with "Asked and answered." Ignore negative reactions until she's
finally taken no for an answer.

Once you've established Asked and Answered, there's no need to respond with anything else when your child challenges your answer. In
fact, if you answer the question again or change your answer, you'll
only encourage her to keep up the badgering in the future.

After you've used this tool once, you can simply say, in a calm and
pleasant voice, "Asked and answered" whenever your child attempts to
change your decision. Pretty soon she'll get the picture that no matter
how many times she asks, the answer is always the same—and she'll
stop asking quite so relentlessly.

Tips and Scripts

- If your child repeatedly makes the same unreasonable request,
  there's no need to answer it with anything but "Asked and answered." She'll learn that going to the pool alone is never up for
  discussion.
- Don't get caught in the trap of offering endless explanations as
  your child tries everything in her power to convince you. "Asked
  and answered" is all the response he needs after your initial
  answer.
- If your child asks a question you don't yet know the answer to—
  for instance, ten-year-old Max wants to camp out in the backyard
  with a friend—it's okay to say "I'll have to think about that. Let me
  get back to you this evening."
- Asked and Answered is most effective when you don't use it for
  every single question or request. Switch it up with the other power-
  diffusing tools throughout the book.

YES, BUT . . .

What if my child makes a reasonable point and I want to change my mind?

Carefully consider your initial answer before you give it. If it's something that might be up for discussion, turn it into a conversation to see if an agreement can be reached. If you need time to think about it (or consult with your spouse), say "I need time to talk it over with your mom. I'll let you know when I have an answer." This will keep you from putting your foot down unnecessarily.

And if your child really does change your mind with some new piece of information, it's okay to switch your answer. Give the green light, but be sure to explain why. Say "It really sounds like you've thought through your plan for walking home from school and a backup plan if anything goes wrong. I have confidence that you can handle it." Your kids will feel empowered when they see that it's not their whining or negotiating that got you to change your mind, but instead their thoughtful consideration and respectful communication style.

I know from experience: it can be *really* hard to say no to our kids. Let's revisit the examples from the first part of the chapter, apply a few of the tools and see what it might look like for John's and Cadence's parents to avoid giving in.

Scenario 1: John and the Dinosaur Cup

The scene is the grocery store. You've got your kids, a grocery list a mile long and dozens of other people who are just as desperate as you are to get home for dinner. Then the tantrum happens (you're not going to buy the overpriced plastic dinosaur cup for three-year-old John that the store has so conveniently placed in the breakfast cereal aisle). As the tantrum ramps up, you tune in to your grocery list. You've warned John in advance that you're not going to pay attention to whining and that you expect him to use his calm voice. While you're prepared to park your cart and take John and his sister outside to cool down, you're relieved when John recognizes your glazed-over, unresponsive eyes and tries a different tactic: negotiating. To which you respond with an "Asked and answered." He knows what that means, too, having tested you on it several times already. He grumbles, and you gently start a game of I Spy, as you expertly wheel away from the dinosaur cup (figuring that Controlling Your Environment can also work in the grocery store), having grabbed your breakfast cereal at lightning speed. Soon he's helping you find the pasta, and the dinosaur cup is (mostly) forgotten.

Then you hand John and his sister each a few whole-wheat crackers you'd stashed in your purse. You know they're hungry and have had a long day, and that John's tantrum is a signal he's at the end of his rope. You grab the necessities—involving them in your decisions on which apples and how many plums to buy to help boost their significance and prevent future episodes—and hightail it out of the store.

Scenario 2: Cadence and the Designer Handbag

Sixteen-year-old Cadence is apparently the only girl in her group of friends without a designer handbag. You know that's not true, but she nevertheless reminds you of this statistic every day. You realize it's time to take action. You warn her in advance that you will no longer pay attention to whining about what she doesn't have, and instead you'll simply walk away (Sail Out of the Wind). You also work on cutting back on your own obsession with jewelry, and model healthy ways to take an interest in fashion (and expand the interest to things other than acquiring more fashion—for instance, learning how to make jewelry or checking out fashion design magazines from the library to explore a potential career). On one of your mother-daughter trips to the mall, she falls in love with a handbag that's far beyond your price range (or her allowance). She begins to beg and plead, even after your initial no, so you end the negotiation with an "Asked and answered." You ask if she'd like to put it on a wish list for the next holiday (she does). Meanwhile, you find some to-die-for sunglasses that would be perfect for vacation next month and they're even on sale. But you opt to put them on *your* wish list, even though you can afford them, to model that it's okay to leave a store empty-handed. Later, as you enjoy smoothies at the food court, Cadence finds herself having a good time despite her "ugly old purse." And you find that you feel pretty good about your shopping trip, too.

The tools in this chapter work together to help you give up giving in to your kids—and the sooner you put them in place, the sooner you'll start seeing the results you're looking for. In no time at all, your kids will get used to the new arrangement and quit pestering quite so much. Can you imagine a trip to the store without endless requests for new toys, gadgets and junk food? It's entirely within your reach with a little work (the tools in chapter 8, Money and Sense, will help, too)—and a great start toward ridding your home of the entitlement epidemic.

3

They're Not Helpless

At three years old, Kyle had never put on his own shoes. He always had help—shoes can be tricky. At four, he had never put together a puzzle all by himself—he'd get frustrated, so Mom or Dad or the baby-sitter gave him a hand every time. At five, he'd never poured himself a glass of anything or a bowl of cereal. He'd just make a mess, so his parents did it for him. He still rode with training wheels even when nearing the end of his sixth year. He wasn't scared, but his parents were afraid he'd fall and get hurt. At seven, Kyle had homework most nights, but had never completed so much as a worksheet without the careful eye of his parents watching every stroke of his number two pencil, just to make sure he was getting it right. At eight, he was still unable to make his bed, and by nine he was entirely unwilling, so his parents gave up trying to get him to. Kyle at age ten looked away whenever a grown-up asked him a question and practically whispered his responses. Eleven-year-old Kyle needed help writing thank-you notes. Twelve-year-old Kyle was still deemed incapable of taking out the trash—what if he spilled it or didn't wash his hands afterward? At thirteen, his parents cleaned his room for him because they grew tired of reminding him over and over. At fourteen, when Kyle's parents tried to get him to empty the dish-washer, he let the dishes sit in there for two days until his dad finally relented. And at fifteen, his mom got him a paper route, which she did for him most school days so he could sleep longer. When Kyle turned sixteen, his parents decided to shuttle him around instead of teaching him how to drive. They figured he was still too young—after all, he didn't even know his way out of the neighborhood very well. At seventeen, Kyle's mom routinely called his teachers to make sure his grades were good so he could get into a good college. And in Kyle's eighteenth year, his dad outlined all his college application essay questions for him and reviewed every word of what he wrote—after all, getting into college is so competitive. By the time Kyle was an adult, he'd never done a load of laundry, never learned about home finance, never used a map and never scrambled himself an egg. Kyle was, in fact, still a child.

Why We Do What *They* Should Do

We hear about kids who feel entitled to be served at every turn but we don't expect them to grow up in our own house. That's because the process happens so slowly that we barely notice it. Kids naturally start out on a very gradual trajectory from complete dependence to complete independence—but parents unknowingly, and often lovingly, hamper this very important process. The result, as we see in the news all the time, is that kids lack the skills they need—or the desire—to function in the real world. Their parents argue grades on their behalf and eventually secure internships for them; they bring their laundry home from college; they eat fast food three very unsquare meals a day; they ask for help with car payments on a monthly basis; and far too often, they simply give up and move back home, where their needs are, once again, entirely attended to.

I don't think any of us actually wants this for our children. So let's make sure it doesn't happen. In this chapter we'll cover a type of entitlement that doesn't have anything to do with a new video game system or fake-diamond-studded gold sandals: the need to be served.

We all talk the talk about kids nowadays who never feel the need to lift a finger to help around the house or face the pressure and hard work that come along with real life. But do we really know what's going on?

It's true that we're only a couple of generations away from a lifestyle that required kids to put in long hours working the family farm or contributing heavily to the family in other ways. But how did we jump from kids who rose before dawn to milk cows, to children who can't be bothered to move aside so we can vacuum the rug under their feet?

The change is certainly due in a major way to the me generation mentality, as described in the first chapter. Kids who have constantly been told they are special expect to be treated like royalty. What's more, media and our culture as a whole are all too anxious to tell kids they needn't worry about anything except their own pleasure. But the other fundamental change is simply the fact that we actually don't *rely* on children's contributions the way people used to. We won't starve this winter if our kids don't weed the garden.

But that's not to say parents are not frazzled by busy lifestyles—and that our kids don't need to be pulling their weight. We may not be canning apples and drying beans to eat in February, but we are involved in the PTA, stressful jobs and our kids' activities. So while we will survive our busy schedules, we would certainly appreciate our kids' pitching in once in a while. Beyond that, children actually do need to know how to navigate a successful adult life, and they'll be paralyzed if they don't get plenty of practice in childhood. We're not doing our kids—or ourselves— any favors if we help them too much. While parents of over-entitled kids often shoulder all their children's responsibilities in a well-meaning effort to provide them with a carefree, magical childhood, they're actually depriving their youngsters of a fulfilling adulthood.

> Never do for a child what he can do for himself.
> A "dependent" child is a demanding child. . . . Children
> become irresponsible only when we fail to give
> them opportunities to take on responsibility.
> —Rudolf Dreikurs and Margaret Goldman,
> *The ABC's of Guiding the Child*

I know what you're thinking: surely hanging up our kids' towels after their shower for them or drawing a horse on a poster for 4-H can't possibly entitle them to a lifetime of the royal treatment. After all, don't we all shove our kids' hands into mittens when we're running out the door, fill out forms for them at the dentist or even do the lion's share of a finicky dinosaur diorama project for school? In an ideal world, we'd be cheering our kids on from the other room but enabling them to do the work themselves. Reality strikes, however, and the ten-year-old has a head cold and loads of other homework, so we consent to color tiny prehistoric plants and tape them in place. And we know the hygienists will be annoyed if our thirteen-year-old is still penciling in her address while in the dental chair (and dotting every "i" with a heart). It's not that it's wrong to help out. The important thing is to set our kids up for success by enabling them to contribute to the family and to their own lives whenever possible, and building the feelings of belonging and significance that are so crucial to our kids' emotional well-being.

Of course, most parents of over-entitled kids aren't proud that their seven-year-old can't seem to remember to say thank you, or that the seventeen-year-old hasn't made a meal from start to finish. And it's not that the kids intended to keep their heads in the sand. This type of entitlement is usually the product of well-meaning moms and dads who are very concerned for their kids' safety, comfort, convenience, self-esteem and so on. So how do parents commonly miss the boat on the job of raising capable, responsible, independent kids? There are plenty of reasons and traps that even the most conscientious parents fall into. Let's take a look and put an end to them.

First, we should note that it's entirely possible that our kids don't take on these tasks because they feel entitled to be waited on hand and foot, in the same way they feel entitled to an expensive phone plan. As we saw in the previous chapter, these kids have been coddled since birth—with the best of intentions—and aren't used to pulling their own weight, making their own decisions or doing their own dirty work. Parents commonly make excuses for them: "Jordan was late because he was out late last night and I didn't want to wake him" or "Cora is too little to be expected to remember her gym shoes" or do the work themselves. It doesn't take much of this special treatment to teach kids that they shouldn't have to step up. Someone will be there to take care of them, every single time. Even to the point of being ridiculous—from spoon-feeding a two-year-old to running a fourteen-year-old's class president campaign for her. In fact, kids *love* to be waited on hand and foot. Here's another page from the Entitled Kids Manual:

ENTITLE ME! TOOL: PERSONAL SERVANT

No one likes to load the dishwasher, take out the trash or dust the furniture—there's too much other fun stuff to do. And if you don't want to,` you shouldn't have to! With Personal Servant, you can have your parents jumping to do what you ask—or better yet, doing everything for you without your having to so much as say the word. It might take a little work at first, but soon your days will be filled with fun!

Put It to Use

Turning your parents into Personal Servants won't happen overnight, but the task is well worth the effort. First, use Whining (from the previous chapter) to make a big stink about whatever your parents ask you to do—no matter how small. Pick up the napkin you dropped on the floor? "But why can't *you* do it?" Use the hose to water the bushes? "I don't *want* to!" Remember to whine *every time* or it'll take longer for the tool to work.

Whenever your parents find a way to convince you to do something, negotiate every step and act really annoyed. "Fine, I'll water the bushes if you bring the hose from the backyard" or "I'll pick up the napkin but I won't put it in the trash." Make it sound like your parents are asking you to fly to the moon, and pretty soon they'll take you seriously.

Then, be sure to take *forever* to do the job. It's even better if you

---

can make your parents late for something by not getting your job done or making them stand there and nag you every step of the way.

Fighting back every time will really wear your parents down. But this final tactic will seal the deal: you need to do the job badly every time. When you load the dishwasher, leave tons of chunky food or melted cheese all over the plates so they'll never get clean. Leave water all over the bathroom floor when you clean the tub. Let your parents see you not wash your hands after emptying the trash or not cleaning up after the dog. Pretty soon, your parents would rather do all the work themselves, rather than face the chore of asking you! And if they ask you if you think they're your Personal Servant? Don't say a word. It's best not to let them in on the plan.

Sound like anyone in your house? A Personal Servant mind-set is a hallmark of an entitlement problem, but it's entirely curable. Kids use it because it works—wouldn't most of us find it easier to clean up after our kids than to make them do it? But just as you can un-entitle your kids from a handbag more expensive than yours, you can un-entitle them from making housework a spectator sport.

Sometimes our kids expect special treatment because they feel entitled to it—but sometimes we give them no other option. By doing everything for them and discouraging their efforts, we tell them, "You'll only mess it up" or "You're too little to be any help." Put yourself in your kids' shoes—literally.

Five-year-old Sydney is learning to tie her shoes. Meanwhile, her dad is trying to get her out the door to the new exhibit at the science museum before the lines are monstrous. Sydney fumbles with a knot. "Come on, sweetie, do you want me to do that for you?" Sydney doesn't. She slowly and deliberately starts over. This time she loses a loop. "Honey, we need to get going. Let me help." Sydney jerks away, insistent. She starts over again. Dad checks his watch. Finally, Sydney finishes the first shoe and then starts on the second. The laces get twisted. Dad's doing his best to be patient but is picturing the crowds. We're all human, aren't we? "Hurry up! We need to get going!" Finally, Sydney gives up. "*You* do it," she tells her dad. We don't know whether she's more exasperated with her laces or her dad's impatience—either way, she's learned more about the fact that Dad does things better and faster than she does than about tying her shoes.

Then there's nine-year-old Brady offering to wash the family's car on a bright Saturday morning. He asks his mom if he can. "I don't know, honey—can you even reach the top of the car?" she questions. "I could use a step stool!" Brady responds. "But can you remember to wash all the windows—inside and out, the right way?" she wonders. "I'll remember!" he says. "It barely needs washing—I did it just a week or so ago," Mom mentions, thinking the whole project is going to be more of a big mess than a big help. "Do you even know where all the supplies are?" Brady begins to doubt his abilities, as well as his desire to do the job. "Um, I'm not sure. Maybe I'll just go over to Tristan's house instead."

And at thirteen, Adrianna wants to be trusted to babysit her three-year-old sister at home while her mom runs an errand. "I'll watch her, Mom, don't worry!" she assures her mom. "I don't know—you're awfully young to be babysitting a toddler all by yourself. I'm not sure that's a good idea," Adrianna's mom responds. "It's okay, I can get help from Mrs. Howell across the street if I need anything. And you won't be gone long, and I know where everything is." Mom still isn't sure. "She's awfully young, and still potty training. I think I'd better take her along. Maybe when both of you are a little bit older, then you can babysit her."

If we faced doubt, impatience and the third degree every time we wanted to take on a new task, we'd probably give up, too. We certainly wouldn't feel empowered or motivated to take matters into our own hands. Pretty soon, kids take these messages seriously. And phrases or actions that say "Be careful!" or "Let me do that!" are tremendously discouraging to kids, who are, quite rightly and naturally, grasping for independence. After hearing these phrases over and over, they begin to lack confidence in their abilities to take on new challenges or solve problems.

And then there's the fact that because our lives are so full, we often can't find the time to help our kids take on new challenges. We're chronically running late—so the bathroom really does need to be cleaned *this minute* before our houseguests arrive, and we can't spend a Saturday afternoon showing our teen the ins and outs of lawn care, because we have to attend our boss's kid's birthday party or take the Boy Scouts camping. These are all good things, but we can't let them rob our kids of the opportunities they so greatly need.

And finally, we'd be remiss not to pay proper homage to the fact that many kids *hate* washing windows, changing a tire, discussing a lost book with the librarian and the like. While they might appreciate these skills later on, chances are they won't enjoy practicing them in the short term. Even if they do think running the lawn mower or wrapping the family's holiday presents is fun at first, they're likely to lose interest and want to ditch the tasks next time you ask for help. So in order to give our kids the gift of independence, we have to use our tools to quell the whining (or at least ignore it) and motivate them to pull their weight, persevere and work as a team. (I won't leave you hanging—there are plenty of tools to do just that!)

DITCH THE DON'T

"Don't leave your towel on the floor." "Don't talk like that to Grandma." "Don't wear your shoes in the house." We so easily tell our kids what not to do, but in so doing, we leave our kids in the tricky position of having to double process our request. First, they have to remember not to wear their shoes in the house, and then they have to figure out what to actually do (hang the towel on the hook, put your shoes on the shoe rack, "Why don't you tell Grandma about the giant worm you found outside?"). Next time you're tempted to use a "don't," switch it to a "do." Your kids will more quickly learn the positive behavior you were looking for in the first place.

How Too Much Helping Hurts

When we do for kids what they can do for themselves, we rob from them the extremely rewarding opportunities to learn from their mistakes, work toward and achieve a goal, tackle a challenge, collaborate, take pride in their work and build confidence for taking on future challenges. We also rob from them the crucial feelings of belonging and significance—both of which are bolstered by contributing to the family—they crave on a regular basis. Kids raised without these rich experiences will be less likely to put themselves out in the future and work through obstacles—or even leave home, where they have it so easy. What a shame!

A shame becomes a tragedy when it reaches epidemic proportions—like the entitlement bug that's raging through our families. We're at risk for facing a generation's worth of young people who can't hold a job, manage their finances, vote their opinion or nurture a relationship. After all, jobs take work (sometimes yucky work), finances are confusing, politics are boring and relationships are complicated. It's easier to play video games all day while someone else worries about all that—and more fun, too. Entitled kids turn into entitled adults who continue to want the world handed to them on a silver platter. Except they're not so cute anymore.

Kids who are constantly helped gradually fall behind in the ability to look after themselves in practical, everyday matters. While folding and putting away laundry, for example, seems simple to us, it actually takes plenty of practice to learn to do the job efficiently and effectively. Same with a hundred other daily household tasks. If they don't learn the fundamentals of these jobs in childhood, they'll feel overwhelmed in a one-bedroom apartment in a few years—or turn it into laundry mountain, dish mountain and the entire range of undone chore disasters. And then there are the not-so-common jobs, such as changing air filters, finding the best rate on car insurance or opening a bank account. It's not that these can't be learned in adulthood, but won't our eighteen-year-old feel empowered when she's left home if she can already navigate tasks like these? When parents miss opportunities to teach kids important life skills—everything from behaving at a wedding to managing credit cards to unclogging a toilet—they set their kids up to be rather helpless later on. All this extra service does kids no real favors. Not only do we entitle our kids but we make it harder and harder for them to escape their condition since they lack the real-world experience they need to take on their own responsibilities.

In fact, giving kids too much help with things they can and should do for themselves not only robs them of opportunities, it also erodes their self-confidence. If you've never so much as made a sandwich, you'll be overwhelmed by the proposition of planning healthy meals, shopping for food and cooking them for yourself when you're on your own. It's easier to pick up takeout—every night. And if you've never had a difficult conversation with a teacher about a grade, you'll quit your job down the road rather than face the troubling task of asking for a raise.

Worse, by giving our kids a free ride, we unknowingly tell them that we have little faith in their ability to solve a problem or stick to a task. We would never say that to them outright—but don't we think it a million times a day? We'd always rather face a sink of dirty dishes ourselves than unleash our six-year-old on them. (They'll get broken! The floor will get wet!) We don't actually want to entrust the important duty of setting the table for a dinner party to our accident-prone nine-year-old, do we? (The table will be a disorganized mess and the guests will think I'm a terrible hostess!) It's far less nerve-racking to get our sixteen-year-old a cushy job babysitting our friend's napping children than to send her out job hunting on her own, isn't it? (What if she has to work on a school night? What if she has a mean boss?) So we take matters into our own hands and tell them, "I don't think you can do this the right way, so I'm just going to do it. Go play—at least you're good at that." Ouch! Next time, they'll just pass on the opportunity to take responsibility.

Kids quickly get into the habit of not lifting a finger and feel entitled to a free ride. Children who are expected to empty the silverware tray of a dishwasher, clean up their own spills, negotiate simple disagreements with a sibling and make their bed at age four will be much more likely to do their own laundry, write a polite thank-you note, interview for a job and navigate using a real map by the time they leave for college. And kids who aren't in the habit of contributing will flounder on their own in the real world, where the amount of work required far surpasses the time for play. Their relationships will be affected, too. Kids who aren't used to putting in the time will add plenty of stress to future roommate, romantic and spouse situations. Would you want to share space with someone who didn't understand what is meant by "It's your turn to clean the bathroom this week"?

Along those lines, if we don't allow our kids to contribute to the family, we erode their feelings of belonging. How can you belong to a group if your most meaningful role is that of couch warmer?

The line between simply helping our kids out when they need it and letting them get away with a free ride can seem like a very thick gray one. So how do you know if you have a problem? You might have a free-ride entitlement problem at your house if:

- Your kids constantly expect you to do things for them that they can easily do themselves.
- You ask your kids to help out with something and they rarely do— or it takes an inordinate amount of time (or a bribe or a reward) to get them to cooperate.
- You often find the need to rescue your kids from their commitments since they so often feel overwhelmed.
- Your kids rarely seem genuinely appreciative of your help—since they *expect* your help all the time, they're not grateful for it.

Helpful Helping

If you're like most parents, your head is probably spinning right now. Is it okay to straighten your kids' rooms every so often before company comes? Or walk your tenth grader through her economics assignment to help her gain a better understanding? When is it helpful to help, and when does it become too entitling?

The tools that follow will help you train your kids to take on everyday tasks—and motivate them to complete their responsibilities. When they're actively helping with regular contributions, you'll no longer feel so put-upon when you're cycling everyone's laundry through on a weekly basis, because you know they're taking the load off your back in other ways. And when you see this balance start to take shape, you'll know when your kids are asking too much ("Mommy, I left my princess pony in my room, can you please get it for me?") and when their requests are legitimate ("My alarm clock lost power in the thunderstorm during the night and I'm running late—can you pleeeaasssseee pack my lunch?").

If your child does cross a line (like asking you to drop what you're doing and retrieve a princess pony from an upstairs bedroom so she doesn't have to budge from the family room), simply say "That sounds like something you can do yourself." Then, use the tools from chapter 2 (Sail Out of the Wind, Asked and Answered, etc.) to deflect any further inquiries on the subject. As an alternative, you can let your child know what *would* be reasonable. If he wants help finding a missing puzzle piece, for instance, tell him, "Sure, I can keep an eye out for it," so you're neither scouring the house for the next twenty minutes until it magically appears in his pocket nor outright denying him *any* assistance.

Be sure to consider the situation when gauging how much you should help your children on a day-to-day basis. It's certainly not out of line to help a three-year-old with a raging ear infection into her coat and shoes as you're headed to the doctor or to aid your eleven-year-old in scooping up handfuls of the cereal he accidentally spilled all over the kitchen floor. As a rule of thumb, it's okay to help if:

- You'd help an adult in a similar situation in a similar way.
- Your child truly lacks the skill to complete the task on her own—either because she's not developmentally ready or because she

hasn't learned. In the second instance, use Take Time for Training (page 73) to teach her in the near future.

- If your help is within reason. Work to find good balance of work and free time for your kids and family as a whole.
- There are special circumstances (illnesses or something far beyond your child's control). But if these happen too often, you may have an entitlement problem. A minor head cold can't always be a reason for an eight-year-old to get out of practicing the piano. Likewise, particularly difficult math problems shouldn't mean that Mom completes the assignment by herself.

The First Eighteen Years

While we all make mistakes and let things slip, doing things for our kids becomes an entitlement *problem* when it happens all the time or becomes a pattern. As a rule of thumb, remember that ideally, by the time your kids leave your house, they should have at least a little experience—and sometimes a lot—with *every single thing* you manage for your home or family, from performing simple car maintenance to navigating health insurance to scheduling activities to avoiding food-borne illnesses by cleaning out the fridge every so often. It's a lot easier for them to get practice with household tasks in their own home, benefiting from your experience, than on their own.

On a daily basis, this looks like expecting your kids to perform age-appropriate tasks in self-care, household jobs, schoolwork, relationships and all the rest. You'll find a chart as part of the second tool (Family Contributions) in this chapter to help you figure out where your kids can be helping. Other tools will help you get cooperation to ensure that teeth get brushed, the dog gets walked and that there's plenty of quality time for homework to get done.

As your kids grow, you'll need to actively look for more opportunities to involve them in managing the household and their own lives. Once you've become more mindful of your kids' contributions and independence, you'll see more and more things for your kids to take on. Childhood lasts eighteen years for a reason: there's so much to learn! You'll also find that your kids will gradually accept their important role in the home as status quo, and you won't face quite as many arguments about who should dust the furniture or weed the garden.

You can also encourage independence in other ways. For instance, the next time you find yourself wanting to say "You'll slice your finger off!" when your four-year-old asks to help chop vegetables for dinner, instead offer to let him tear lettuce. When five-year-old Sydney wants to tie her own shoes, as in the example on pages 64–65, do your best to bite your tongue and wait through all the start overs. As for nine-year-old Brady and his idea to wash the car, so what if he doesn't do a perfect job? Encourage his desire to help out, even if you end up washing the top or digging out the soap and bucket for him. And even if you're not comfortable with Adrianna home alone with her little sister while you run errands, find a way to let her contribute on terms you can both agree to—for instance, letting Adrianna babysit while you have coffee with the neighbor across the street. Yes, you're inconvenienced now— but the dividends will pay off down the road as your children assume more independence and willingly take on trickier tasks.

And be sure to catch your child in the right when she lends a hand voluntarily (or without complaining) around the house. Let her over-hear you tell your spouse, "Maggie really saved me some time this after-noon by putting away the Halloween decorations!" You can use Control the Environment from chapter 2 to help prep your house for little help-ing hands and further encourage your kids to take on new responsi-bilities. And of course, you can take every opportunity to make it fun—perhaps a special bathroom-cleaning playlist will lighten the load a little.

Are you all set to un-entitle your kids from a free ride at home? The tools in this chapter will not only help you get them off on the right track but also motivate them to get the job done. Your little ones will gain independence, confidence and so much more as they tackle tasks and learn real-world skills. And you might just regain your lazy Sunday afternoons.

Un-Entitler: Take Time for Training

A fifteen-year-old who does his own laundry? Who cooks dinner for the family every Sunday night? Who balances his own checkbook to keep track of his income from the computer work he does for the neighbor's small business? Whose child is this? While this situation sounds magical, it's not—it happens from years of taking time for training. Even little things we take for granted, like making a piece of toast, can be overwhelming for a young child. Picture this, for instance:

You're six years old and you've never made a piece of toast. In fact, toast is more mystical than practical—you've seen bread go in, but how do you make sure toast comes out? And then what? You'd like to make yourself a piece, but you have more questions than answers. How do you get it out of the toaster when it's done? How do you even know when it's done? And what about the toppings? You know you prefer butter and honey to jam most days, but when it comes to actually getting them onto the toast, the honey is almost gone and hard to squeeze, and the butter is all chunky because it's been in the fridge. The toast gets torn up as you try to spread cold butter, and you drop both the knife and the toast on the floor (facedown). Do you start over or just give up? Or ask Dad to make it for you?

Everyday tasks like this are simple to us with our vast experience, but the number of tiny decisions to be made really add up (and besides, aren't cold butter and sticky honey still a challenge for us all?). The same goes for putting away laundry, uploading photos and watering plants—we all had to learn these skills at one time or another.

A key step to reversing our kids' notions that we need to do everything for them is to empower them to do it themselves. Use Control What You Can from chapter 2 to set up a household environment that invites everyone to participate. In tandem with those efforts, use Take Time for Training to build your kids' confidence when it comes to anything from cleaning the microwave to staying safe during a tornado to choosing a new cell phone plan.

This tool is power packed for ridding your house of the entitlement epidemic. Yes, you and your child will be spending some quality time with the toilet plunger together, but it's also a way to teach them more efficient routines, how to lose the whiny voice, the manners you'd like them to use when your boss comes over for dinner, how to make a good first impression and everything else they need to know for a successful, independent adulthood. When we do our job training our kids, we'll see dramatic jumps in our kids' levels of self-sufficiency and responsibility. At high school graduation, we'll feel confident that our kids will, actually, be prepared to survive and thrive without us *still* nagging them to put their dirty laundry in the hamper.

You'll love the results you'll see with this tool. Soon, your kids will be feeling independent and enabled instead of entitled.

PUT IT TO USE

The first time you use this tool for each child, choose an age-appropriate task that you think they might enjoy. The list at the end of this tool has some suggestions. Consider your kids' personalities—a six-year-old who loves anything loud might be thrilled to get to push around the vacuum, while a fourteen-year-old with an eye for style would enjoy learning to properly—and artistically—set the table for a special occasion.

Find a time to train when both you and your child are low on stress and there will be minimal distractions. Learning to sweep floors properly right before company comes over would probably not be an ideal situation. Then, develop a plan. Break up large jobs into smaller steps for young kids, and be sure you have all the tools for the task handy.

Dive in! Start training and encourage every success (see more about encouragement in chapter 7). Don't make your child feel guilty for not helping out before and remember there's no such thing as a dumb question. In fact, go out of your way to explain the why behind everything from tossing out expired mayonnaise even though it hasn't developed green fuzz yet to the reasons we don't just hide spilled peas under the kitchen rug. Recognize that both you and the child will make mistakes and keep the mood light.

Once you've built your kids' confidence and gotten them excited about learning new things, continue to train them to complete tasks that will help take responsibility off your back. Also, be on the lookout for future training opportunities—as your kids grow, they'll find themselves in new situations and able to learn more challenging skills. Consider making it a goal to train young kids on one new task (or experience, or behavior) each week. One per month is reasonable for older kids.

Tips and Scripts

- Marketing is everything for this tool. If you treat it like a drag, so will your kids. Encourage them that they can take on these new responsibilities since they're really growing up, and make sure they know you have complete confidence in their abilities.
- When you use this tool, make sure you and your child are both well rested and fed and in a positive frame of mind. You'll need to be able to communicate patiently and calmly even if powdered laundry detergent ends up scattered to the four corners of your laundry room floor, or half the still-growing carrots get pulled from the garden while half the weeds remain.
- Occupy siblings elsewhere so there's no added pressure on your child. Both older and younger siblings can cause distractions and be less than supportive when your child makes mistakes.
- The first couple of times you use this tool, be sure to choose something they'll be excited about. Once they realize you're not trying to ruin their lives, they'll be more willing to take on the not-so-savory tasks.
- For young kids, teach a new skill over several sessions and move on to the next step only when they're ready.

- Be creative and make it fun. Dolls and action figures can help role-play with young kids as you teach table manners or conflict resolution (perhaps T. rex can even be convinced to set the table). Then switch roles, and have T. rex teach *you* where the napkins go.
- Whatever you do, don't criticize! You'll put your child on the defensive and set her back. Instead, encourage any bit of progress you see or even a helpful attitude.
- Once your child has mastered a self-care task, hold him to it. When he learns how to make his bed, tie his shoes, wrap birthday presents and so on, he should always be expected to. Other jobs can be rotated among family members, but ensure that each child has the opportunity to practice what they learn regularly.
- Remember that this tool can be used for responsibilities and skills beyond the household. Think about training kids in everything from interviewing for a job to getting the car inspected to respectfully disagreeing with an adult.

YES, BUT . . .

My child doesn't want to learn new responsibilities.

Remember that you don't have to train your kids in household tasks only—this tool can be for anything. The first few times you train your child, make sure it's something he is interested in (and that you're able to do!). Cake decorating? Pounding nails? Basic self-defense? Once your child has seen that training can be fun and produce useful skills, she might be more open to learning things that will help you out around the house.

And when you really do have to teach Shower Cleaning 101, for instance, try to find ways to make it interesting—like letting your child put on his swim trunks to do the job. You could also motivate him by reminding him that once he's learned how to make a shower shine, he'll soon be ready for other tasks that are more interesting—washing the car, for instance, or baking muffins. For the truly reluctant learner, offer to let him keep a list of responsibilities he'd like to learn and alternate them with some he's not as excited about. If, however, you're considering rewards or bribes, think again. They may seem like a good idea at the time, but this kind of practice always backfires down the road. We'll talk more about the perils of rewards in chapter 7.

Keep in mind that once your kids have gotten used to learning new things and contributing to the household, they'll accept the added responsibility as the new norm. They'll also get a kick out of being able to do grown-up things—not to mention a huge boost of positive significance. When they recognize these wholesome payoffs, they'll be less likely to drag their feet.

Once I've trained my child to do a task, it loses its luster and she never wants to do it again. Sometimes I can't even get her to finish it in the first place.

You mean you don't love scrubbing the toilet on a weekly basis? All jokes aside, you can hold your kids to their commitments and contributions using several of the tools following this one in this chapter, as well as others throughout the book. Again, your kids won't enjoy painting a wall after the first few strokes, but that doesn't change their need to finish the job.

Un-Entitler: Family Contributions

What happens when a free-ride situation gets a bit out of hand? I once worked with a mom who had three teenage boys. She came to me for coaching because her kids balked at any kind of work—from cleaning their rooms to getting part-time jobs. She told me that the kids didn't want to help out around the house, preferring to play video games instead (wouldn't we all?). She nagged, she reminded, she yelled, and they apologized, but nothing changed, and she and her husband ended up doing all the work. It soon became clear that Mom had never really expected them to lift a finger—in fact, she had been pampering them and picking up after them since they were toddlers. These boys had Mom well trained. Eventually, the housework became too much for Mom and Dad to handle. Their solution? They hired a housekeeper to come in three times a week to clean up after the boys. Kind of an expensive free ride, if you ask me, even though the family had the means. And since most of us can't afford to hire extra help, we instead fall into the nagging, reminding and yelling cycle—or canceling our weekend plans to do it ourselves. While it's easy to chuckle at this story, we also know it's easy to see how this could happen. After all, much of the time it's simpler to do the job ourselves than convince our kids to do it. Pretty soon, that becomes our lifestyle. And with our busy lives outside the home, how can we keep track of what happens inside? Enter entitled children who think the world revolves around them.

One of the best tools for avoiding the it's-all-about-me mentality, and getting the work done around the house, is Family Contributions. These are the responsibilities that belong to each member of the family, for the good of the family. Without everybody contributing, the home wouldn't function.

Essentially, these are chores—but they're also so much more. According to the late H. Stephen Glenn, PhD, the difference between a chore and a contribution is the *difference it makes to someone else*. When kids get used to acting as a team to keep the household running, they not only achieve a great sense of belonging and significance, they also lose a little bit of the I'm-the-center-of-the-world attitude that plagues entitled youth. Your kids will learn teamwork and life skills at the same time, as well as the expectation that everyone has something to contribute. Not only will this give them a big boost of positive power and capability, but it'll go a long way toward curing feelings of entitlement. They'll also learn to maintain a base level of cleanliness and organization (future spouses will thank you), and develop problem solving, resourcefulness, perseverance and many additional valuable skills.

PUT IT TO USE

With this tool, the earlier you start, the better. Ideally, your kids will be helping out with assigned, regular contributions, as soon as they're old enough to match socks. But even if your youngest is of legal driving age, you can set up the expectation that they'll be helping out.

First, develop an age-appropriate list of contributions you think your kids can handle (you can use the list at the end of this tool for suggestions). Think about jobs that need to get done routinely or things you could really use a hand with. To start, you'll need at least a couple of contributions each child can do on a daily or weekly basis. For example, a four-year-old might be responsible for making her bed, putting away her clean laundry and setting the table for dinner every night. A nine-year-old could be required to clean the bathroom counters every week, take the dog out twice a day and change his own sheets. And a seventeen-year-old may be asked to prepare a family dinner every Tuesday, empty wastebaskets and put out the garbage every collection day and shuttle a younger sibling back and forth to soccer practice.

CHILD'S NAME	DAILY JOBS	WEEKLY JOBS
Jeremy—age ten	Make bed, walk dog after school, clear dinner dishes and help put food away.	**Wednesday:** Take trash bins and recycling to the curb **Saturday:** Rake leaves **Sunday:** Dust and vacuum bedroom
Becca—age four	Make bed, unload silverware from dishwasher, feed the dog, set the table	**Tuesday:** Empty small trash cans **Saturday:** Fold towels and match socks **Sunday:** Wipe down bathroom sinks and countertops with a disposable wipe

Tell your kids about the new system. Say that since we all enjoy the privileges of a safe house, good food and warm clothing, we all need to contribute to keep the family running. And be real—your kids know you won't toss them out on the street, so there's no need to make it sound like you will. Then, use Take Time for Training to teach new tasks, if your child has yet to learn them.

You can add to and remove contributions from your child's list on a weekly, monthly or as-needed basis—but personal-care items (making a bed, putting away one's laundry) should remain once your child has learned them. It's also a good idea to include a task or two that helps the whole family, so kids can reap the benefits of contributing to the greater good.

In addition to regular contributions, you can ask your kids to help out with special jobs, or just when you need an extra hand. For instance, you should be able to ask a playing child to find a good stopping point and take ten minutes to fold the towels. Likewise, you can expect a teenager to work raking and bagging leaves into her weekend plans.

Now, I know you're thinking it: "How in the world am I going to convince Jordyn to empty the dishwasher *every single day?*" Relax. The next two tools will actually make this easier than doing the job yourself. I promise.

And finally, fight the urge to pay or reward your child for completing his contributions. A job well done is a reward in itself, and rewards actually erode the positive payoffs such as pride in one's work, working as a team and more. We'll talk more about the detriments of rewards later on; for now, help your kids understand that family contributions are part of living under your roof.

Tips and Scripts

- Try to include at least one task a week that your child is likely to enjoy—or at least doesn't flat-out hate.
- Let your kids have some input as to which tasks to take on, and

when or how to complete them. You can ask "Would you rather use a vacuum or a broom to clean the kitchen floor each week?" or "What day would work best for you to mow the lawn every week?"

- Make sure the contributions are reasonable. For instance, if Daniel is supposed to prepare a simple side dish for dinner every night but isn't home from football practice early enough to complete the job before everyone reaches for the cereal out of desperation, table the task until spring. Or if Marla just doesn't have the dexterity or patience to iron shirts, there's no sense in frustrating her. Wait six months or so while she develops a bit more skill.

- Plan for fewer contributions on school days, and extra jobs during the summer and on weekends.

- Be sure to rotate contributions often enough that each child gains the experience to do the task well.

- If your kids want to trade tasks, let them—as long as each child ends up with the capability to do each contribution.

- While you do want your kids to step up to a challenge, be sure not to overload them—especially if they're busy with schoolwork and activities. If your child's schedule leaves virtually no extra room for helping out at home, it might be time to have a serious talk about cutting back on the extracurriculars. Contributing to the family is nonnegotiable in an un-entitled home.

- Keep in mind that when you first begin implementing family contributions, you can expect a lot of pushback. Your kids won't like the new system, but the longer you stick to it, the more accepted it'll become.

- Remember the reason to have your kids contribute to the household is to un-entitle them from a free ride and to take some of the load off your shoulders. Use that newly found time to care for yourself—take a walk, read a book. Not only will you nourish your soul, you'll set a good example for your kids about balance.

YES, BUT . . .

Whenever my kids help out, they just mess it up, and it's more work for me.

I hear you. That's where training comes in. If your kids still have trouble completing a job correctly after they've been trained, it might be time to reevaluate their skills and try something simpler. If you're confident of their abilities and you're pretty sure they're simply slacking, use the next two tools to hold them accountable for a job well done. So if they spill laundry soap all over while running a white load, be sure they know that completing the task involves leaving a clean washer and dryer for the next user.

Also, bear in mind that when you're just starting to implement family contributions, your kids might show their disapproval by doing sloppy work. Show them that the new system is here to stay, and they'll (eventually) get with the program.

It seems that whenever I want to hold my kids to contributions, something comes up—they get sick, they have a giant project, we have company, etc.

Find small jobs that have to get done no matter what—like dishes, making beds and laundry—and start with those. If your kids never have the thirty minutes it takes to clean the kitchen, break it up into five- or ten-minute tasks (such as wiping out the microwave, disinfecting the sink or tossing the expired food from the fridge). Adjust expectations or shift deadlines for sickness and unforeseen circumstances—but if Thomas has put off a book report until the final night and thinks he doesn't have enough time to sweep the floor, you'll need to hold him to it. He'll be less likely to procrastinate next time.

When it comes to your kids' family contributions, think beyond making the bed. Check out the list below for some ideas and then pick jobs that suit your kids' abilities and development. Be sure to provide appropriate supervision (without being a helicopter), especially for dangerous jobs or the first few times your child words on a task.

AGE-APPROPRIATE TASKS

Two to Three Years Old

Wipe down kitchen chairs and stools with a damp sponge.
Carry in the newspaper or mail with help from parent.
Pick up toys and clothes.
Wash tables and counters with a damp sponge.
Fold washcloths.
Wash vegetables, tear lettuce, stir.
Help set the table—napkins, silverware.
Feed the pets and refill water. (Be sure to provide training and
    measuring cups so kids know just how much food and water
    to offer.)
Help clean own place at the table.
Help put groceries away at kid-friendly level.
Unload spoons and forks from dishwasher and put them in a
    drawer with the help of a step stool.

Four to Five Years Old

Same as previous list, plus:
Wake up using an alarm clock.
Make own bed (use a simple comforter).
Help fold towels and washcloths.
Match socks.
Clean own bathroom sink with wipes.
Water plants (provide training on how much water).
Prepare simple breakfast/lunch and clean up.
Polish silver (wearing gloves).

Empty small trash cans around the house.

Sort white clothes from dark clothes for laundry.

Help with vacuuming, sweeping and dusting.

Transfer clothes from the washer to the dryer.

Dust mop the floor.

Disinfect doorknobs and remote controls.

Use handheld vacuum for spills and messes.

Six to Eight Years Old

Same as previous list, plus:

Wash dishes; load and unload dishwasher.

Prepare simple dishes, such as salads and desserts.

Peel vegetables.

Help change bedsheets and put dirty sheets in laundry.

Pack lunch for school.

Iron cloth napkins.

Fold simple laundry items and put them away.

Dust baseboards.

Vacuum and dust furniture.

Walk pets daily.

Get up in the morning with an alarm clock, and self-manage
    the entire morning routine.

Pull weeds.

Put groceries away.

Nine to Eleven Years Old

Same as previous list, plus:

Change lightbulbs, batteries and other household maintenance.

Fold all of own laundry and put it away.

Clean refrigerator, toilets and other more detailed household
    tasks.

Wash car and vacuum inside of car.

Plant flowers and garden items at change of season.

Assist younger siblings with homework and reading.

Bathe and groom pets.

Gather trash, organize recycling, take trash bins out and perform other weekly trash duties.

Organize closet and drawers monthly.

Twelve to Fourteen Years Old

Same as previous list, plus:

Change bedsheets independently.

Do laundry start to finish.

Iron clothes.

Wash indoor windows and lower outdoor windows.

Mow lawn with supervision, rake leaves, spread mulch.

Help with administrative tasks in parents' business.

Prepare family meal one day a week using a simple menu.

Manage family recycling efforts.

Babysit siblings for short periods with adult nearby.

Have total responsibility for family pets.

Clean shower and tub.

Fifteen to Eighteen Years Old

Same as previous list, plus:

Deep cleaning—garage, attic.

Trim bushes, heavy landscaping.

Babysit independently.

Car maintenance.

Complete meal preparation.

Weekly meal planning.

—Adapted from Kathryn J. Kvols, *Redirecting Children's Behavior*

Un-Entitler: When-Then

If you've ever had the simplest of requests (anything from "Please empty the dishwasher" to "Please remove your muddy boots from the white carpet") get completely ignored, When-Then is the tool for you. Your words will no longer disappear into thin air, and instead your kids will listen and obey as if by magic. How does this amazing tool work? You'll structure your child's less-desirable tasks to occur before a highly desirable activity, like a snack, media time or a ride to a friend's birthday party.

At the same time you'll let your child know that not only are you not his personal servant but also that privileges go hand in hand with responsibilities. You'll nix the idea that he's entitled to coast through life without lending a hand now and then, and you'll go one step further, introducing and supporting the idea that everyone's expected to help, and no one's entitled to slack off.

PUT IT TO USE

First, simply state your reasonable request. It might sound like "Rebecca, could you please help me dust the living room?" If Rebecca jumps up to help or reasonably indicates that she just needs to let her recently polished nails dry, you don't need this tool. If, however, Rebecca has decided that she'd rather act like you don't exist than come near a dust rag, you'll need to restate your request. Calmly and clearly inform her that "*When* you have finished dusting the living room, *then* you may enjoy your phone time for the day." The when-then phrasing is key. Keep it in the same format every time, and your kids will take the cue that *when* you phrase a request like this, *then* you mean business! Here are a few other examples:

- When you finish your family contributions, then you can go over to Miguel's house.

- When you clean up the playroom, then we'll have lunch.
- When you finish your homework, then we'll leave for practice.

After you deliver your When-Then statement, leave the room—or find another way to tune out the "But Moo-oom . . ." that's sure to follow. Ignore protests, whining and negotiations, and be sure to follow through with the *then* part of the tool.

Be aware ahead of time that this tool relies on a desirable then item to get your child moving. This is something *normally occurring* in the future—not a special treat or reward. When you use other tools in this book to give your child a strong sense of significance, you'll get much less pushback from them when you present them with reasonable requests, so you won't need to use a When-Then every time you ask your child to help you gather up the week's library books. At the same time, if you expect an argument, it's helpful if you have a deadline you can live with (like a meal or a privilege your child looks forward to) in mind before the request leaves your lips.

Also, remember that this system leaves a little wiggle room for your kids to do the job on their terms and with their timing. But this is a good thing. Your kids will get a boost of positive significance in deciding to do the task—and when—and then accessing a privilege. If they don't get the job done, it's true that you'll be stuck with it. On the bright side, however, is the knowledge that your child will be much more likely to comply in the future after losing the privilege of playing outside with friends, enjoying a snack or updating her Facebook status. To help repeat offenders get with the program, you'll learn how to effectively set up a system of consequences in chapter 5.

Tips and Scripts

- It's completely fair game to put a deadline in place. Some thens will have a natural deadline—the start of ballet class, for instance. But others will need a limit: lights go out at eight, technology is off-limits after nine, no snacks after four thirty, be inside by dark and so forth.

- Savvy parents learn quickly that they can motivate their kids more easily by making their requests shortly before a normally occurring privilege would be expected. In other words, if you want the front step swept, ask your twelve-year-old twenty minutes before dinner. Then, if you get pushback, state "*When* you've swept the steps, *then* you can join us at the table—but remember, the kitchen closes at six thirty."
- Don't forget to vacate the scene after stating your When-Then; otherwise, you are providing an audience for moaning and groaning.
- It's not okay to use Mind, Body and Soul Time as the then. Your child needs her daily dose of undivided attention, and losing out could create more problems than it solves. You can, however, use other fun activities such as a family bike ride, movie night or board game you were already planning on.
- For younger kids, be sure the then occurs in the near future. Older kids can handle more delay. In general, the bigger the project, the more time you can (and should) allow before the then. For instance, you could tell your fourteen-year-old on a Wednesday, "*When* you've cleaned out the garage, *then* you're free to attend the sleepover on Saturday."
- If you generally ask your kids to help out at specific times every day, you might benefit from a When-Then Routine and a short list of family contributions for each child to complete.

YES, BUT . . .

I can never think of a then.

Next time you pose a request to your child, take the extra minute beforehand to decide what your then will be, if needed. Remember that snacks and meals make great thens (most hungry kids won't want to miss out even on tuna casserole surprise). Media time is also a natural then. Anything you can put a limit on that would be considered a privilege is an option. If you just can't think of anything, you might want to save your request for a different time of day. Alternatively, you can use some of the other power-diffusing tools in chapters 3 and 4 to get the job done.

What if my child complains, whines, fusses or has a total meltdown when I use When-Then?

While When-Then might soon become your favorite tool, it will not be your kids'—power struggles and negotiating have worked in the past to get them out of the tasks you've asked them to do, and they see no reason to change things now. You'll need to completely ignore all complaining, negotiating and disrespectful comments you're bound to receive. Appear completely unfazed, and they'll soon get the point that their bad behavior won't change your mind.

What if she follows me around the house when I try to disengage?

Be unimpressed. As long as you are consistent in ignoring the grumbling and complaining, she'll soon realize there's no point. If she keeps at it, go into the bathroom and close the door, letting her know that you'll be happy to talk once she can have a respectful conversation.

Un-Entitler: Let When-Then Routines Be the Boss

If your day is like most families', many of the battles are concentrated at certain times. I'm talking about morning, after school, homework time and bedtime. Do you dread them even more than your kids do? If so, this is the tool for you.

Let When-Then Routines be the Boss will have your kids taking the responsibility for themselves to brush their teeth, finish their math problems, walk the dog and more—with absolutely no nagging from you. Sound impossible? This homework-bath-bedtime dream is well within your reach.

The problem with these tricky times of the day is the fact that parents not only nag, remind, threaten, yell, etc. to move their (usually highly unmotivated) kids through the motions, stripping the youngsters of any sense of independence and personal power, but they often change the standards midstride. Take bedtime for instance. If lights go out at eight on Monday, but that time migrates to nine thirty by the weekend, what is a kid going to expect the next night? If there are no set standards, kids will decide that bedtime is always up for negotiation.

What's more, if your kids' daily responsibilities aren't on their radar, they feel entitled to a play-all-day lifestyle. Why should they comb their hair, water the plants or study for their spelling test? You can't make them! By putting the ball in their court for these types of activities, however, you keep the responsibility squarely on their shoulders, all while removing the entitled attitude.

When you let When-Then Routines Be the Boss of your kids, you will no longer have to be the bad guy as you attempt to herd your kids through their daily activities. If they push back on washing their face or feeding the dog, you will have the amazing freedom of simply referring them back to their routine and leaving the room before their complaints hit your ears. Ah, bliss.

And even better, once your kids are well established in their routines, they'll gain a huge boost of significance every time they follow it through, and learn that enjoying privileges means keeping up with responsibilities. This novel idea will cripple the entitlement epidemic that's been infecting your house.

PUT IT TO USE

For each nagfest of your day, plan out a routine for your kids to follow. And this is key: the routine has to end with a desirable activity, whether that's breakfast, media time, play time with friends or a ride to soccer practice. Be sure you're not dangling a reward in front of your kids, however (see chapter 7 to learn why rewards do more harm than good).

The desirable activity should be a normally occurring privilege or event, not a treat.

A chart like this can help you plan your day:

THINGS I NAG JESSICA TO DO EACH MORNING: OUR WHENS	THINGS JESSICA ENJOYS IN THE MORNING: OUR THENS
Get dressed	Eat breakfast
Make bed	Play before the bus arrives
Gather backpack and lunch box	
Put on shoes and socks	

Then, let your kids in on the plan. Tell them "You're growing so fast, and you no longer need me to tell you what to do in the morning before school. From now on, you get to be in charge of your own routine. So, *when* you're dressed, your bed is made, your hair is combed and your backpack is ready and waiting by the door, *then* you're welcome at the breakfast table. But the kitchen closes at seven thirty so you have time to brush your teeth and make it to the bus." Or "*When* the dog has been walked, your homework is finished and you've completed your piano practice, *then* you may enjoy your thirty minutes of computer time. But all technology is off-limits after eight p.m." For younger kids, write the routine on a checklist and post it in a logical location (the bathroom mirror, for instance). Use pictures if necessary and set a time limit, using a timer if necessary.

Do a practice run to make sure your kids have plenty of time and know what's expected of them. Make the practice fun and positive— allow plenty of time so no one feels too pressured and avoid nagging. This will get you off to a great start.

And yes, you read that right—your child might miss breakfast. You can bet it'll only happen once or twice, however, before he gets with the program. Resist the urge to hand him a banana on his way out the door, as rescuing him will only mean he'll dawdle and delay in the future. Remember that you're teaching him valuable lessons that will serve him for a lifetime, and that's well worth going hungry for a few hours. Soon, you'll be sipping coffee while your kids efficiently complete their morning tasks, no nagging required. And if your kids aren't motivated by breakfast, or have health needs that absolutely require a balanced meal in the morning, choose something else, like playtime or computer time.

Stick to the routine every day—if you allow negotiation once, your kids will feel entitled to negotiate every time. Of course, special circumstances (a birthday party, a football game, illness, etc.) might occasionally disrupt your routines. If these become common, remember that the routine is in place for a reason. You and your kids will benefit if you can keep your usual schedule most days.

Tips and Scripts

- Keep weeknight and weekend bedtimes the same. Kids' (and adults' for that matter) internal clocks aren't meant for big fluctuations. If you let them stay up late a couple of nights a week, they'll suffer for it Monday—and Tuesday and Wednesday.
- It's okay to enjoy a slightly later bedtime in the summer as long as your kids aren't losing out on any sleep. But keep it consistent each night, or you're opening the door for constant negotiation, not to mention cranky kids.
- The preschool set might enjoy switching roles and practicing their routine by taking you (or Spider-Man) through it.
- After you've trained your kids in the routine, there's no need to nag. Keep any comments limited to "What's your next step in your routine?"

My three-year-old still needs help with a lot of everyday tasks.

Evaluate your routine and make sure it's reasonable—really young kids can handle only a couple of items on a list. Help her along by using colorful pictures, using Control the Environment to keep everything she needs at her level and patiently practicing a few times. If there's a skill she's still working on, make sure you use Take Time for Training to help her along. If she still needs help, you might need to temporarily remove the responsibility from her routine and use other positive-power-boosting tools in chapters 3 and 4 to help move her along.

Un-Entitler: Empathize and Appreciate

So you've finally gotten your kids to help out around the house. Fantastic! But you have yet to figure out how to get them to help without griping, moaning, complaining and all the rest. And frankly, can you blame them? There's not a person alive who actually enjoys dusting baseboards. One strategy is, certainly, to ignore most of the whining that goes on. But for the child who's just letting off a little harmless steam, you can Empathize and Appreciate to help him internalize the fact that he matters, and so does his hard work.

With Empathize and Appreciate, you'll help your child feel the significance of her contribution and take her mind off the negativity. This tool allows you to express understanding of the fact that turning the compost pile does, indeed, stink—as well as your heartfelt appreciation of your child's help. It entitles him to his feelings—including pride in a job well done—but not to skipping out on the task.

PUT IT TO USE

Empathize and Appreciate is a simple tool, but it will make a difference in how your child views her contributions. To use it, you first voice your empathy for your child and then comment on the impact your child is making. Here's an example:

Fourteen-year-old Sara has been asked to dust all the blinds and ceiling fans in the house. She drags her feet all the way to the Swiffer duster but gets to work. Sara soon realizes that everything is hard to reach and she has to drag around a step stool with her to use. She's aching from having to reach so high and getting grumpier by the minute. It's only a matter of time before she mentions, "I hate dusting the fans! The dust keeps falling in my face!" You totally know what she means: you've done the job plenty of times. But you also know she's old enough to handle the responsibility, and there's no need to rescue her. To empathize, say "I know! I hate when that happens! Yuck!" Then, be quick with your appreciation: "You know, I really appreciate your help—I've been so busy getting the garden planted and the windows washed that I haven't had time to do it, and it really helps that you're getting the job done before it gets worse."

Sara knows that she's been heard and her instincts are correct: dusting blinds and ceiling fans are, in fact, crummy jobs. But at least her hard work isn't going unnoticed or underappreciated.

Tips and Scripts

- You can also use this tool without prompting. Say "I know that organizing the pantry is no fun, but I really needed the help. Thanks for pitching in!"
- For particularly arduous tasks, try telling a story about that one time when *you* were painting the storage shed as a kid and ended up with an entirely gray shoe (or whatever). Not only will chatting help pass the time, but your child will recognize that he's not the

first sixteen-year-old in the history of the world to be expected to
complete a difficult job.

- If your child continues whining after you Empathize and Appreciate, it's time to ignore her. Calmly involve yourself elsewhere so
your child doesn't start to think that being asked to mop the
kitchen floor entitles her to stage her own gripefest every time she
does this job.

YES, BUT . . .

Do I have to use this tool every time I ask my kids to do something?

Nope. A thank-you, however, is always warranted

But what about the whining, badgering, complaining, moaning, groaning and my-life-sucks drama?

Oh, the drama! We're all thinking it: how do we handle all the
griping we can anticipate coming from our kids when we start
asking them to lend a hand? The tools we covered in chapter 2
are perfect for cutting through the complaints. Here's how to put
them to use:

BEHAVIOR	TOOL	WHAT TO DO
Whining, complaining	Ignore Undue Attention	This tool will help you ignore your kids' complaints about cleaning dirty dishes and more. Be sure to warn them in advance that you're not going to pay attention to whining and tell them that "Just because you aren't happy with this situation does not mean I'm going to change my mind."

BEHAVIOR	TOOL	WHAT TO DO
Negotiating	Asked and Answered	If your kids try to get you to do their work for them, simply say no. Then use Asked and Answered to derail their further attempts.
Fighting or trying to get a rise out of you	Sail Out of the Wind	Remember that it takes two to argue. Remove your sail, and the wind will soon fade away.

4

Overcontrol

It's a rainy morning in April. Hailey, a second grader, has been shopping for spring clothes with her grandma and wants to wear the new pale yellow sundress her grandma bought her. "You are *not* wearing your new dress, young lady. You'll get it wet and muddy," her mom points out. But Hailey isn't about to put on the jeans and T-shirt her mom is handing her. "Grandma bought it for me. It's mine and I want to wear it!" She stomps off. But her mom plays the trump card: "Fine! No TV for a week if you wear your new dress!" Hailey groans, glares and eventually wilts, and although she pointedly picks out *different* jeans and a *different* T-shirt, it's clear Mom has won this match. Not only has she rescued the pretty dress, but she's shown Hailey who's in control.

After school, Hailey is playing kickball in her backyard with some friends when her older sister, Phoebe, grabs the ball away from them. "Hey!" yells Hailey. "We're playing with that!" The older girl looks back, then kicks a different ball back in their direction—but this one is deflated and covered in mud. "You can use this one. I need the good one for *my* game." But Hailey knows what's right. She charges over to Phoebe and spouts, "We had it *first*! Give it back *right now*!" Phoebe just laughs. "You can't make me, little baby!" She knows that'll get Hailey really mad. As it turns out, however, Hailey *can* make her. Picking up a handful of mud, she splatters it onto the bigger girl's hair and clothes. A surprised Phoebe drops the ball and screams all kinds of not-nice words at her sister, but is, in fact, forced to go inside and clean up rather than play kickball. Worse, she can't even complain (too loudly) to Mom, seeing as she'd stolen the ball in the first place. Chances are she'll find a way to get back at Hailey, but for now, Hailey's scored a home run.

Okay, so we all know that Hailey shouldn't have thrown mud at her sister. But which of us isn't secretly cheering for the plucky youngster? Both of these incidents deal with control. Hailey's mother and her big sister both wanted to be in charge of what happened to Hailey. In the first case, we can certainly relate to Hailey's mom wanting to protect Hailey from mud splatters on her brand-new dress. And any of us who have grown up with siblings knows that they sometimes get the idea that they can call the shots.

News flash: Hailey does *not* want to be told what to do just because she's littler. She wants to feel in control of what happens to her. She wants to be in charge of her own seven-year-old life. And guess what? Wanting to feel independent and in control are not only inborn characteristics of being human, but they're positive desires in a child's life. In fact, the purpose of childhood is for kids to learn to be independent. Yet the autonomy they need so much can so easily be snatched away if we're not careful, leading to a whole host of problems.

Control is something that every parent has (whether we feel like it or not) and every child wants, and it's the source of most of the struggles between parents and kids. Because the issue of control so permeates a child's life, it's worth a deeper look. One of the best ways to curb the entitlement epidemic is to give kids more of what they are truly entitled to: age-appropriate, positive power and control, along with dignity and respect. When we give them more of what they *are* entitled to, they will be less likely to demand what they *aren't* entitled to.

To do this, we'll gradually turn over more of our parental control to our kids. The more age-appropriate control kids have, the more practice they get in making decisions and taking responsibility—and the less likely they are to depend on their parents to make everything all right for them.

This chapter is devoted to giving kids more age-appropriate power and helping you step back from the need to control everything. I'll give you the tools you need to hand off control in appropriate doses so that your kids can seek independence in positive, helpful ways, rather than resorting to throwing mud.

Who's Really in Control?

I think it's safe to say that control is a hot-button topic. Parents and kids regularly struggle for control, as do spouses and kids on the playground. It's also a misunderstood topic, with parents often feeling—understandably—that they need to be in control of their kids' lives for a whole variety of reasons. But is that really what's best for our kids? Let's start at the beginning to see why control is so important in the first place and why it affects your kids' behavior in a big way.

Everyone, no matter their age, needs to feel a sense of control, or power, over their own lives. This need is hardwired into us, as we saw in chapter 1. Our kids, whether they're eighteen months or eighteen years, don't actually *choose* to seek power—the drive is built-in, and nothing we do can change it, even if we wanted to. Most can't articulate this need for power, but every child feels it. And it's something they're entitled to on a psychological basis (just like being entitled to a safe environment, a loving family, food and other basic necessities).

Kids need to have control over their own world, but don't worry—they don't need to play the part of a little dictator in your home. A child shouldn't feel entitled to decide what kind of car the family will drive or whether to continue his education past third grade, but picking out the kind of cereal you buy at the store or deciding whether he'll do his homework before or after snack will give him just the kind of power boost he's looking for. On the other hand, if kids—and adults, too—can't feel in control throughout the day in positive ways like choosing a breakfast cereal or having input on daily routines, they will resort to negative ways to get the same feeling of control. Like flinging breakfast cereal all over the kitchen or refusing to do homework altogether because they know it'll get a rise out of Mom. More about this later.

Hailey's attempts to gain control of her situation are not misguided. She's right that it's her dress, and her turn with the kickball. She is tuned in to a well-developed sense of fairness, and she knows she deserves to be respected as a person. The fact that she spoke her mind to her mother and her sister (albeit with a bit of a tantrum) when her sense of fairness was violated is actually a good thing.

But kids haven't always felt free to stand up for themselves (for better or worse). When we were growing up, or at least when our parents were, the saying "might makes right" was the order of the day. In this authoritarian environment, bosses could berate employees for showing up five minutes late, and husbands could demand to sit down to a roast at five thirty every night—cooked by a housewife wearing an apron and high heels, no less. Kids were expected to toe the line and be seen and not heard. While it sometimes managed to get good behavior at the time, in a dysfunctional sort of way, this top-down model of authority is not today's reality.

When we look around us in the twenty-first century, we see that respect has become a big part of family life, work life and school life. The fact that Hailey knows her rights and is willing to speak up about them shows that society has undergone a massive, and welcome, shift, so that everyone deserves respect, no matter their size or status. When Mom feels like she can tell Dad, "I would like to watch a movie instead of the game tonight," and Dad responds with a reasonable compromise, Hailey learns that power is often negotiable. She learns to stand up for herself, with a keen eye for fairness. As annoying as it might be when you really want the yellow dress to stay yellow, Hailey knows subconsciously when she's within her rights and is due a little control.

The problem is, when it comes to actually controlling our kids, we can't. We want to and we try to. But it never really works. The principles of Adlerian psychology (see chapter 1) remind us about the reality of control. It goes like this:

1. We can't control another person.
2. All we *can* control is ourselves and our environment.

This applies to kids as well as to adults. The problems we face when we try to overcontrol our kids stem from the fact that by trying to hold all the power, we actually produce children who rebel against all our attempts to civilize them. Overcontrol—including micromanaging, bossing around, punishing, trying to assert our control and all the rest—doesn't work. But giving them bite-sized pieces of personal power does, since we work *with* their inborn need for significance rather than *against* it.

We can't control our kids—at least not without a power struggle. But we can control our reactions to them, and the environment in our homes. All of the tools in this book are grounded in these tenets, which is one reason why they're successful. And admitting these principles is the first step toward creating an empowered home that will help kids gain the independence they need, in addition to training in positive behaviors. In an empowered home, while each person might not have an equal vote, everyone can share opinions, just as they should share in the responsibilities and privileges.

"So wait a minute," you might be thinking. "I need to let my kids do whatever they want, just because they want to? Talk about entitled!" I'm certainly not saying you have to be a doormat for your children, and in fact, you shouldn't. You will still set the rules, and you'll have the tools you need to make sure your rules are followed. But within your nonnegotiables (for instance, bedtime, curfew, family contributions, which activities may and may not be enjoyed in the living room, etc.), with the strategies and tools in this chapter, you'll be able to empower your kids with the opportunity to take charge of their lives in littler ways. Remember your long-term goal: to raise responsible, resilient, un-entitled people who can successfully function in an increasingly complex adult world. To do that, you must let go of some of your power, and use it to help your kids learn life lessons while building their sense of significance, getting better cooperation from them along the way.

This chapter will discredit the popular parenting tactics that *don't* work to control kids, and give you the tools to let your kids have the control they crave without running rampant over your rules.

Out of Control: Parenting Techniques That Flop

We know that kids *are* entitled to be respected in today's society. As mentioned earlier, this was not entirely the case when we were kids, and even less the case in our parents' and grandparents' days. Kids were expected to obey—*or else!* For no reason other than the fact that Dad said so. (Okay, and the fact that the yellow dress really might be ruined—which is an excellent Natural Consequence, a term you'll learn more about in chapter 5.)

Truth be told, even as grown-ups, that hardwired need for control is still within us—especially as it relates to controlling our kids. Appropriately, we want to control our kids to keep them from putting postage stamps all over their stuffed animals or dying their hair with Kool-Aid right before their cousin's wedding or doing all the other things they think up. But for the same reason our kids are no longer paddled for passing notes in school—because they're respected as people—the old command-and-control parenting tactics we often turn to no longer work. Which is more than a bit frustrating for those of us who grew up with them! Why can't we keep our kids in line with the same techniques our parents used on us? After all, we turned out okay, didn't we?

Spanking, washing mouths out with soap, giving the look and all the rest of the intimidation tactics used as attempts to control kids' behavior rely on the idea that might makes right, or bigger is better or Father knows best. But our kids see firsthand every day that these outdated ideas don't always hold up. Father, while he certainly does know a thing or two, might be (rightly) contested by Mom, who may win. Schools have a zero-tolerance policy for bullying, and children are accustomed to being treated with respect by teachers, coaches and others in authority. The mantra of the day is "be nice," and we discourage our kids from overpowering others. We encourage them to share, take turns, talk about their feelings and generally be fair. Today's kids are not regularly being bullied into submission by people bigger than they are, simply *because* they are bigger. We're glad things have changed—we're all better for it. When parents attempt to use overpowering strategies at home, however, kids instinctively know it's out of sync with today's norms.

All the same, in our well-meaning effort to make sure our kids behave, many of us continue to use these outdated parenting techniques based on floundering philosophies, to fulfill our own need for power. It's true: parents are also entitled to a sense of control. It's natural that we want control, especially when we know that what our kids are doing is wrong. Besides, it's *our* house, *our* money, *our* family and *our* rules. And wouldn't it be easier on everyone if they'd just obey? And when we feel disrespected by our kids, we demand respect by resorting to the same techniques that our parents used on us, in hopes that they'll work on our own offspring, all the while escalating the power struggle.

Because kids need a sense of control, our attempts to *make* them behave only makes the situation worse. If you're grinding soap into Devon's teeth because he told a lie, I guarantee he's not thinking, "Gee willikers, Mom's right; my mouth really is dirty with all those lies I told! I'd better always tell the truth from now on!" This type of treatment only teaches kids to fear their parents, to lash out or to do a better job of not getting caught next time. Sure, many of us endured this tactic and survived. But chances are nothing about our actual punishment helped us make a more positive choice next time.

Punishment, or demanding respect out of a sense of fear (the look), only serves to widen the gulf that so often separates us from our kids. It relies on the outdated idea that parents can wield authoritarian control over their children, and fails to empower kids to make the right choice next time.

But physical punishments like spanking and soap aren't the only ineffective discipline techniques still commonly in use. Threats, time-outs, yelling and counting 1-2-3 might seem to work at first, but they also come up short in actually teaching kids proper behavior. Threats, like missing out on a friend's birthday party, TV time or dessert, might needle our kids into cooperating this time, but in the long run, they fall short at actually changing behavior because they don't teach the child to do anything differently next time. Time-outs, seen as a milder form of punishment than a spanking, rarely get kids reconsidering their actions as they're intended to do. At best, they cause a momentary delay in the disruptive behavior, and at their worst, they incite a massive power struggle between Dad and a four-year-old, as Dad tries everything in his power to convince her to actually *stay* in time-out. Counting 1-2-3 also relies on shaky power to make it effective. After all, kids know that when you start counting, they have *at least* three chances before they need to listen (1 . . . 2 . . . 2 ½ . . .). What's more, if they don't obey, you still need some sort of consequence to put into effect—which is where many parents falter, hoping that they sound serious enough to convince their child they mean business. In the end, sometimes it's just easier to give in, adding fuel to the entitled kids' belief that they can get their way by refusing to cooperate and guaranteeing the behavior will be repeated in the future. Parenting this way is exhausting and unsustainable, because the tactics are based on the parent overpowering the child, which fights *against* our kids' natural need for power. As a result, they fall short in gaining the long-term cooperation and positive choices we're looking for.

Sometimes it doesn't feel fair to us that we can't wave a magic parenting wand and have our kids taking orders, but it's just not the way parenting works. The bottom line is, we can either work *with* our kids' built-in psychological need for power or we can work *against* it. But along the same lines, our kids can always choose whether to cooperate with our rules or to dig in their heels every step of the way. And guess what? They *will* choose to fight us if we don't fulfill their requirement for significance in positive ways—because their desire for age-appropriate control over their world is nonnegotiable.

That's why we must choose strategies that actually work *with* our kids' need for power. If we set aside our command-and-control mentality and instead give them the age-appropriate power they crave, we will not only teach them how to make their own positive choices, but we can alleviate all the pent-up frustration that comes from their never feeling like they have a say in their own lives. We can un-entitle them from negative, power-seeking behavior by making a few modifications to our parenting style. And here's the clincher: once our kids' power baskets are full from being treated with fairness by us, rather than threatened into submission, they'll be much more likely to take action without a fuss next time we ask them to "Please hang up your jacket."

Micromanaging, Nitpicking and Overpowering: A Recipe for Disaster

While it's true that some parents try to control their kids' lives simply because they want their kids to obey, others do so in a well-meaning attempt to shield kids from the consequences of their poor choices, give them a smooth ride through life or make sure the job gets done right. We want our kids to do things *our* way. In fact, our constant nagging and reminding are ways we overcontrol our kids, as we try to get them to do things they don't really want to ("Pick up your napkin." "Have you finished your project yet?" "Don't forget to pack extra socks for the sleepover!" and so on). Some of that ordering, correcting and directing is necessary; however, if we're not careful, the bitter aftertaste of these well-meaning interactions build up over time, overcontrolling our kids and annoying and frustrating them at the same time.

Here's what this might look like:

For his fourth birthday, Lucas receives the superhero, big-kid, training-wheeled bike of his dreams. He couldn't be more excited to ditch his trike (only babies use trikes—never mind he was riding it around yesterday) and take his new ride for a spin. He snaps on his helmet with a little help from Dad and starts to get on his bike.

"Wait!" Dad says. "We need to take it outside." The pair somewhat awkwardly carries the bike together to the driveway. Lucas starts to swing his leg over the seat.

"Oops, don't you want to take the price tag off so you don't sit on it?" asks Dad. "I'll get the scissors." The seat is now devoid of a price sticker, and Lucas, rolling his eyes, starts to climb on.

"Actually, Son, you don't have much experience riding a bike. I'd better give you a lesson." After Dad has explained the pedals, steering and brakes (most of which Lucas already has a full understanding of), Lucas positions himself to get on his brand-new bike.

"You know, the seat might be too high, let me fix it," Dad cautions. He adjusts the seat for a now-fuming Lucas and the boy is ready to hop on.

"Wait, let's point you in a different direction—there are fewer rocks this way," Dad suggests. Lucas sighs loudly as he helps turn the bike, then gets set for his first ride.

"You don't want to wear those pants while you ride it, do you? They don't look like they'll be comfortable to ride in." Lucas furiously rejects this idea but runs inside anyway to change into different pants and then starts to get on.

"Here, let me hold your arm so you don't fall," Dad says, worried. Dad helps Lucas onto his bike while Lucas tries to yank his arm away from his parent's grasp.

Lucas is finally ready for his first ride! And he can't wait to ride as far away from his dad as he can get.

As Dad nips away at Lucas's opportunity to ride his new bike on his own terms complete with the chance that he'll make a few mistakes, Dad also erodes his son's sense of empowerment. When Lucas no longer feels a strong sense of significance, he gets feisty—don't we all? Whatever Mom and Dad's intentions, it's easy for kids to start to feel overpowered, as though they have no control over their own lives. After just a few hours of this type of treatment—maybe much less—you'd be ready to snap and lash out. Kids are no different. There's only so much bossing around they can take, even if it's spread out throughout the day. Only when kids snap, it doesn't sound like "Mom, I love your ideas and really appreciate your help, but I think I'm ready to clean and organize my room by myself. Why don't you stop by a little later and we can talk more about it?" No, when a child lashes out on a mission for power, the dialogue is usually a lot louder, to say the least.

Overcontrol breeds power struggles, tantrums and all the rest of the nasty, entitled, power-seeking behaviors you'd rather start your new diet early than face. And as you know, Lucas won't time his power struggle in accordance with your convenience—it'll happen when you have a nasty head cold, the baby is crying and you're just getting on a conference call with your colleagues on the other side of the country.

The Struggle for Power

The ongoing quest for power, often negatively manifested in our kids through behaviors like talking back, throwing tantrums, negotiating and fighting, is exactly why power struggles happen. You want Isaac to sweep up the mess he made eating a cupcake, and Isaac would much rather go play outside. Jayla is planning to paint her nails on the living room carpet, refusing to see the logic in doing the job in the (easily washable) bathroom instead. These first-world problems are not on your kids' radar screen—they are *your* priorities. If your kids are feeling overpowered, you now have the perfect storm for a battle. If your kids are feeling empowered with a strong sense of significance, they'll be much more likely to go along with your requests to get the broom or move the nail polish—even though they may not see the point—because they're not on a subconscious mission to gain the control they don't have. But if they're not feeling a strong sense of significance? You can watch the cupcake crumbs fly.

I talked about tantrums in chapter 2. Sometimes they happen because a child is having a meltdown (because he's been pushed past his limit) or because she feels entitled to something she's not receiving. Tantrums (and power struggles and battles of all kinds) are also a quest for control. You've heard it from me before: when a child doesn't get power in positive ways, he will resort to negative ways to achieve it. That's what all the yelling is about—and the bedtime battles, homework strikes, slammed doors, teenager rages and preschooler screaming fits after not being allowed to put sprinkles on their mashed potatoes at dinner. These are often the result of a child who feels chronically over-powered and just can't take it anymore. She's subconsciously saying, "Just let me make my *own* decisions and live my *own* life a little bit! Back off!" even as she kicks the sofa and pounds the floor.

When power-seeking bad behaviors surface—anything from refusing to do homework to purposely splashing water all over the floor at bath time—our best bet is to take the fuel out of the fire by *not* responding in kind. It might be tempting to respond to their "You can't make me put away my shoes!" with a "You wanna bet?" but you'll only escalate the argument. Use the tools from chapter 2 to defuse the situation. Leave the room or otherwise tune it out. Remember—they can express their feelings, but we don't have to participate.

You can prevent future flare-ups by providing plenty of opportunities for power and control in advance, using positive tools such as Mind, Body and Soul Time and the tools at the end of this chapter. We'll get to the new tools next—but first I want you to see what's in store for you when your children *are* feeling empowered with a strong sense of significance—and a few strategies to keep in mind as you turn over the reins.

The Empowered Child

It's five o'clock and the grocery store is packed. You were hoping to avoid stopping for groceries on your way home from picking up your four-year-old from day care and your eight-year-old from tae kwon do, yet here you are.

But tonight, you've put in the extra effort to make sure the trip goes smoothly. You spent quality time with each of them in the morning before school, and in the van on the way to the store you continued to engage them by talking and really listening to them about their days. You also get them started on brainstorming ways to celebrate the four-year-old's upcoming birthday. As you enter the store, you show them that there's room on the list for them each to pick one healthy snack food for the pantry this week, and you write down their selections.

Next, you let them pick a job to do—the eight-year-old chooses to be the cart loader, and the four-year-old decides to cross items off the list as you find them. They're both so busy with their jobs—stacking boxes and cans so they'll all fit and making a straight line all the way through "vegetable broth"—that they walk right past the doughnut display.

Inevitably, the freezer section, with its wealth of frozen goodies, holds them up. And they are a united front: "Can we *pleeeze* get ice-cream bars? We haven't had them in *forever*!" You bring up the point that they are welcome to add them to the list next time they get to choose a treat, but this time you have to pass them by. But look! It's time to choose what kind of frozen juice to get. With their power baskets full, the kids don't feel the need to pitch a fit about the ice cream, and instead start discussing the pros and cons of grape, apple and orange-pineapple blend.

Nearing the checkout, you ask the four-year-old if there's anything left to get. He consults the list, then confidently tells you there's one item not checked off. You read it, and then everyone heads back to the salad dressing aisle to pick up some ranch, thanking your four-year-old, who beams with pride.

In line, the candy selection looks tempting. Your kids eye it, but you mention that you could really use some help unloading the cart. You ask your eight-year-old if she thinks she can fit everything on the conveyor as well as she fit it in the cart, and she's up to the challenge, not giving the candy another thought. She's feeling empowered, and doesn't have the need to pick a fight. Meanwhile, you let your four-year-old choose whether to have green beans or broccoli with cheese sauce as the dinner vegetable, and promise to let him push the buttons on the microwave to cook his selection.

Ta-da! You've made it through a grocery run that could've been long and painful. Your kids are feeling like contributors rather than troublemakers—and much more likely to pitch in without a fuss when you ask for help unloading the bags.

This is just one example of how empowering our kids sets them up for success. Multiply this by all the tricky times in your day and you'll see that even though handing over control can take a little more time and effort in the short term, it'll pay off when we're not facing a battle over ice cream in the grocery store (or over homework or walking the dog or not drinking milk out of the jug).

When we *overcontrol* our kids, we do it with the good intention of wanting to make them behave and act wisely. We want them to obey our rules, respect us and others, take care of their things, clean up after themselves, do well in school and all the rest.

When we *empower* our kids by handing over some of the control, we actually get the behavior we're looking for more often than not. Kids aren't perfect—and neither are we—but when we work *with* our kids' natural inclinations, we're a lot more effective in teaching them and encouraging them to use appropriate behavior.

In my years of parenting experience (both with my own kids and by coaching other parents), I've seen plenty of overcontrolled kids and plenty of empowered kids whose parents consistently use the tools in this book. While the overcontrolled kids are fixated on getting power any way they can, the empowered ones show lots of positive characteristics and behaviors. When you start empowering your own kids, you have a lot to look forward to.

Empowered kids are:

- Happy and content. They're not on a mission to seek control wherever and however they can get it.
- Obedient. Yup, you heard me. Kids who are receiving regular doses of positive power are much more likely to go along with what you say rather than turn it into a power struggle.
- Able to get along well with others. Because they're not storing up

frustration stemming from overcontrol, they don't have a (big) problem sharing, taking turns and generally being kind to their friends and siblings.

- Confident and prepared. Since they've been allowed to practice wielding control over their own lives, they can make positive decisions for themselves.
- Assured that their parents are on *their* team. They don't feel like their parents are out to get them and are less likely to respond to their parents' suggestions and rules with a fight.

Empower, Not Overpower: Strategies for Handing over the Reins

First, let me say that we all do it. We all try to manage our kids' lives. Sometimes it's because we're running late to the school concert and we just have to get our ten-year-old into his tie and out the door so he makes it on time to be onstage with his cello rather than watching from the audience. Sometimes it's because we are worried that the dishes will be speckled with dried-on cheese if we don't hover and give step-by-tiny-step instructions. And sometimes we simply want our kids to respect us—because having respect is, in fact, a good thing. It's a natural part of parenting to want to make sure things go well for our kids—and it's something we'll talk more about in the next chapter. For now, let's look at some surefire ways to loosen the reins and begin empowering our kids rather than overpowering them.

First and foremost, be sure that you're providing regular Mind, Body and Soul Time to your kids. This tool provides lots of positive power and attention to your kids, so they won't feel the need to resort to negative behaviors to achieve a strong sense of belonging and significance.

Next, recognize that you have a need for control in your own house, just as your kids do. In fact, your kids *need* you to control some things—but by using the tools in this book to set reasonable limits, not by flashing them the look. If you feel like your kids are out of control, write a plan for instituting some rules over the course of the next few weeks and months. Take one thing at a time, and soon you'll be well on your way to regaining control over important things like the pantry, the TV and the family car. As you see your kids stepping up with good behavior and positive actions, you'll be better prepared to let go of things you *don't* need to control.

Determine a few things you can let go of, and that your kids can take over. Often, handing over control comes in the form of building a Decision-Rich Environment (the first tool in this chapter). Sometimes, it'll mean letting your kids take on new privileges and responsibilities, like walking the dog around the block alone, learning simple car repair, being allowed to go to the mall with a friend or taking homework to the park to work on rather than doing it at home. And many times, giving your kids power will simply mean holding back from nit-picking their decisions, methods and actions. For instance, if your seventeen-year-old is turning the ten-minute job of vacuuming the stairs into a thirty-minute chore by using the tiny dust vacuum, it's okay to gently offer, "We also have the bigger handheld vacuum if you want to use it." But leave it at that—no need to needle him as long as he gets the job done.

Aim to give power to your kids many times a day. Remember that you won't always like their way of doing it—so if you just can't handle the fact that they would rather go to a friend's house one Saturday than go with you to visit Aunt Jane in the hospital, don't leave the choice up to them ("Do you think we should bring Aunt Jane flowers or chocolates to help cheer her up?").

Hand over appropriate control. You don't want your rambunctious four-year-old pushing the shopping cart at rush hour, but he can pick out the flavor of kids' toothpaste, even if it's not your favorite brand. Likewise, you probably wouldn't trust your fourteen-year-old to grill hamburgers for the backyard barbecue you're hosting, but she could decide how to arrange all the condiments, sides and utensils on the table (if you're worried about traffic flow, train her in the task ahead of time, then let her do a practice run before guests arrive—plus, be prepared to let it go, and realize your guests won't mind as much as you think).

Remember that completing important (if minor) tasks boosts your child's feeling of significance, too. Your kids may outwardly groan when you ask them to mop the kitchen floor, but if you let them accomplish the task on their terms (assuming you've trained them and they know what steps need to take place), they'll inwardly love the sense of power they get from contributing to the household. Consider letting them choose *when* they do the job (before their snack or after their snack) and *how* they do it ("Would you rather vacuum or sweep it first"; "would you rather use gloves and a rag or a mop?").

UNDERCONTROL: WHEN LIMITS ARE IN ORDER

It's one thing to know that our kids need to feel a sense of control over their own lives. It's another thing entirely to know *when* to hand over the reins and when to keep them firmly within our grasp. How do we know when our kids are taking advantage of our willingness to let them have some power and when we really do need to put our foot down? Here are a few rules of thumb:

- It's never okay for kids to hurt people or things. If your kids do so, they're out of line and you need to put a stop to it. Your first priority is trying to understand the why behind the behavior. What is your child trying to tell you by acting out and hurting others? Once you know the reason, you can focus on fixing the problem.
- You're letting your kids control *themselves* but not other people. Help your kids understand that they shouldn't be bossing you, their siblings or their friends around. If they do, you need to take back some of the control using positive tools.
- Too much power will go to your kids' heads. If they start acting entitled to having whatever they want, whenever they want, you'll need to un-entitle them using the strategies and tools in this book.

Assuming more independence is a very important part of growing up. As you hand over control in positive ways—more and more as kids get older—you'll have the opportunity to watch your little ones turn into responsible adults before your very eyes. As much as you love having a big say in how, exactly, the dishes get washed, what they wear to school or how they interact with others, won't it be more rewarding to empower them to be successful on their own? That's what parenting's all about.

The rest of this chapter is packed with the tools you need to make it happen. Then, in the next chapter, you'll learn the ins and outs of letting your kids fly on their own and how to enjoy the ride—even when they come crashing down from time to time.

Un-Entitler: The Decision-Rich Environment

The best, simplest way to avoid overcontrolling your kids is to let them make their own decisions whenever you can. Letting your kids decide everything from how they wear their hair to which jobs they'd rather do to help out around the house to what the family should do for fun on Friday night will boost their sense of significance, as well as let them practice decision making in the real world. This practice entitles them to some things they legitimately need: a feeling of control over their own lives, the ability to change their circumstances and the feeling of being capable.

And at the same time, by letting your child choose which kind of toothpaste to buy at the store, for instance, you're letting him know that you *do* expect him to brush his teeth. When you tell your teen she can pick whether to make a salad for dinner Tuesday night or Friday night, you're telling her she's not entitled to a free ride at home but that she can pitch in on her terms.

And that's where The Decision-Rich Environment tool comes in. Yes, you've given your child choices before, but the guidelines that follow will help you make sure you're using decisions throughout the day and throughout the years to empower your kids on an age-appropriate level as a strategy to build their sense of significance as well as their decision-making skills. By setting up your home and family life so that your kids are entitled to feel in control as often (and appropriately) as possible, you'll cut back significantly on negative entitled behaviors and create an environment that will prepare them for a positive future. They'll love it, too, as they begin to see themselves in control of their world—and able to use their power for good.

PUT IT TO USE

Creating a Decision-Rich Environment can be as simple as asking your four-year-old what he'd like for breakfast. In fact, it doesn't get much more difficult than that. The possibilities are endless: would you like your rocket ship pajamas or your dinosaur pajamas? What would you like to do for your birthday? Where should we go for dinner? Would you rather help me address holiday cards or help with the outdoor decorations? Should we get granola bars or fruit snacks for lunch boxes this week? What colleges would you like to visit, and when? What are some goals you have for your summer? How can we make mornings run more smoothly? Think of decisions they'll enjoy making—everyday life decisions, big things and little things. As you use this tool, you're likely to find more and more opportunities to give your child a say in what's happening.

In fact, parents often find that the most challenging part of The Decision-Rich Environment is to be able to let go of the outcome themselves. We might have to watch our kids walk out the door having mixed plaid and polka dots, or we might have to eat tacos when we were in the mood for Thai.

If you're not used to giving your kids much control over what happens in their lives, it's okay to start small. Aim for one new choice a day. Then gradually add new decisions whenever you can, scattered throughout the day so their significance basket remains full. Rotate the privilege of making family decisions (such as what kinds of flowers to plant this spring) among all your kids. Pretty soon, your kids will be feeling more empowered than ever as your Decision-Rich Environment builds.

Of course, there's also no need to let our kids walk all over us—and not every decision is up for discussion. But the more you can let your kids have a minisay, the more likely they'll be to cooperate when they don't have a choice, and the more practice they'll get in making good decisions.

Tips and Scripts

- Younger kids might only be able to handle having two choices, while teens might benefit from being presented with a wide variety of options, or an open-ended question.
- Leave the question open-ended only if you can handle the response. Saying "Should we buy orange juice or apple juice?" will facilitate a better decision than a broad "What kind of juice should we buy?" Unless, of course, you like tomato-pear juice that costs $4.50 a pint.
- For bigger decisions, let your kids know it's okay to take some time to think. If you've asked your sixteen-year-old "What state park should we camp in as a family this summer?" hand her some brochures or let her lead you through the state park Web page, so she can make an educated decision.
- You can offer decisions during the trickiest parts of the day to distract your kids from the fact that they have to wash their hair ("Would you like to shampoo your hair, or should I?"), help clean up ("Would you like to sweep the floor before or after dinner?") and go to bed ("Would you like to read in the living room or your bedroom before lights out?").
- Remember that this is a tool for *you*, too. It'll take practice—and guts—to hand over the reins to your kids. Start small with something you can easily handle ("Should we have green beans or peas with our salmon for dinner?") but be willing to raise the stakes.

You might not be thrilled that your thirteen-year-old would rather take tennis lessons than join the debate team or that the living room will get dusted on Sunday afternoon instead of Saturday morning but you also might find that you're relieved to hand off a little control and the responsibility that goes with it.

YES, BUT . . .

My child takes forever deciding.

Part of the beauty of The Decision-Rich Environment is that your child will get lots of practice making decisions, so the more you use it, the faster she'll learn to decide. Try setting a time limit ("I need your decision before dinner," for instance) or telling your child in advance what she'll need to make a decision about, especially for something that might take a little thought ("What kinds of summer camps do you think you might be interested in?"). If even deciding which underwear to put on takes ten minutes of deliberation, you can end it with a simple "I see you're having trouble deciding. I'll pick this time, and you can decide tomorrow." Then stick to your word—and it won't be a problem next time.

If my child doesn't like the choices, he refuses to make a decision.

As in the previous example, end it with a simple "I see you're having trouble deciding—so I'll choose." You can also use a When-Then or a When-Then Routine to get your child moving, especially if it's something that happens every day (like refusing to do homework). This attitude might be a sign that your child needs to feel a positive sense of significance in other ways. Keep offering lots of decisions in situations he'll be more amenable to, plus use other significance-boosting tools, such as Mind, Body and Soul Time, Family Contributions, Empathize and Appreciate, and others you'll learn later in this book.

The bottom line is that kids learn to make good decisions
by making decisions, not by following instructions. If we
want them to take responsibility for making the world
a better place, then we need to *give*
them responsibilities.

—Alfie Kohn, *The Myth of the Spoiled Child*

Which decisions can my child make?

In a perfect world, our kids would increase their authority
over their own lives, as well as their responsibility, each year,
with the goal of a smooth transition into the "Should I take the
job on the other side of the country or the one in the next town?"
decisions of the adult world. After all, if we make the decisions
all along, the move to college is going to challenge much more
than our child's knowledge of calculus.

Here are some age-by-age examples of choices your kids can
make as part of your Decision-Rich Environment. Of course, this
is only a start—the possibilities really are endless!

AGE	DECISIONS YOUR CHILD IS PROBABLY READY TO MAKE
2	Breakfast cereal (two options); color of bath towel; which books to read at night
3	Which shirt to wear; which crackers to buy at the store; paint or Play-Doh
4	What to buy for a friend's birthday (two or three options); who to invite over for a playdate; what healthy option to have for a snack
5	Vegetable selections for weekly dinner menus; whether to dust the bookshelf or set the table; whether to play in the backyard or the basement
6	What to pack in lunches for the week (within parameters)
7	Whether to take a shower or a bath
8	Which summer activities to do as a family (within budget and time parameters)

AGE	DECISIONS YOUR CHILD IS PROBABLY READY TO MAKE
9	Whether to shower in the morning or before bed
10	Which musical instrument to learn
11	Whether to see a movie or go to the swimming pool as a family on Saturday
12	Whether Mom or Dad should come along on the class trip
13	Which activities to do on a family vacation (within a set budget)
14	Which stocks to invest in with allowance money; what kind of (caged) pet to get
15	What time to go to bed; which charity to volunteer with over the summer
16	How to earn money during the summer; which colleges to visit
17	Which colleges to apply to
18	Where to attend college; what kind of transportation to use; where to live

Un-Entitler: What Is Your Plan?

This is the tool you'll use when you'd normally be inclined to yell, "Go clean your gerbil cage *now*!" It's a way to keep your child on top of a task without nagging or reminding (or shouting), while letting him know you have confidence in his abilities.

With What Is Your Plan?, you'll give your child the chance to save face and complete a task or project on his own terms. At the same time, you're not entitling him to coast by doing the work for him or letting him skip out on it. Likewise, you're not overcontrolling him by reminding him constantly, demanding he do it your way or needlessly bossing him around. Your child will get the significance boost of being in control of his own responsibilities and get the job done, too.

PUT IT TO USE

Next time your fifteen-year-old is kicking around a soccer ball in the backyard when you know she has a big project for Spanish class due the next day, pull out this tool. Calmly ask her "What is your plan for getting your Spanish project done?"

Simply mentioning the project might be enough to get her going—you'll jog her memory without being (too) annoying. It's also entirely possible that you'll get an I don't know. If so, you can ask if she'd like help coming up with one. Either way, she'll soon be working away on her poster of Peru.

Tips and Scripts

- Much as you might want to, you can't use this tool every five minutes, or it becomes the nagging and reminding that you're trying to avoid. Use it no more than once per task, and no more than one or two times a day, at the very most, or it'll get as tuned out as your attempts to figure out their latest crush. Try to save it for when you need it most.
- Allow your kids their own plan, even if you're pretty sure it won't work. Chalk it up to a learning experience, and be willing to help your child figure out a new plan if something goes wrong with hers (if for instance, her little sister *isn't* willing to fold all the laundry for her for five cents).
- If you must offer a suggestion (maybe your child is errantly assuming that the big project is due on Monday instead of Friday), do it in a respectful, nonthreatening way. Pretend you're talking to a coworker. You don't have to feel like you're walking on eggshells—this tool is to simply help you avoid the communication pitfalls that tend to escalate power struggles.
- Recognize, too, that if your child has been avoiding a big set of math problems, he might just need to sit down and do them. In this case, What Is Your Plan? helps remind your child in a non-

threatening, nonnagging way to take time to finish her responsibilities.

- If you're met with a blank stare, you can follow up with a choice. "Would you rather get your Spanish project out of the way now or after supper?"

- Many parents use this tool the day before a homework assignment is due, but remember that you can also use it to help your child start off on the right foot or make steady progress once she's begun. If there's a beaver diorama due on Friday, try asking on Tuesday or Wednesday.

YES, BUT . . .

My child just ignores me when I ask about his plan.

It's probably not wise to use this tool when your child is wading through aliens in a video game or intent on another activity. Get his attention first by saying "Can I talk to you for a second?" Then ask the question, and you'll be more likely to get a response. Remember, too, that the response and exact plan aren't always as important as the fact that your child knows you're not letting him off the hook with regard to a particular responsibility.

My kids try to convince me that they are done when they're actually not.

If it's rather obvious that the outdoor toys have not been put away even when your child insists that they have, make sure the problem isn't a simple oversight by mentioning that you noticed a scooter in the driveway, sidewalk chalk on the patio and a bunch of buckets and shovels out by the sandbox. No need to sound accusatory, just state the facts. This should be enough to jump-start the plan or the action—either one is fine.

In some cases (homework, for instance, when you have to take your kids' word for it) you might need to let it go and allow them to experience the Natural Consequence of missing the due date, a tool you'll learn about later in this chapter, or use a When-Then. Part of not overcontrolling our kids is to let them take the reins—and the consequences, too. We'll learn more about the positive side of letting your kids fail in the next chapter.

Un-Entitler: Invite Cooperation

No one likes to be bossed around all day long—but what about the times we really do need our kids to clean under their beds, help us pack for a family picnic or shovel the driveway? Sometimes the difference in whether we (readily) get cooperation from our kids is simply in the way we ask. Invite Cooperation will help you rephrase your requests to appeal to your kids' need for control and significance. You'll get the help you're looking for and un-entitle your kids from a free ride, and your kids won't feel nagged.

PUT IT TO USE

When you need help getting together a picnic to enjoy before the big game, you might be tempted to bark orders and demand that your kids pitch in. But as you probably have experienced, things can get ugly really fast with this kind of system. Instead, Invite Cooperation by enlisting your kids' help *on their terms*. Switch your demands to a polite request that sounds like "Kids, I'm having trouble getting everything ready for the picnic. Anything you can do to help put together the food or load the car would really help us get out the door!" Chances are your kids will be more likely to put peanut butter on bread and lawn chairs into the car than if you'd assigned tasks and nagged them all the way.

Other times you might say "I noticed the sandbox is overrun with toys. Anything you guys can do to tidy that would be awesome." "If anyone has some time this afternoon, I would love some help with the lasagna for supper!" "Any help you can give me painting the family room this weekend would really be appreciated!" Essentially, state your request respectfully and invitingly, as you would to a group of friends or coworkers.

Then be open to the help your kids decide to give. Be prepared for the fact that your five-year-old might offer to help in ways that aren't 100 percent helpful (scrubbing the bottom half of the guest shower to prepare for Grandma's visit, but not the top, for instance). If the task you're up against really needs skilled labor (tying purple ribbons on 250 tiny picture frame favors for your sister's wedding), this might not be the best tool. This isn't the tool to use with an agenda—the help needs to feel organic and happen on your kids' terms. The more you let them pitch in as they see fit, the more likely they'll be to contribute in the future.

Be sure to thank your kids for any effort they put in, and let them know you appreciate their help. "I really appreciate the time you spent hosing off the deck furniture. That's a huge job I don't have to do today!" Remember, the difference between a chore and a contribution is the difference it makes to someone else. Any time you can phrase a request by Inviting Cooperation instead of handing down orders and show sincere appreciation after the fact, your kids will get the significance they crave, even while you get the work done.

Tips and Scripts

- This tool works best for medium or large jobs that are somewhat out of the ordinary. If you try to use it every time you need someone to take out the trash, your kids will pass.
- Keep the mood light to show your kids it can be fun to work together. Making the job an interesting challenge can also help engage your kids—setting goals is a great way to do this. "Do you think we can have the flowers planted by the time Mom gets home?" "Can we get everything we need for the pool into one beach tote?"

- Always remember: the minute you start demanding, nagging, bossing around or nitpicking, your kids will check out. Don't use this tool during high-pressure times.
- Even if only one child jumps up to help, try making the job fun (without pressuring the other kids), and you might get more hands pitching in next time.
- Consider setting the stage for this tool by using it with your spouse, a friend or a relative ahead of time. Be sure to let the other adult know what's going on, then find ways to have a blast doing anything from vacuuming under the furniture to packing for a vacation.

YES, BUT . . .

My kids start out helping, then ditch the task before it's done.

The stronger their sense of significance, the more likely they'll be to stick with it. Help them find tasks that offer a meaningful contribution but that aren't overwhelming. Allow them to take breaks if they need to. If it's clear they're running out of steam—maybe the job has gotten really involved or all the tasks at their level are completed—you'd be best served to dismiss them with a "Thanks so much for all your help. I feel so much better about being able to get this finished now!" before they start griping so they're left with positive associations about pitching in. Encourage them to do as much as they can do well and leave it at that. If the job is one that you know they can finish, and you want to hold them responsible for it, use a different tool, such as When-Then or a When-Then Routine.

Un-Entitler: Convince Me

Kids, especially tweens and teens, are fully tuned in to their blossoming need for control and freedom. As they grow toward adulthood and complete independence, they're bound to ask us to allow them to do things that wouldn't have been possible a year or two ago. And they're never afraid to ask: Can I cross the street by myself? Can I ski down the slope alone? Can a friend and I go to the outlet mall in a town an hour away? This is tough on parents, seeing as we're used to calling the shots and, admittedly, micromanaging to make sure things go smoothly for our kids. Convince Me, a strategy developed by Madelyn Swift, author of *Getting It Right with Teens,* is the tool you'll use to partner with your child and determine whether she's ready for this new burst of independence. Even if inside you're shouting, "No way on earth!" you can allow your child the opportunity to convince you why your instant no to her request to camp in her friend's ten-acre backyard might be upgraded to a yes in a way that will help both of you feel comfortable with the possibility.

Convince Me links freedom with responsibility. If your kids can convince you that the new freedom they're proposing can be managed responsibly, they get the go-ahead from you. If not, the *no* remains.

PUT IT TO USE

When your child confronts you asking for a new type of freedom, Swift suggests you consider three different responses: yes, no and Convince Me. When possible, say yes. But if you can't comfortably give a green light, and if there are any circumstances at all under which the request might be reasonable, say "Convince me," instead of resorting to no. This puts the burden on your child to figure out a safe and rule-abiding way to carry out his plan.

Then lay out your concerns—let your child know why you don't think it's a good idea and the specific things you're worried about. Give your child the floor for a response.

As your child does his best to convince you that what he's suggesting would work, listen with an open mind. Remember that kids have a growing need for independence, and if they can handle a new freedom with a responsible plan in place, they should be allowed to. If your child comes up with a plan you can agree to, fine-tune the ground rules or conditions and give the go-ahead. If, however, the risks are still too great or it's clear your child hasn't thought it through, it's okay to say no. Plan to revisit the idea in a few months or a year.

Here's an example of how this might play out:

Your sixteen-year-old, Tyler, approaches you and asks if he can leave his high school's campus for lunch with friends. Your first reaction? Absolutely not! Lunch is only forty minutes long. There's no way he could safely leave campus with a car full of friends and return in time for class without racing at the speed of light! Plus, he'd have to take a left onto a busy road and lunch out is expensive. Instead of giving a flat-out refusal, however, you decide to use Convince Me and present your concerns.

Here's Tyler's response:

We will only go off campus for lunch two days per week and I'll pay for it with my own money. When we do go out, there will be no more than three kids in the car. We'll pick a restaurant within a three-mile radius of the school. We'll all have cell phones with us and the phones will be on at all times. If anything in the plan goes wrong or we're running late, I will call you and the school immediately to let everyone know what is happening. I've never been tardy for school; I've never had a speeding ticket and I'm a responsible driver.

Are you convinced? With this plan laid out, you'd probably be inclined to say yes because Tyler has thoughtfully considered your concerns and come up with a good plan. You might add that he needs to stay on campus if it's snowing, and possibly set up consequences for returning late to school (losing off-campus lunch privileges for a month).

Tyler gets the yes he was looking for, and you get peace of mind. Plus, not only does Tyler get a huge boost of significance, but also he's learned a valuable lesson about the power of responsible planning.

If everything goes well with Tyler's plan, make a mental note when considering future freedom and his growing sense of responsibility. If it doesn't, he loses ground in your mind and needs to earn it back.

Tips and Scripts

- Convince Me is not and should never be an outlet for whining or badgering, which are only meant to wear you down. Let your child go ahead with the plan only if his ideas are reasonable and well thought out.
- "Because I really, really want to and everyone else is allowed" is not a sound argument.
- Remember that it's your child's job to convince you, not the other way around. This tool works best if you let your kids come up with their own plans and resist the urge to take over.
- It's okay to give your child time to formulate a plan. Ask "Would you like time to think this through?" Hint: it's a good sign if she does. You can even offer to write down your concerns to help her address them completely. Remember that it's in everyone's best interest if she's successful.
- Practice runs and trial periods are good ways to make sure your child is up to the task and spot any potential problems.

YES, BUT . . .

I can't be sure that my child is following the rules we've set up and/or completely safe.

If your child truly lacks the responsibility to follow through on his plan, give a no answer and then work on other positive ways to build his sense of responsibility. Tools like Take Time for Training, When-Then Routines and The Decision-Rich Environment will help with this. The same thing goes for safety: it's something you can train your child in, but part of handing over the reins is allowing your kids to experience the world without a parent hovering over her at all times. Once your child has the training, practice, tools, skills and physical capabilities she needs to be safe, it may be time to let go. If you need to see the plan in action, consider a practice run with you along so you can look for potential pitfalls and make the best decision for your family.

Un-Entitler: What Can *You* Do?

You've always told your kids that they can come to you for anything, right? And sometimes they take you at your word a little *too* much! "I have a hangnail!" "Kara won't stop bugging me!" "I'm scared of the basement because I heard a *thump* and I think it's a tiger that's going to eat me!" If this sounds at all like your home, this tool will soon become a classic. It shifts responsibility and control away from the parents, empowering the child to realize that he can be in control of, or at least influence, his own situation. Your child will no longer play the victim of his circumstances and will be un-entitled from needing Mom or Dad to make everything better. It's not that you won't play a supporting role, but What Can *You* Do? will boost your kids' sense of significance, and get them taking responsibility for their own solutions.

PUT IT TO USE

When your kids voice their concerns over everything from worrying about summer camp to feeling bored to getting picked last for kickball every time, simply ask "What can *you* do?" Then be prepared to listen to their answers.

For example, five-year-old Avery is afraid to go to sleep at night. If it's not a monster hiding in the closet, it's a thunderstorm or the shark she saw on TV ("But what if it swims around on the floor and tries to eat me while I sleep?"). We might normally be tempted to try to rationalize with the child: There are no monsters. Thunder can't hurt you. Sharks wouldn't survive on carpet, and besides, we wouldn't let them in the house. But that rarely works, as we all know. A pattern begins of Mom lying down with Avery until she falls asleep, and it never ends.

It's time to ask Avery "What can *you* do to help yourself feel less afraid at night?" She might suggest using a night-light and leaving the door open a crack—or possibly drawing a picture of herself fending off sharks and monsters and hanging it on the wall or leaving out fairy potion so that the nighttime fairies will protect her. Whatever works—as long as they're her ideas, right? Try her plan (assuming it's reasonable). She'll be more likely to comply if she came up with the solution. Avery will get a big boost in her sense of significance from solving her own problems, and you'll get your evenings back.

You can use this tool for all kinds of challenges your kids face, including:

- What can *you* do to feel less homesick when I drop you off at preschool?
- What can *you* do if your brother is teasing you?
- What can *you* do to be less bored when it's technology-free time?
- What can *you* do if you aren't happy about the amount of time you're spending on the bench?
- What can *you* do to feel less anxious before your speech?
- What can *you* do if the neighbor kid never gives you a turn on your own swing set?

As kids gain confidence using this tool, they'll begin to solve their own problems from the outset rather than run to you.

Tips and Scripts

- You can start using this tool when kids are really young—around age three or four—and all the way through their teens.
- Reinforce the fact that feelings are okay—everyone feels scared, frustrated, angry at times. But we can address those feelings in positive ways and often improve our situation for the better.
- Don't give an inordinate amount of attention to fears, anxiety,

etc., as that reinforces those behaviors. So in Avery's case, while you need to acknowledge her worries and briefly reassure her that she's safe, you'll want to move quickly to solutions.

- Empathize with feelings ("That must have been hard for you.") but shift the emphasis to the fact that your child has the power to influence his own situation.
- When you first ask "What can *you* do?" you'll get blank stares and an "I don't know," particularly if it's been your job to make it better up until now. It's okay to offer up a few suggestions ("What do you think would happen if . . . ?") but avoid telling or directing. Your child should be in control of the plan.
- Express confidence that your child can work through it.
- Be there for ongoing, age-appropriate support, but not as a crutch.
- Be patient. It may take a while for your child to embrace being in control of her own situation, especially if you've been rescuing her in the past. Stick with it, and the positive results will help your child gain momentum in solving her own problems.

YES, BUT . . .

Sometimes my child's solutions don't work, and he gets so discouraged he doesn't want to try anymore.

First, give him a little time and space to cool down. He'll be able to approach the problem with a more positive mind-set in the morning or even after he's played a few games of backyard soccer with his friends. Then let him talk about his frustration but don't dwell on it. If it helps, remind him of past success he's had solving problems—including other times his first solution didn't work out. Talk about when you've had to really work to get the result you were hoping for, too. Then gently ask if he has any other ideas and offer suggestions if he's stuck, while still letting him be in control. Consider the fact that you might need to ramp up your support, especially if he's tried and failed more than once. For instance, if other kids at school are picking on him and he's already tried using assertive techniques to get them to stop, it might be time for you to get more information from the teacher and draft an action plan. Finally, if your son continues to have trouble, it could be that the problem is beyond his control, and you'll need to explore other options.

Un-Entitler: Family Meetings

This is a tool I love to talk about, because it's one of the great un-entitlers—it inherently reinforces we versus me. Family Meetings are also a way to give everyone—from the toddler to the college student—a fair and equal voice in matters that pertain to the whole household, while doling out heaping helpings of belonging and significance. Family Meetings are held weekly with everyone who lives in the house, but don't worry—they're fun, short (if necessary) and very empowering.

Of course, Mom and Dad still call the shots on the big stuff, but we'll get better buy-in when we involve the kiddos in the decisions. What's more, we'll teach our children about problem solving, cooperation, conflict resolution, leadership and more, giving them real opportunities to practice. Kids learn that they're entitled to have a say—and sometimes their own way—but that their voice is no more important than anyone else's.

PUT IT TO USE

Family Meetings can be short and sweet or they can include lots of topics and discussion. To begin, choose a time and a place (away from the TV, and not during dinner, which can be too distracting) that everyone in the house can commit to. Many families find that Sunday afternoons or evenings are a great time, but choose something that works for your whole family. It's okay to reschedule every so often, but the tool works best if you can stick to it every week, so kids know there's always a time and place to connect as a family.

While you're still getting used to Family Meetings, keep them simple, with the following elements.

Compliments and Appreciations

Kick off your Family Meeting by having each person say something nice about every other person. It can be anything from "Thanks for cheering me up earlier with that joke you told!" to "Thanks for all your help taking care of the little ones this week." While your kids might draw a blank at first when trying to come up with an appreciation, they'll not only get the hang of it very quickly but also soon really look forward to this part of the meeting as they hear the kind things everyone has to say.

Calendar

Every family is busy and each one of us can benefit from reviewing the weekly schedule before it hits in full force. If you sort out business trips, car pools and softball games at the Family Meeting, you can make sure no one's left waiting for a ride or missing out.

Snack

Make Family Meetings even more fun—and official—by serving a special snack. This also gives kids even more of a chance to contribute, as they can help prepare it, serve it and clean it up on an age-appropriate basis.

Allowance

Family Meetings are the perfect chance to pass out your kids' allowances—plus, it's an extra motivator (if necessary!) to get them to make an appearance.

Fun

Here's the best part of your family meeting: a fun activity for the whole family to enjoy together. Make this the last thing you do and keep it as short or as involved as you'd like. Consider reading a chapter of a funny book, playing a board game or even going on a family walk. Whatever you choose, be sure it involves everyone.

Roles and Jobs

To enhance feelings of significance, it's important for everyone to have a role to play in the meeting. Rotate positions such as Meeting Leader, Taskmaster, Calendar Holder, Snack Server, Snack Preparer, Fun Planner and Note Taker every week. Even really young kids can help hand out napkins for the snack or decide the order of topics to talk about, and a four-year-old would get a huge boost of his sense of significance from leading the meeting. Everyone should be included—make up as many positions as there are members in your family.

Once everyone's on board with a basic Family Meeting (which could take a few months or more, especially with younger kids), feel free to add any of the following elements:

Topics to Discuss

Post an agenda where kids and parents can see it and add to it, then review the items during your weekly meeting. You might ask for suggestions for when and how to tackle spring cleaning, discuss your upcoming houseguests or decide on a few fun things to do as a family during summer vacation. Anything is fair game. To avoid having your meeting drag on, however, rule that any topics for discussion have to be on the agenda before the meeting starts.

Problem Solving

This is the opportunity to bring up issues plaguing your house—such as the fact that Thomas keeps borrowing Maggie's headphones without permission. Let your kids air their grievances in a considerate fashion but hold them to the following guidelines:

1. Use respectful language, such as "I feel" statements. No accusatory statements or impolite comments are allowed.
2. Everyone can contribute their opinion, and only one person should talk at once.
3. If you bring a problem to the meeting, you also need to bring a proposed solution.
4. Stay on topic. Also, once a topic is closed, it's closed at least until a new rule or arrangement has been given a fair chance to work (generally, until the next Family Meeting).

While your kids should have the opportunity to talk about what's on their minds, don't let them dwell on it. Instead, focus on solutions, then move on.

Training

Family Meetings are the perfect opportunity for quick training sessions on topics from fire safety to wedding etiquette to how to frost a cake without the frosting getting all crumby. But keep it short—no matter how much you'd love to teach everyone all at once how to scrub grout, huddling over a toothbrush and grout cleaner in the crowded bathroom won't make for a positive family experience.

> Could any company or professional organization work
> very well (or last very long) without a recurring, regular
> meeting where needs and solutions and schedules
> are discussed and resolved?
>
> —Richard and Linda Eyre, *The Entitlement Trap*

Tips and Scripts

• Set a no technology rule. A Family Meeting is like Mind, Body and Soul Time for the whole family, so make sure everyone tunes in.
• Make sure everyone has a chance to speak up and go out of your

way to solicit opinions from quiet kids. Don't let anyone—
including yourself!—dominate the discussion.

- Stick with any new ideas or rules agreed upon during a Family
  Meeting for a minimum of one week. Not only does this time
  limit give your new rule a fair chance to either flop or succeed (or
  need a little tweaking), but also your kids will take decisions more
  seriously when they know they'll have to live with them for a
  while.
- Resist the urge to meet only when something is wrong or your
  kids will learn to dread Family Meetings! Meet weekly, if possible.
- If life gets in the way and you miss a few weeks, don't give up—get
  right back on track. Your kids will thrive on the ritual of weekly
  Family Meetings.
- It might be in everyone's best interest to allow a new rule your
  kids suggest rather than shooting it down, even if you're pretty
  sure it'll be a disaster. They'll learn much more by picking up the
  pieces, revising their plan and reaching a new agreement than
  they would if you swooped in and set them straight.
- Keep it fun! Family Meetings should be a time for bonding above
  all else. Keep them upbeat, and don't let them become a gripe ses-
  sion or a nagfest.

YES, BUT . . .

My work schedule is inconsistent.

Make it a goal to meet four times a month. As soon as you get
your work schedule, decide on times when you can meet as a
family. Even if you can manage only twice a month, try to keep
it as regular as possible and post the meeting time and date in a
highly visible place so your kids know attendance is not optional.

My kids are too cool for Family Meetings.

Your kids might have their doubts at first, but chances are
they'll soon see the value of giving their input on how to share

the family car or what flavors of ice cream to stock the freezer with. Stick to it—even if they never love Family Meetings, the lessons they'll learn are still valid. Make sure the snacks and the fun activities you plan are enjoyable, to get them excited. If your kids are truly obstinate about attending and contributing, make sure you're doing Mind, Body and Soul Time and using the other tools in this book to provide plenty of opportunities for increasing their sense of belonging and significance. If they're fulfilled emotionally, they'll be more likely to cooperate.

5

Creating a Consequential Environment

Oh no! It's 7:43 a.m., and eleven-year-old Jackson forgot to set his alarm! The bus will arrive in fifteen minutes! But not to worry: Jackson's mom would hate for him to have to rush, so she quickly assures him that she'll drive him to school. Jackson meanders into the kitchen, butters a piece of toast using his left hand instead of his right and standing on one leg, just to see if it's possible, and then proceeds to discover how many tiny bites it takes to finish the whole slice. His mom nags him to hurry up with his breakfast, gets him to brush his teeth, reminds him to grab his lunch and puts a hat into his backpack, just in case.

Oops! As soon as Jackson steps foot out of the car, he realizes he's left his gym shoes in his room, under his beanbag chair and with last Thursday's socks inside. Poor Jackson—he won't be able to play kickball in gym class if he doesn't have his shoes! His mom telephones his dad, who hasn't left for work yet and says he can deliver them in time if he skips his coffee run.

Not cool. At recess, Jackson is in line for the slide when another kid steps ahead of him. Jackson does the only thing that makes sense at the time: he pushes the other child—who is half a head shorter than he—harshly off to the side and takes his place back. The child falls and skins his knee, and a worried teacher soon appears to rush the injured party off to see the nurse and, presumably, choose from her amazing collection of Star Wars bandages. The teacher, in her haste to staunch the trickle of blood, only half listens to the answer to her rushed, "What happened here?" and mildly suggests Jackson say "I'm sorry" next time he sees the smaller boy in the hallway. Three seconds later, it's Jackson's turn on the slide and he's forgotten the entire incident.

Too bad. After school, Jackson is standing on a rubber ball in the kitchen while drinking a glass of milk, and—huge surprise—it spills all over the floor. Jackson's mom shoos him outside to play while she cleans up the mess.

Shoot. It's chicken and rice for dinner, and Jackson likes neither—he wanted hamburgers. Eventually, Dad catches him stealthily feeding his meal to the thrilled family dog and after gently scolding him, makes him some macaroni and cheese so he doesn't get hungry later.

Yikes! As he's getting ready to turn out the light, Jackson remembers that his poster on picking up litter to save the environment is due tomorrow! He hasn't even started—he never found a time when he wanted to do it. Jackson's dad promises to e-mail his teacher to get an extra day and then proceeds to start sketching out the title and a few pictures for Jackson to simply color in. After all, Jackson knows how to pick up litter like the best of them, so why should his grade suffer over a pointless poster?

It's been a day full of errors—but the biggest tragedy? Jackson has gone another entire day without facing a single consequence for his negative actions.

At some point, we all need to learn to follow through on our responsibilities, remember our gym shoes and show up on time—and that includes kids. If they are to flourish rather than flounder in the real world, that is.

And we all want the best for our kids—so much that we do everything in our power to make certain the homework gets done, gym shoes are remembered and alarm clocks are set. Unfortunately, we often feel we have no other option to achieve this goal for our kids than to resort to nagging, lecturing, reminding, yelling, punishing, bribing—you name it.

Here's the thing: we can't count on parental rescuing and other not-so-helpful parenting tactics to get the message across. Sure, we can remind our kids every day to remember their lunch box—but we're only teaching them that they don't need to take responsibility themselves. Same goes for nagging them to clean their pet turtle's cage, giving the good-grades-will-get-you-into-a-good-college-and-get-you-a-good-job-and-a-good-life lecture, engaging in daily battles about whether to wash their hair and taking away dessert for a week to teach them a lesson about leaving the park when Dad says to. None of these methods reliably achieve good behavior and most only create a wall between parents and kiddos. Simply telling our kids "Please don't let your new red shirt land in the white load" won't get them to internalize the message. They might get lucky and toss their shirt into the pile of dark laundry that's waiting to go into the washer this time, but never having had their whitest whites turn pink, they aren't likely to actually learn anything.

Indeed, if we want our kids to internalize good behavior, we have to find a way other than badgering them into it. That's where consequences come in.

Actions have consequences. Kids learn this from an early age: I drop the cup, it falls to the floor. Most also learn that Mommy picks it right back up again. The child quickly learns that she can repeat this behavior until Mom finally decides she has better things to do and either takes the cup away or chains it to the high chair.

Experiencing consequences teaches us that if we sleep late, we'll miss the bus; if we don't eat, we'll get hungry; and if we try to drink a glass of milk while balancing on a ball, we'll have a big mess on our hands. These lessons and countless others are important well into adulthood.

But what happens if consequences are diverted or avoided? Take Jackson, for example. His day was full of excellent lessons—but will he learn any of them? Each consequence he could've faced was removed, virtually ensuring he would make his bad choices again sometime. His parents meant well with all their rescuing and reminding—they wanted Jackson to have a worry-free and pain-free day. That's all fine and well, except when this becomes a habit, expectation or lifestyle (which it quickly does), and Jackson grows up without having to think for himself or be held accountable for his actions.

Think of it this way: What would happen if you didn't complete an assignment at work—and nothing occurred? Or what if you showed up an hour late, and no one batted an eye? Or told your boss exactly what you thought of her management style, and she simply smiled and asked if you would like the rest of the day off? It wouldn't take long until you realized there was absolutely no reason to put in any effort, because nothing would happen if you gave it your worst. Pretty soon, work would be something you squeezed in between your midmorning coffee and lunch, but only if it was convenient.

When kids like Jackson enjoy an entire childhood that's virtually consequence-free, their behavioral maturity gets stunted and their internal compasses waver off-kilter. As they age, they become less and less ready to face big decisions. If they don't really learn *for themselves* to wear a coat when it's cold, for instance, they will have less experience and ability to draw on when they're deciding what to fix themselves for a snack, when (or whether) to study for the geometry quiz or where to go after the prom.

And that's why a lack of consequences creates a huge entitlement problem. If the burden is not on our kids to make good decisions, they get used to a pain-free lifestyle. And when they're used to it, they expect it—and when they expect easy living, they feel they're entitled to it.

Facing consequences might not be enjoyable to us or to our kids but it's one of the most effective ways to learn positive behavior. And frankly, wouldn't we rather they learn that there are consequences for dawdling and missing the bus at age six instead of being put on notice for tardiness at their first real job? In fact, your kids *will* learn that actions have consequences at some point in their lives. Our goal is to teach them about real consequences safely and effectively when the stakes are still low. By the time they're out in the real world, as we know, the consequences of their poor choices might result in anything from prison time to an unwanted pregnancy to losing a job they love. Letting our kids face consequences now could save them from much bigger problems in the future.

This chapter is all about how we often get sucked into the trap of rescuing our kids from the consequences of their negative choices (and we all do it!), and how we can institute carefully monitored consequences in a way that best helps children of all ages learn valuable lessons from their mistakes and make fewer of them down the road.

We'll learn how to set up a *consequential environment* in our home. Essentially, to the best of our ability, our kids' positive choices will be met with positive outcomes and negative actions will be met with negative consequences. But that doesn't mean we're dishing out punishment for every single misstep. A consequential environment is one that often simply allows consequences to take place, without rescuing or diverting them. We don't have to watch our kids like hawks—we're better served, in fact, if we watch *our own* actions to make sure we're not letting our children off the hook rather than allowing them to be held accountable.

When our home becomes a consequential environment, there's less nagging and reminding, and more accountability and responsibility. Parents always tell me what a welcome change it is. Yes, kids will mess up and face the consequences, but then the incident passes with a lesson learned and a higher likelihood of success next time. Sound good? Read on to learn the ins and outs of consequences, and how to get started.

Not Inconsequential

Consequences are the steamed broccoli of the parenting world. We may initially *love* the idea of our kids learning valuable lessons from their mistakes and beginning to step up to their responsibilities. But when it comes to serving them up every day, consequences can be hard to choke down.

What actually constitutes a consequence, anyway? Think back to your high school physics class. Every action creates another action. In the case of perfect parenting (and in a perfect world), a positive action (like helping a younger sibling build a marble track) would produce a positive reaction (the younger sibling shares his favorite marbles). A negative action (feeding leftovers to the family dog) would produce a negative reaction (family dog throws up all over the perpetrator's shoes).

Of course, the parenting world is not perfect, and sometimes our kids see no consequences at all for their actions (they decline to practice their presentation on Neptune, only to be saved by a fire drill) or face a positive consequence for a negative action (they forget their PB and J lunch and a friend shares his pizza) or vice versa (they stop to pick up litter from a flower bed in a neighbor's yard, only to be scolded for trespassing). These things happen, but that's why it's all the more important to allow consequences to play out when they may. Why? Because they pack a valuable punch when it comes to teaching our kids about life in the real world.

Consequences adeptly teach lessons when parents cannot. Consider this situation, told two ways:

Thirteen-year-old Hannah is heading out with friends to a nearby park for an afternoon of tennis. It's supposed to warm up, so you remind Hannah to bring a water bottle. She mindlessly agrees, then wanders off to check her ponytail. You nag her again when she comes back downstairs, but she dismisses you as if you aren't even there. While she's out of the room, you fill up a small water bottle and put it into her tennis bag where she'll see it when she takes out her racket—you wouldn't want her to get thirsty, after all. When Hannah comes back into the room she's in a hurry, her mind elsewhere. She grabs her bag and heads to the park. Sure enough, she gets warm while playing tennis and is glad for a drink. Does she thank you? Of course not. Does she remember a water bottle next time? Not likely.

Thirteen-year-old Hannah is heading out with friends to a nearby park for an afternoon of tennis. You mention that it's supposed to warm up and ask if there are drinking fountains or if she'd like to bring water.

Hannah wanders out of the room mumbling something about "maybe" and "there are drinking fountains." When she returns, she's in a hurry—she grabs her bag and leaves. Sure enough, she gets warm while playing tennis. But instead of reaching for a water bottle, she has to cross the park multiple times to drink from the water fountains. Is she annoyed when she gets home? Of course. Does she remember a water bottle next time and every time thereafter? You bet.

Hannah is going to learn much better from being inconvenienced than from being relentlessly reminded and nagged. Not only has she learned to bring water along when she plays tennis, but also she can apply the lesson to other areas of life. It'll put her in a mind-set to prepare more thoroughly for her activities in the future because she knows you won't take the responsibility from her. Cruel? Not at all, considering she'll be making much bigger decisions than that in a few years.

Of course, we wouldn't expect our four-year-old to remember his preschool field trip permission slip, but we can expect him to remember his backpack when he hops out of the minivan (or suffer the indignity of walking in without it). Just as a seven-year-old can use a checklist to remember gym shoes and library books on the correct day, a thirteen-year-old can keep track of her own music lesson and sports practice schedule, and an eighteen-year-old can reliably pack for an overnight trip. But without the practice at a young age, even an older child will flounder with simple responsibilities.

Lessons Learned from Life's Mistakes

When we look at consequences primarily as a *teacher* for our kids, we get less worked up about the fact that the six-year-old opened half her birthday presents when we weren't looking or the eleven-year-old gave himself a haircut that won't look nearly as cool the next day as he thinks it will. Instead, we can calmly let the consequence (fewer surprises on a special day, the necessity of wearing a hat for the next month) do the talking for us.

The fact of the matter is that our kids *are* going to mess up. We can either make the best of their mistakes by letting them see the direct results and offering guidance or we can throw away learning opportunities by rescuing them. Rescued kids do learn something, but it's "If I mess up, I'll always get rescued. I can do what I want without worrying about what will happen."

This quickly and easily leads to a feeling of entitlement: "I *deserve* to do what I want without worrying about consequences." Pretty soon, this attitude leaches into every area of life.

When consequences play into your child's growth and development, however, she first learns, "When I throw my cup on the floor, I don't have it," and then, "If I don't wear mittens my hands will get cold," and then, "If I don't share my toys, my friends won't play with me," and soon, "If I don't practice my free throws, I won't get much playing time," and finally, "If I don't study for finals, I won't get into med school." Kids who are used to choosing for themselves can manage bigger and bigger decisions throughout childhood and eventually adulthood with relative ease. If, however, a child hasn't learned that throwing sand means he's done playing in the sandbox, he's less likely to realize that if he fouls too much in a big game, he'll be sitting out the rest of it on the bench—star player or not.

And, inevitably, there will still be times, even as adults, when they *don't* make the right choice. After all, don't we all own a treadmill we use to hang our coats on, shoes that give us blisters every time we wear them, or slightly ugly throw pillows we regret? But that's okay, too. Kids who grow up facing consequences will not find themselves debilitated by the fact that they didn't keep track of their favorite goggles and beach towel at the pool—they'll quickly realize that a phone call to the pool's office might secure the lost goods until they can return to pick them up. A child unused to facing the results of poor decisions and forgetfulness might instead have to resort to whining to a parent to buy her new goggles and a new towel. After all, Mom should have reminded her.

Consequences will hone kids' critical thinking skills as they learn to evaluate their options based on possible outcomes, their resourcefulness as they figure out new solutions when one goes awry, their ability to accept responsibility as they learn that mistakes aren't the end of the world and even their empathy as they experience firsthand what it's like to be in hot water. These are the lessons that only life itself can teach them. Rest assured your kids would actually *rather* learn from life circumstances than from daily nagging throughout their childhood. And what they learn *from* life, they will learn *for* life.

With consequences, your kids will learn not to fear setbacks but to use them to make a better choice next time. What a powerful tool! When you employ consequences in your home (and you'll learn how soon), you'll feel the pressure fall away as you let life teach your kids how to live. And while your kids might not like the system initially, they'll soon feel empowered by what they're learning—especially once they start to make good decisions on their own and see firsthand the results of positive choices. You'll see less of the entitled I-can-do-whatever-I-want attitude in your kids, and more of the what-I-do-makes-a-difference mind-set that will serve your kids well down the road.

A Consequential Environment

The first tools in this chapter are called Natural and Logical Consequences, and they'll give you the ins and outs of how to set up consequences to play out when poor choices are made, plus how to make sure your child has every opportunity to learn from mistakes. The rest of the tools similarly un-entitle your kids from the feeling that their actions don't matter and they can get away with any kind of behavior. Put them to use, and your home will soon run smoother as your kids get used to being held accountable for their actions.

But how, as a whole, do you get kids who are used to being rescued from their poor decisions (or not allowed to make them in the first place) on board to make better choices and take responsibility?

First, prepare *yourself* for the shift. It's hard to watch your kids make choices you know will cause them problems, no matter how pint-sized! The good news here is that once your kids start to realize they won't be rescued from making bad decisions or from their consequences, they'll soon be more careful about the decisions they make. In time you'll hear less "I don't get to play in the next game because I was late to practice too many times," and more "Coach said I could start next game since my free throws improved with all the practicing I've been doing!" And won't that be music to your ears? When you look at your kids' errant behavior with this kind of perspective, you'll be less apt to yell, lecture, nag, remind, punish and break out all the other negative parenting behaviors we all use from time to time. In fact, the more patiently you can respond to your kids and their problem situations, the more effective the consequences will be.

One of the things I like most about employing a system of consequences is that I'm not the bad guy! Allow the consequence to do the talking—whether you're keeping your teenager in next Friday night because he missed curfew tonight, or turning off the light without a bedtime story for your four-year-old because she was too busy making faces in the mirror to get to bed in time. Then you get to be the good guy by offering plenty of empathy for the missed night out or rendition of *The Little Engine That Could*. There's no power struggle (remember, you can just walk away and ignore any protests), so your child has only himself to blame. Your child will learn his lesson, and you get to keep your composure.

You'll also need to prepare your kids for the new status quo. The tools put the words in your mouth to help you deliver the news to your youngsters, but you'll also need to keep an eye out for ways to Take Time for Training to get the behavior you're looking for. Training in good behavior is important in a consequential household for two main reasons. For one, the more your kids know what to do, the less they'll be left to their own devices and open to bad behavior. What's more, when your kids do make mistakes, they'll feel less overwhelmed and better able to do damage control if they have a few skills under their belt.

Finally, use Control the Environment, When-Then Routines and other positive tools to further aid in setting your kids up for success. An after-school When-Then Routine and an organized, quiet homework spot will go much further toward getting your twelve-year-old to finish his math homework than any lectures you could deliver. Seek their input to get buy-in (do you have any ideas that would help you keep track of your homework every week?), then let your child adjust as needed, as long as it gets the job done.

Are you ready for a dramatic change at your house? Consequences will soon take on the heavy lifting when it comes to helping your kids get over their forgetfulness, irresponsible choices and downright bad behavior. Your kids will no longer feel entitled to a what-I-do-doesn't-matter lifestyle, and you'll all be happier for it.

Un-Entitler: Natural and Logical Consequences

What happens when you try to balance juice on your notebook, stay up watching an awards show the night before a big presentation or go out for a walk without an umbrella despite threatening clouds? You spill, you bomb and you get wet. These, as we all know, are the consequences of somewhat poor decisions. Even worse than an orange stain on your new shirt, however, would be growing up *without* any consequences for negative actions. You might learn that you can do whatever you want—even if it's detrimental to your health, relationships, finances or future.

The attitude of "I can do anything I want" is a hallmark of the over-entitled generation, and these kids often grow up being rescued from their bad behavior, not allowed to face the consequences. As a result, they give little thought to how their actions will affect others and feel entitled to a worry-free lifestyle even if they make choices that wouldn't normally allow for one.

That's why it's so important to set up a consequential environment for your kids—and these strategies are a great place to begin. Natural and Logical Consequences are teaching tools that will help your kids learn firsthand the results of their negative behavior, and give them a good reason to make a better choice next time.

PUT IT TO USE

Consequences will always be a very important part of an un-entitled home. That being said, they are not meant to be the *first* line of defense against bad behavior. If you find your kids are constantly faced with negative consequences, you might need to do some more groundwork in other areas of positive parenting. Your first action should be to increase your child's feelings of belonging and significance using Mind, Body and Soul Time and other positive tools (Decision-Rich Environment, What Is Your Plan?, Take Time for Training, etc.) to prevent bad behavior from happening in the first place. Also, since you'll be setting up consequences in advance, consequences work best for repeated misbehaviors— you'll use other tools to address first- and second-time offenses.

There are two types of consequences: natural and logical. It's important to understand the difference so you can use them both effectively.

Natural Consequences are something you *allow* your child to face. Essentially, once you've warned your child in advance about the possibility of an unsavory outcome, you do nothing and let the consequences play out. If your child refuses to wear a coat, she gets cold. If he leaves toys out in the yard, they get dirty, lost or broken. If she refuses to eat the apple you brought her for a snack on the way to her clarinet lesson, she'll get hungry. Once these have played out, you can discuss the consequence *if your child is open to talking.* But resist the urge to drive your point home with a "See? You didn't wear your coat and now you're cold!" The lesson will evaporate as your child fumes.

To put Natural Consequences to use, follow these steps:

1. In a calm moment, briefly warn your child in advance what could happen if she keeps up the negative behavior. For instance, if your nine-year-old has been bossing around her friends, you can gently

let her know, "Your friends probably don't enjoy being told how to play all the time. If you keep trying to boss them around and control what they do, they might not want to play with you anymore."

2. Let the Natural Consequence happen. Next time your daughter is telling her friends exactly how to dress their Barbies for the big dance, keep quiet, even if you can tell her friends are getting annoyed.

3. Skip the "I told you so" and offer empathy and guidance as needed. When your daughter is bemoaning the fact that her best friend doesn't want to come over, empathize. Then, instead of saying "Of course she doesn't—you always boss her around!" ask "What could you do differently the next time you have a play-date?" and role-play how respectful conversations with friends can sound. Your daughter will soon get the memo to play nicely.

Here's another example of how this might work:

It's a cloudy day, and you've seen in the forecast that there's a 70 percent chance of rain. You mention to your seven-year-old over a bowl of Cheerios, "You might want to wear your raincoat and boots, Evan— it's supposed to rain today."

"I hate my raincoat," he replies.

You've done your job—but the tricky part comes later. When Evan's on his way out the door in flip-flops and a T-shirt, keep your mouth shut even though he's walking to his friend's house down the street, and you can practically smell the rain.

Sure enough, an hour later, while Evan's on his way back home, the skies open up. He's dripping wet by the time he arrives at home—but chances are he'll take your forecast more seriously next time.

Your final act is to continue to hold your tongue when Evan comes back home, except to offer sympathy if it seems warranted with a "Wow, you look miserable! How about some dry clothes?"

While Natural Consequences are those you let play out, Logical Consequences are those you *impose* on your children. Not as a punishment but as a direct result of a negative action. You might want to put a Logical Consequence in place when:

- Facing a Natural Consequence would be harmful to your child (for instance, your child would contract a mouth full of cavities from her refusal to pick up a toothbrush).
- The misbehavior doesn't usually produce an effective Natural Consequence (for example, your child will hardly notice if the toys in the family room aren't picked up).

NATURAL AND LOGICAL CONSEQUENCES: THE PICKY EATER

"Ew, gross!" "I won't eat that!" Nope, that's not roasted raccoon and steamed crabgrass on the table—it's a lovely spread of colorful (and nutritious) stuffed peppers, green beans amandine and sliced mangoes. That you spent an hour and a half assembling. Your kids would rather eat frozen chicken nuggets forced pathetically into dinosaur shapes. In fact, that's what they're begging for now, lest they have to eat real food. Meanwhile, you're asking, "How do I make my kids eat?"

Here's the thing: you can't. Hunger, however, is the most basic Natural Consequence there is, and your best bet for getting your kids to eat more than just a dinner roll. In fact, picky eating is likely a classic example of an entitlement issue. While some research suggests that a certain percentage of kids could be considered supertasters, with more taste buds than the average person and thus predisposing them to an aversion to various fruits and veggies, most picky eaters don't start out fussy. Their limited palettes are nurtured by years of having their tastes catered to or being rewarded for cleaning plates or trying new things (and can we blame them for gagging on cauliflower?). On the other hand, if you don't eat, you get hungry—quickly. I'm not suggesting you starve your kids, but I am offering a different solution than cajoling, bribing or punishing them to get them to force down just one more mouthful of salmon or spinach.

If you've been preparing multiple meals or trying to force your kids to eat, make dinner different tonight. Tell your kids in advance, "You're old enough now to eat what the whole family eats. Dinner is from six to six thirty. At six thirty, the kitchen closes and plates get cleared until breakfast." Then be sure they're not filling up on snacks too close to dinner. At the meal, try to provide at least one option that your kids will probably like but don't go overboard. Then let them eat at will—no "Eat your peas!" necessary (in fact, even commenting on good eating might produce a power struggle because it lets them know you are invested in what and how much they eat). If you're worried they'll fill up on corn, serve only enough for everyone to have one serving. Even if your best baked potato soup isn't enough to tempt them tonight, you can bet that spending one night with a rumble in their stomach will have them digging into tomorrow's beef stroganoff. They won't starve—but they might just learn to try new things.

Unlike Natural Consequences, the parent creates and institutes Logical Consequences. To be fair and effective, a Logical Consequence must follow the five Rs, which are adapted from the work of Jane Nelsen, EdD, and H. Stephen Glenn, PhD. They are:

Respectful
Anything that is intended to cause suffering or shame, such as physical harm, humiliation, yelling, withholding affection or expressing your disappointment in her as a person is not a positive Logical Consequence.

Related to the Misbehavior
Kids think more logically than you'd guess sometimes—so if you set up Logical Consequences that restrict TV privileges for talking too

loudly in the library, they won't get the message. Additionally, they're more likely to learn the lesson if it feels fair to them and they can see the connection between their errant behavior and the consequence. Instead of restricting TV privileges, discuss the do's and don'ts of library behavior and inform your child in advance that you will leave without any books if he talks too loudly—and follow through. One or two occurrences should ensure a better volume for future visits.

Reasonable
Remember that young kids especially can only handle so much. You want the Logical Consequence to get their attention so they'll think twice next time, but not to the point that they'll get discouraged.

Revealed in Advance
This tool only works if you let your kids know the Logical Consequence ahead of time, and when everyone's calm. Otherwise, your consequence will come out of the blue and feel like punishment, and your child will be more inclined to lash out than to shape up.

Repeated Back to You
Ask "To make sure we're clear, can you please repeat our rule for sitting at the table and what will happen if you get off your chair at dinner?" Then you can follow through on your Logical Consequence confidently knowing that your child was fully informed.

Let's look at an example of when and how to use Logical Consequences. Sixteen-year-old Jasmine can't seem to bring her texting conversation to an end before your 8:00 p.m. phone curfew. Your first step is to make sure she's getting plenty of belonging and significance through Mind, Body and Soul Time and other positive tools so she won't have to use negative behavior to meet these needs. If there's still a problem, tell her (and her siblings) in a calm moment in advance, "You're really growing up, and part of being older is being responsible for our phone curfew by making sure you're done *before* eight p.m. If you're still on your phone or texting after eight, you will lose phone privileges for the next week. Now, to make sure we're on the same page, can you repeat back to me our rule for phone privileges, and what will happen if you are still using your phone after eight?"

Keep in mind, a child who is old enough to have a cell phone is old enough to remember the rules associated with its use. That means no reminders from you are required. Even a "Remember what I said about the phone curfew?" just before curfew robs her of the opportunity to take responsibility herself.

If you are concerned about her ability to remember, it's okay to say, "Jasmine, I'm not going to be reminding you about the curfew—it's your job to get off the phone by eight every night or lose phone privileges. What do you need to do to help you remember our new rule?" Jasmine can create a few sticky-note reminders strategically placed around the house or set an alert on her phone to remind her at seven forty-five. The key is it's her job to remember the rule—not yours.

After that, keep an eye on your kids at eight—Jasmine may either not believe your intentions or forget the new rule and stay on the phone past eight as usual. If so, calmly ask her to end her conversation, and let her know that her phone privileges are now revoked for the next week. No matter what kind of a fit she pitches (or how politely she asks), resist the urge to fold, even if she wants to call Grandma. She is welcome to use your landline to call Grandma before 8:00 p.m. tomorrow; however, access to her cell phone is restricted for the next week due to the choice she made. And since you revealed the rule in advance and confirmed her understanding by having her repeat it to you, Jasmine can only be mad at herself.

Natural and Logical Consequences work best if you think them through ahead of time and use them only after you've tried other attention- and power-boosting tools. Mind, Body and Soul Time, Take Time for Training, When-Then Routines, Decision-Rich Environment and other tools will help your child achieve a strong sense of belonging

and significance and will cut down on the misbehaviors you see. For
the recurring misbehaviors that remain, a chart like this will help you
organize your Consequential Environment:

MISBEHAVIOR	CONSEQUENCE	REVEALED IN ADVANCE?
Won't brush teeth	Logical Consequence. Restrict sugary foods. No crackers, treats, sugary cereals, fruit snacks, etc. until child is regularly brushing teeth without a power struggle.	
Never ready for Saturday morning soccer on time	Natural Consequence. Let her know that you will no longer remind, nag or rush. You will leave when she is fully ready. Your child will arrive late and have to explain to the coach and other players why she wasn't on time. She may even lose playing time in the next game.	
Loses or forgets library book	Natural Consequence. Book will accrue a fine, which must be paid from allowance.	
Breaks a sibling's toy	Logical Consequence. Must help fix toy, replace using allowance money or replace with one of her own toys.	

Tips and Scripts

- When implementing either type of consequence, be sure not to
  allow suffering or shame. That includes not letting Natural Consequences play out if you think your child will endure these. For
  instance, if your child refuses to take his medication, giving him
  more control over how the medicine is taken (dropper or spoon)
  and other creative measures would be safer and more effective
  than natural or logical consequences.
- If, however, you warned your kids in advance about the perils of
  leaving craft projects out where the toddler can smash them, fol-

low through by letting the consequence happen. No matter how inconvenient it may seem in the moment, don't rescue—you're laying the groundwork for a consequential environment and the change you're looking for. What's more, your kids are watching—if they see that you don't follow through, they won't take you seriously next time.

• Since you'll be following through, you might want to be very deliberate about when your advance notice takes place. For instance, you probably don't want to institute new consequences about sneaking junk food the day before your child's birthday or before your in-laws visit for the weekend.

• When you do have to implement consequences, be sure to use them as discussion starters. Without judgment, remind your kids that everyone makes mistakes and ask "If you had a redo of the situation, what would you do differently?" This will help unentitle your kids by letting them see mistakes as learning opportunities.

YES, BUT . . .

I can't think of a good Logical Consequence.

First, take a step back. Is it possible you could use a Natural Consequence? If so, do. Natural Consequences have the advantage of not requiring your involvement, plus they do a better job of teaching the lesson. But if not, the appropriate Logical Consequence should be fairly obvious. If you can't think of a Logical Consequence that makes sense and meets the five Rs, it probably means another tool will be more helpful to your child. Perhaps you need to Take Time for (More) Training, improve the consistency of Mind, Body and Soul Time, revamp When-Then Routines, seek their input on solutions to solve the problem or offer Encouragement when they demonstrate positive behaviors (see chapter 7). Try some different approaches until you discover what works.

It seems mean to let my child go outside without a coat.

First and foremost, you certainly don't want to put your child in actual danger. If your eight-year-old refuses a coat and the weather is actually freezing (and not just a chilly forty-seven degrees), try some different strategies. One of my favorites in this case is to ask him if he'd like to test his plan by standing outside without a coat for a few minutes. Chances are he'll soon be headed back indoors to bundle up. This type of arrangement can work for other situations, too.

But to address the big question of "Is it mean to let my kid face consequences?" rest assured that as long as you're on the lookout for his safety—and not putting him in the way of shame or suffering—you're doing your job as a parent. You are teaching him valuable lessons about consequentiality. As we learned in this chapter, it's irresponsible *not* to let consequences play out since our kids will only learn that their actions have no consequences and make poor decisions down the road.

I've tried using consequences and my kids couldn't care less.

If your kids don't care about the consequences, you should view this as a red flag that there's something else going on. Very likely:

1. The consequence feels like punishment to the child because it includes a dose of blame, humiliation or I told you sos. If the intent of the consequence is to make the child suffer or pay for his mistake, he will retaliate by acting as if it doesn't bother him at all.

2. The consequence wasn't related to the original misbehavior, and as a result it feels unfair to the child. Haphazard punishments that aren't related to the original infraction usually result in the child turning her anger against her parents. If we expect our kids to take responsibility for their behavior, we have to make sure the consequence feels fair, even if they don't like it. Using the five Rs

to create your consequences will ensure the process makes sense to your kids, and they'll be more likely to make better choices in the future.

Un-Entitler: Either-Or

Let's face it—there's no way we were going to be able to set up effective consequences and warn our kids in advance about what will happen if they choose to toss a football around in the living room or paint themselves purple. We can't entirely prevent what we can't predict, can we? But that doesn't mean we have to allow the behavior to continue, resort to using punishment or yell until we turn purple ourselves. For those unexpected, unusual and unnerving behaviors that crop up from time to time (or possibly daily), you can use an Either-Or to put a quick end to it without losing your cool (or your sanity).

PUT IT TO USE

An Either-Or takes a bit of quick thinking on your feet, but the results are immediate. Let's say you walk into the living room, only to find that twelve-year-old Nate is tossing a football to himself over your coffee table. Instead of freaking out, take a quick moment to think about what you'd like to see happen. Say *"Either* you can put your football away and find a different activity *or* you play with it outside." Then, leave the scene (watching out of the corner of your eye to make sure your instructions are followed) so there's no room for negotiation.

And how did you come up with that smooth sentence that gets your child hopping to do the right thing? Essentially, you're giving your child two choices: one focused on stopping the behavior at hand and rectifying it (by putting the football away) and another focused on the appropriate way to continue the behavior (taking it outside). Structure it the same way every time so your kids know you mean business when you break out the Either-Or.

Here's another example. What if you catch your four-year-old purple-handed in the middle of an art project? In your calm voice, say "*Either* you can clean the purple paint off your hands now and keep your paint on your paper *or* you can be done painting." Your child has two viable choices, and each would solve the problem.

Remember to avoid anything that causes suffering or shame as part of your Either-Or and follow the five Rs of an effective consequence. As much as you might be tempted to spout "*Either* you can quit blowing your whistle in the house *or* I will step on it until it shatters into a million pieces," that only puts your child on the defensive and does nothing to teach proper behavior.

Tips and Scripts

- An Either-Or is for behavior you didn't anticipate and allows you to address it in the moment. To address a repeated misbehavior, use a Natural or Logical Consequence instead and, of course, reveal the consequence in advance.

YES, BUT . . .

My kids just ignore me without choosing the Either or the Or!

First, be sure you're giving them plenty of positive attention and power in other ways—keeping their baskets full meets their psychological needs so they're more likely to cooperate when you need them to.

If they still ignore you, choose for them—whichever option is easier for you to work through. Say "I see you haven't decided, so I will pick for you." And then put the football away where they can't get to it.

Anatomy of the Follow-Through

For consequences to be truly effective, they have to be implemented the right way. Read on to learn how to stick the landing as you follow through on the consequences you set up.

THE CONSISTENT IMPLEMENTATION

An effective consequence is *followed through consistently.* As you begin to implement consequences of any kind, remember that they won't be effective unless you follow through *every time.* When I was first learning about Adlerian child-rearing strategies, my mentor, Vivian Brault, would illustrate the importance of consistency by facilitating a discussion that went something like this:

"How many of you have ever driven on a military base?" (Hands rise.)

"If the speed limit on base is twenty-five miles per hour, and you drive thirty miles per hour, what will happen?"
You'll get pulled over and issued a ticket.

"For those of you who drive on base, do you ever drive faster than the twenty-five-miles-per-hour limit?"
No way!

"How many of you have driven on I-95?" (Hands rise.)

If the speed limit on I-95 is sixty-five miles per hour and you drive seventy, what will happen?"
Usually nothing. Usually, you won't get pulled over for going five miles per hour over the limit.

"What happens if you drive seventy-five miles per hour and you pass a policeman?"

Well, it depends on the officer. Some will stop you and issue you a ticket; others will let it go.

"So what happens if you exceed the speed limit on I-95?"

It depends. There is no hard and fast rule.

The same concept applies to kids. If parents issue rules but don't consistently follow through each and every time, then the rule isn't hard and fast—in a child's mind, it doesn't really exist. Whether Mom follows through often depends on:

1. the chaos in the house at the time,
2. how tired Mom feels, and
3. how much pushback, whining, begging and throwing tantrums she can expect after enforcing it.

The problem is when we let things slide after we've clearly set up and warned our kids about a consequence, we set the expectation that the rules aren't really the rules. In so doing, we fuel an attitude of entitlement: "If I 'got away with it' last time, I should this time, too!" On the other hand, parents often find that when they follow through a few times, overall behavior quickly improves. When you start implementing consequences, expect to be tested. But once you're tested, and if you've consistently followed through, your kids will begin to take you seriously—which means you'll be faced with fewer misbehaviors in the first place. Even if new misbehaviors do come up, you'll find that your kids won't be as likely to test your resolve since they *know* you'll stick to the rule. It's hard at first but will get easier as your kids learn you mean business.

This might mean you wait to introduce new consequences until after your spouse is home from a weeklong business trip or after the stress of high school midterms is over. At the same time, while you want to feel prepared to follow through you can't put consequences off forever, and the sooner you start, the sooner behavior will change.

And in fact, as chaotic, exhausting and unbearable as things seem now, family life will improve once consequences are consistently followed. Even if following through ruins your afternoon once or twice at the outset, you're doing your whole family a favor by making sure the rules stick and creating a consequential (un-entitled) environment in your home.

THE RESPECTFUL DELIVERY

An effective consequence is *delivered respectfully.* Our goal as parents with implementing consequences is to un-entitle our kids from escaping the results of their poor choices and encourage personal responsibility. Setting up a consequential environment, then, means we need to enable our kids to be held accountable with dignity.

Instead of flying off the handle when your twelve-year-old neglects to turn off the television when her time is up, say calmly and sincerely (assuming you've set up the consequence and revealed it in advance), "Since you didn't turn off the TV when I asked you to, I see you choose to lose your TV privileges for the week." Remember that this is not an emotional transaction—it's a rule and a consequence. It's also not the end of the world.

If, on the other hand, we shame our kids with a "What were you thinking?" they'll get defensive and it will take the emphasis off the potential learning opportunity we've set up. Instead of thinking about making a different choice next time, they'll be pondering ways to get back at us or avoid getting caught—both of which do little to foster personal responsibility. Keep the tone respectful to get more bang for your buck with every consequence you deliver.

THE EMPATHETIC RESPONSE

An effective consequence is *allowed to speak for itself.* The beauty of consequences is that they need very little involvement on our part to do their job. So why is it so hard to hold back an "I told you so" the next time our teenager insists on sandals in January? We all struggle with wanting to drive the point home by commenting (sometimes not so kindly) on the fact that we were right about cold feet all along. Unfortunately, any kind of "I told you so" in word or attitude unravels the positive effects of the consequences.

When we rub it in or try to prove we were right, the child gets defensive, and her anger and blame turn toward the parent rather than on her own poor decision. This is classic entitled behavior. If we truly want our child to change his behavior, we have to let him own his choices and take personal responsibility—which is the opposite of entitlement.

We can, of course, offer empathy if our child seems to want to talk by saying something to the effect of "That must've been rough walking around with cold feet all day!" And leave it at that. Your child feels heard without feeling chastised or shamed as well—and the consequence has been allowed to do its job. She'll be more likely to make a different choice next time if you *don't* spout out "See? I *told* you!"

Un-Entitler: Decide What *You* Will Do

We learned in the previous chapter that we can't control our kids much as we'd like to. But we can control our own actions—and we must, as part of setting up a consequential environment. When you Decide What *You* Will Do, you address a specific misbehavior by predetermining your course of action. So instead of cleaning your kids' rooms yourself because they didn't get the job done, for instance, let them know, in advance, "I will vacuum bedrooms on Thursday mornings. If your floor is clear, I'll be happy to do it for you. Otherwise, you'll have to vacuum your own room by dinnertime that same day." You're not trying to control them by nagging and yelling at them to clean up their rooms, but they'll face the consequences of not doing it themselves (gaining an extra chore). This tool helps reinforce the fact that while none of us can control another person, we *can* control our own actions and responses. They also learn their actions (or sometimes lack of actions) affect other people, and that positive behavior gets positive results. These are all key lessons for un-entitled offspring.

PUT IT TO USE

Your first move is to determine a repeated misbehavior that's bugging you. You can use it to get your kids to do a desired behavior (put their laundry in the hamper) or to stop doing a negative behavior (leaving their bikes in the driveway).

Next, since you can't physically force your kids to put their laundry in the hamper or make them finish their homework without handholding them every step of the way, Decide What *You* Will Do about the problem. In the first case, you might decide that you will only wash clothes that are in hampers on laundry day—which means that if a favorite hoodie with a giant ice-cream stain on the front has been flung to a far corner of the bedroom, it won't be clean and ready to wear again anytime soon. In the case of homework, you might decide you can help between 6:30 and 8:00 p.m., after which point you're too tired to focus, and only after the child has put in a solid effort on her own.

Here's the key to making this tool successful: warn your kids in advance about what you will do, so that it doesn't feel like punishment when it happens. Tell them "I'll wash anything that's in the laundry room hamper Wednesday and Saturday mornings" or "I'll be happy to help you with your homework as long as it's before eight p.m., you've completed everything that you know how to do *and* you can explain to me your thought process for the questions you couldn't figure out on your own."

Be absolutely sure to follow through on your plan! Soon your kids will be stepping up to the plate with their responsibilities and limiting their own poor choices without any words from you.

Tips and Scripts

- This tool is best used when there is an action that *you* can take, independently of your children. So it probably won't work to get them to quit jumping on the couch (you can't exactly fit the sofa into the closet for a week), but it will get them to empty out their lunch boxes after school if you warn them in advance that you will only fill *clean* lunch boxes.
- Be sure that you're not using Decide What *You* Will Do to inflict shame or suffering or to make your kids pay for their mistakes. Use the five Rs of an effective consequence to guide you.

YES, BUT . . .

What should I do when I decide what I'll do but my kids whine and act like I'm the meanest parent on the planet?

Prepare for this event, because it will happen. As you work to create a consequential environment using Decide What *You* Will Do, that doesn't mean they'll always like the outcome. Even if they are upset by the outcome, hold your ground. Not only does it teach them a sense of consequentiality, but it also shows that you are not a doormat. You mean what you say and you are not your kids' personal servant.

Un-Entitler: No Rescue Policy

Parents who continually rescue their kids from showing up at soccer practice with no cleats, turning in an English essay full of errors or arriving late to their babysitting gig unknowingly pave the way for an over-entitled lifestyle. Not only do kids get used to having life go perfectly their way but they also become accustomed to having all their battles fought for them and their dirty work done.

Kids who are frequently rescued learn that they can drop the ball and someone else will make it okay. With this lack of accountability, they have no reason to change their ways—to remember the permission slip (Mom will just drive it to school for them), set an alarm clock (Dad will wake them up) or keep track of their tiny toys (Mom will find it or buy a new one). Rescuing becomes a vicious cycle, because each time a child is rescued, she is more likely to need this special treatment again in the future.

The No Rescue Policy, however, puts a stop to all that. Essentially, you'll stop rescuing your kids from the consequences of their forgetfulness and misbehaviors. As part of a consequential environment, this policy teaches kids to take responsibility. What's more, it empowers them to find solutions and make better decisions next time.

The No Rescue Policy tool is simple to use but can be agonizing as it plays out. Once the cycle of rescuing has been broken, however, your kids will be more capable and confident, and you'll be less harried from rushing around to pick up art supplies for a forgotten project or dropping lunches off at school.

PUT IT TO USE

To implement the No Rescue Policy in your house, you'll first need to warn your kids with an announcement: "You're really growing up, and you're fully capable of managing things for yourself. From now on, we won't be rescuing you when you forget things for school." Then make sure they understand that that means no more rushing homework, gym shoes, musical instruments, lunches, permission slips or library books to school. Once you've tackled forgotten school items, move on to something else you rescue them from—such as running late for activities, breaking toys because they're careless, etc.

Next ask your kids to come up with no rescue solutions for the times you've always rescued them before. Say "What ideas do you have for remembering everything you need for school every day?" Or "How can you make sure you make it to practice on time?" Listen to their ideas first and, if necessary, suggest your own—such as marking off a dry-erase checklist by the door, packing backpacks the night before, attaching a laminated list to the hockey bag, setting their own alarm clock, using labeled bins (with pictures or words) to store toys or creating a cubby space for their sports items.

Make sure any new systems and ideas are in place and that you've done a practice run—or two or three—before using the No Rescue Policy for the first time. Then, let your kids know when the rule is in effect. After this point, you won't rescue them from anything they should be able to do or remember themselves.

Once you've laid the groundwork, you're ready for the toughest part of the tool: doing nothing. When you find seven-year-old Abby's lunch bag in the fridge (again!) long after the school bus has pulled away, resist the urge to drop it by her classroom on your way to work. She'll go hungry once and be highly unlikely to leave it behind again anytime soon. And when fourteen-year-old Ben is still only half-dressed in his uniform as practice is starting, don't push, prod or drive one mile over the speed limit. He'll arrive late and have to explain to the coach why, but tomorrow he'll be the one trying to herd *you* out the door. What's more, they'll both lose the sense of entitlement that comes from not taking responsibility and avoiding consequences.

Yes, it's hard to watch your kids walk into difficult situations. And sometimes, knowing that *other* parents *will* rush the lunch to school or blame traffic (again) for the late baseball player is worse than the guilt you feel about not doing these things. It's not easy to let your kids fail, but pretty soon you'll see that the number of times you feel the need to rescue your kids will sharply decline, while your kids exhibit the ability to successfully manage their own responsibilities.

As your children stumble through the new system, be readily available to offer empathy ("Yikes, you must've been hungry all afternoon after you forgot your lunch!") and to talk about solutions ("What do you think you could do to make sure you remember it tomorrow?") but to never say anything in the form of a "Well, that's what you get. . . ." Kids will learn much more from their mistakes than from any lecture you dish out, no matter how well-meaning.

Tips and Scripts

- Use this tool on an age-appropriate basis. For instance, a young child should be able to remember a backpack when leaving for school but might need help the night before remembering exactly what needs to go in it for the next day. Create a checklist in pictures or words so he can be successful without your help.
- Avoid getting upset with your kids as they get used to the new system. If they forget their science project and lose points because of it, it's on them, not you—no matter how much you want them to get into a good college.
- If you feel the need, e-mail your child's teacher (or coach) to let her know about your new policy. Write "We're working with Sophia to take responsibility for remembering her homework. If she forgets, she's prepared to accept the consequences." Chances are she'll be right on board—and appreciative of your approach.
- It's still okay to help your kids out with isolated incidents from time to time. We all make mistakes, but if leaving the lunch box on the counter becomes a habit, you'll need to implement the No Rescue Policy.

YES, BUT . . .

I've done this and my son still forgets his assignments.

Perhaps he needs help with organization (pick up a weekly planner for him) or systems (a dry-erase board that attaches to the inside of his locker so he can write down the books he needs to bring home throughout the day, or reminders or alerts on his smartphone). In an ideal world, we would have focused on other solutions before implementing the No Rescue Policy—but it's never too late. Brainstorm with your son so he can make positive changes before his grades really start to suffer. If his attitude is the problem, however, bringing home a report card full of Cs instead of the As and Bs he's used to might be the wake-up call he needs.

FAILING TO LEARN, OR LEARNING TO FAIL? A TEACHER'S PERSPECTIVE ON LETTING KIDS MESS UP

When parents are too quick to respond to the needs of their children and don't give those children any chance to cope with challenges, consequences or failures, teachers can't teach. Teachers need the space and time to help students wrestle with confusion and to struggle with the challenges inherent in the process of learning.

Teachers get frustrated in the face of these parents, but in the end, parents come and go, and teachers will live to teach another day. The real losers are the students. Those students will likely graduate to the next level of their education, but they can't really learn, can't use the information gathered from the wreckage of their grand mistakes and misfortunes in order to move on to new challenges. Overly directive and controlling parents reap what they sow in that their children age but they don't develop resilience and they can't grow into their ideals through the crucible of failure.

—**Jessica Lahey**, educator, *New York Times* columnist, "Parent-Teacher Conference," and author of *The Gift of Failure: How the Best Parents Learn to Let Go So Their Children Can Succeed*

Un-Entitler: All in the Same Boat

Asking a parent "Do your kids fight with each other?" is like asking "Do your kids breathe?" Where there are siblings, there are squabbles! Whether one sibling received two extra sprinkles on his cupcake or another is monopolizing the water sprinkler, it seems there's always something to fight about.

One key reason is—you guessed it—entitlement. It often happens that if one child feels entitled to the first, the best or the most, her sibling does, too. Which makes sense: they're being raised in the same home and with similar parenting styles, so the entitled chip on the shoulder probably comes from the same day-to-day special treatment they've grown accustomed to over the years.

In this case, entitlement gives rise to rivals. If Briana feels as though she deserves to go first whenever she plays a board game with a sibling, chances are her brother feels the same way. Which means there will be a fight every single time they pull out the Mouse Trap box.

No, you don't need to toss the family's board game collection into the trash, even if you sometimes really, really want to. Once you start un-entitling your kids, the sibling disagreement episodes will start to decline. But they won't disappear entirely, and that's where All in the Same Boat comes in. This powerful tool will help your kids work out their arguments between themselves, or each face the same consequence. It'll show them that fighting has negative consequences that can be avoided through positive efforts. And in the meantime, you'll be able to teach them conflict-resolution skills that will help them pave a peaceful path far into the future.

PUT IT TO USE

All in the Same Boat is a powerful tool, but it relies on quite a few steps. Follow these to make it maximally effective:

1. **Practice peace.** To make this tool work, you'll first need to Take Time for Training with each of your kids, no matter their ages, on how to respectfully voice disagreement, assert their position, use "I feel" statements, listen to the other person, suggest solutions and generally work to reach a resolution without such neg-

ative behavior as calling names, shouting and physical violence. They'll also need to know when to walk away or ask for help from a grown-up—such as if someone is really getting hurt. Try role-playing scenarios or acting them out with stuffed animals to help younger kids catch on. Be realistic, however. Learning conflict-resolution strategies takes years and you can expect plenty of fights and tears along the way.

2. **Prep the plan.** Once your kids have a good understanding of how to reach an agreement, it's time to let them practice on their own. When there are no fights currently raging, tell them, "You are old enough now to manage your own disagreements. Next time I hear fighting, I'm simply going to leave the room so you can work it out between yourselves."

3. **Sit out the squabble.** Then stick to your word. When Charlie stomps like an ogre through the middle of the Lego castle Isabella is building, slip into the kitchen and look really busy (all while keeping a distant eye on the disturbance if you think it might get out of hand). When you first use this tool, chances are Charlie and Isabella will look your way to see what you're going to do. Ignore them and watch the fight play out. With any luck, after the initial screams of "You wrecked Cinderella's palace and now she'll have no place for a ball!" they'll figure out a plan for Charlie to help rebuild the castle, or to let Isabella invite Charlie's coveted knight action figures to the ball. It doesn't matter, as long as both kids are relatively comfortable with the solution and reach mutual peace, even if it's shaky.

4. **Help helpfully.** If the fight escalates to physical violence or the kids just can't reach an agreement even after giving it a good try, it might be time to step in—but not to assign *victim* and *aggressor* labels or declare a winner. Without taking sides, ask each child to tell their story using "I feel" statements. Then restate each child's case: "Isabella, I see you are upset because Charlie wrecked your

castle. Charlie, you're frustrated because Isabella wouldn't let you have any of the Legos. Now, does anyone have any ideas for how we can solve this problem?"

5. **Suggest solutions.** Sit back and listen to your kids' ideas. On a good day, someone will come up with some version of sharing or taking turns—or anything else that settles both kids' minds (and it's okay if it's some strange version of "How about I let you pet my hamster five times and Cinderella can take a ride on the pirate ship?" as long as it leaves everyone happy). If no one has any workable ideas, it might be time to suggest one or two of your own (using a waiting list, finding something else to play with) and let the kids decide.

6. **Put your kids All in the Same Boat.** Finally, if they still can't reach a resolution, it's time to put them All in the Same Boat. Say "If you can't reach an agreement, I will put the Legos into the closet and no one will play with them for the rest of the day." By making your kids face the *same* consequence, you un-entitle them from being able to get what they want simply by fighting about it. Instead, they'll learn that positive behavior—resolving a conflict without calling names, for instance—will bring a positive result.

7. **Do the dirty work.** And if there's still no agreement? Calmly whisk the Legos away, and know, despite your kids' cries of injustice, that the next time they fight, there will likely be a resolution.

Tips and Scripts

- When stepping in to help, use your best sportscaster voice. In other words, without taking sides, simply comment on the situation. Hear out each side, but refuse to favor anyone.
- If the fight has grown heated, give everyone a breather. Have your

kids find a quiet space (e.g., a bedroom, outside) to cool down, then meet up again to find a resolution.

- Resist the urge to critique the resolution. If both sides are satisfied, it works.

- Think of each fight as an opportunity to practice positive conflict-resolution skills. Even if you end up having to step in a lot at first, soon your kids will get the hang of working things out on their own.

- Teach your young kids to use nonthreatening words instead of simply shoving big sister out of the way: "When you're done, can I please have a turn?" Once they've mastered this technique, not only will they relax about who gets to use the swing, knowing that they're entitled to a turn at some point, but you'll cut the number of fights significantly.

YES, BUT . . .

What if I know for certain who was in the right and who was in the wrong? It seems unfair to put them in the same boat and make them both face the same consequence.

Keep in mind that you truly don't know the whole story. Siblings have long histories, and while Molly might look like she was completely unprovoked when she threw Becker's favorite T. rex into the trash can, it could be that earlier in the day, Becker had used her sticker collection to wallpaper his toy pirate ship. The behavior still isn't okay, but by having each child face the same consequence, you encourage them to put the disagreement aside and focus on a solution that works for everyone. Once they've had some practice doing this, they'll default to it next time instead of trashing a favorite toy.

What's more, whenever you get involved and assign *victim* and *aggressor* labels, you escalate competition and risk the behavior's being repeated in the future. After all, Molly will soon learn that "If I pick on Becker, I get attention—even if it's negative," while Becker learns that "If I come crying to Mommy, I'll get her attention." They're more likely to fill those roles in the future, too, if they constantly see themselves as aggressor or victim. It might seem fair to play judge and jury, but this type of ruling does your kids no favors. It's far more important that they learn to work out their own problems than it is to figure out who, exactly, called whom a stink wad first.

And finally, remember that it takes two to fight. When a disagreement is raging, anyone can end it by walking away. Teach your kids that sometimes walking away to cool off, and then revisiting the topic later, can produce a much better result than duking it out.

SHARING: HOW LONG IS A TURN?

Would you say that at least 80 percent of fights have something to do with sharing a coveted object? When siblings share space all day long, sometimes it's hard *not* to push each other off the swing or grab a joystick out of the other's hands. Heather Shumaker, author of *It's OK Not to Share . . . and Other Renegade Rules for Raising Competent and Compassionate Kids,* suggests a very practical tactic to help with turn taking: the waiting list.

It's a simple tool: when someone is waiting for a turn—and especially if they're getting frustrated—you start a waiting list. When the first child is done, it's the next child's turn.

Here's the catch: a turn lasts until the child is *done.* Completely done. Which means the first child gets to *continue* playing with the toy until he is ready to hand it over. A turn can last a minute, an hour or a day—until the child is done.

This might sound like a recipe for disaster, but it's not. You can count on the fact that kids will be voluntarily done at some point (at a crowded children's museum, however, you might have to let your kids know that the rules are different, and limit turn time). What's more, when you allow them to decide when they are done, they'll lose the frustration that mounts every time we set a timer or the sense of injustice they feel when we force them to turn over their toy just because little brother is pitching a fit. Little brother also learns an important lesson in delayed gratification—a crucial skill in an un-entitled home.

In the meantime, though, it's okay for waiting kids to express their own frustration. Teach them to say "I'm waiting for a turn" or "I feel frustrated because you've been playing that game all morning!" In doing so, both kids will learn how their actions make the other person feel. And while turns might be really long at first (especially for kids who have been forced to share their whole lives), as kids relax and feel protected under the new system, they won't hold on to a coveted glitter wand any longer than they're really casting magic spells with it.

Un-Entitler: Making It Right

We all make mistakes, don't we? Hurt people, break things, forget to walk the poor dog on our lunch hour. What matters is how we manage our mistakes—or make it right again. Manners aside, an apology isn't always the best way to fix a problem we've caused. For instance, let's say Dexter breaks off the tentacle of Henry's new alien action figure. A well-meaning parent might force a sorry out of Dexter, but it's certainly not heartfelt, and even if it were, the apology can neither regenerate the missing tentacle nor fix the now-fragile friendship.

In fact, since over-entitled kids aren't used to taking responsibility for their actions, they're likely to shift the blame ("Henry was making it dive off the couch—*he* broke it."), react in anger ("That alien was stupid anyway!"), deny anything really happened ("I don't know what you're talking about!") or preemptively mumble the meaningless apology just to get Mom off his back ("Sorry.").

Making It Right changes the way kids think about their offenses by helping them go beyond saying I'm sorry to actually remedying the situation with a kid-generated act of reconciliation. It holds them accountable for their behavior, helps them learn empathy and teaches them that their actions affect others. All of these will go a long way toward curing the entitlement bug, not to mention improving relationships.

PUT IT TO USE

If your home is like most, you'll have plenty of opportunities to use this tool. Next time ten-year-old Savannah digs into her older sister Julia's jewelry box without permission, instead of demanding that Savannah apologize, sit down with her and go through the steps of Making It Right.

First, skip the lectures, the punishment and the "say you're sorry." Take a few minutes to cool down if you have to, but neither dishing out the Property Rights 101 lecture nor revoking TV privileges will have any real effect on whether Savannah plays dress up with Julia's birthstone necklace in the future. Also, be sure to give Savannah a chance to regain her composure after the incident (which may have involved a tongue-lashing from her big sister), so that she'll be able to work through it in a constructive way.

When Savannah is ready, have a chat with her to help her see the jewelry box raid from Julia's point of view. In a nonthreatening way, induce empathy by asking "How would you feel if Julia had gone through your sticker collection without asking first?" or "What do you think Julia's feeling right now?"

Then ask Savannah what she could do to make it right with Julia. And here's the thing—it's okay (and it's preferable) if saying I'm sorry doesn't top the list. It's more important that Savannah reach out in her own way and in a way that might be meaningful to Julia. Savannah might offer to organize Julia's jewelry for her (or help clean a less-contested area of her room), draw her a picture or give Julia half of her media time later that day. And it's possible that a truly heartfelt I'm sorry is a good choice—but in most cases it needs to be accompanied by an act of kindness that *shows* she's sorry. Actions do, as kids know as well as adults, speak much louder than words. Whatever's decided, Making It Right will help Savannah smooth over relations, practice empathy and learn about the effect her poor decisions have on other people. As for Julia? She'll be grateful to not only avoid the meaningless I'm-sorry-that's-okay routine, but also to see that Savannah took personal responsibility and wants to make up. And when they both win, so do you.

Tips and Scripts

- It could be that a little training would help ensure the offense doesn't happen again, but now is not the time. Instead, Take Time for Training well after the fact, when hostilities have cooled.
- It's okay if you need to give your child some space before Making It Right. We often feel that we have to solve the problem immediately, but by waiting, we can ensure a more positive and meaningful resolution.
- You can (and should) still teach your kids when and how to say I'm sorry. But also teach them that a quick apology doesn't mean they're off the hook.
- Hold your child accountable even if the offense was accidental. Even oopsies need to be rectified.
- If your child is stuck trying to figure out how to Make It Right, it's okay to offer a few suggestions. But be sure your child plays an active role not only in figuring out how to reconcile but also in following through on her plan.

FIVE STEPS FOR A MEANINGFUL APOLOGY

While your kids shouldn't rely on just saying I'm sorry to make amends, this five-step system will help them work through the incident and say the words in a way that will have meaning for both parties:

1. Own what's yours. Your feelings are yours, and it's okay to be angry, upset, sad, etc. But the actions are yours, too. Help your child understand what it means to take responsibility for his errant action.
2. Feel out the other's emotions. Help your child imagine how the other person might have felt about the offensive behavior.
3. Apologize for the action and acknowledge the feeling. "I'm sorry I scribbled on your picture. That must have made you feel really mad."
4. Ask for forgiveness. A simple "Will you forgive me?" will do. This helps both sides understand that letting someone back into your good graces is a choice but an important part of moving forward.
5. Find a fix. Helping with a new picture might be a good solution in the case of wrecked artwork, for instance.

These steps might produce a heartfelt apology that sounds like "I felt jealous because I liked your picture better than mine, but it wasn't okay for me to scribble on it. You must have felt really sad. I'm really sorry I drew on your picture. Can you forgive me? I'll be happy to help you draw a new picture for yourself, or draw one for you."

YES, BUT . . .

My child has learned all the answers to Making It Right and continues to show negative behavior toward others.

You might have a deeper issue. Make sure your child is getting his emotional needs fulfilled with plenty of Mind, Body and Soul Time, and other positive tools. Also evaluate your child's influences. What kinds of TV does he watch? Who are his friends? Is his behavior an act of revenge to get back at someone else for the way they treat him? Determine if any changes need to be made.

Then consider setting up consequences for repeated bad be-havior. For instance, a Logical Consequence for breaking a sib-ling's toy would be to have to replace it using allowance money or with a toy from his own toy box.

The offended child rejected my child's method of Making It Right.

It could be that the offended child simply needs a bit longer to cool down. If she's a sibling, you can gauge when might be a good time for another try, knowing that siblings' attitudes to-ward each other often fluctuate on a daily or hourly basis.

If she's not a sibling, help your child find another time or an-other way to try to make amends. But there's no need to venture into the unreasonable (picking up movie tickets for another child simply because yours called him a snot monster, for in-stance). If you're confident your child has made a solid effort to make up, coach your child to be available to the friend, but let the issue drop. Chances are a good friend will forgive or forget in time.

6

~~Great~~ Reasonable Expectations

Sixteen-year-old Sanjay rolls out of bed on a bright and sunny Saturday morning. He's planning to go for a long run—he's hoping to make the varsity track team, and practices and tryouts are scheduled after school several days this week—and then play tennis with a friend in the afternoon. Between the two activities, he plans to spend an hour or so working on French verbs. He learned yesterday that his good scores on a French exam have made him eligible to participate in an essay competition for area high schools, and three winners will be chosen for a summer exchange program in Paris. Sanjay is really excited about the prospect—he's always wanted to travel abroad and has even been thinking about a career in international business.

As Sanjay is stretching before his run, his dad materializes in the doorway. "Hi, Buddy, good news! I managed to get a French tutor for you to help you prep for your essay! Lucky for us, she had a cancellation today and agreed to squeeze you in! She'll be here in thirty minutes and will spend the morning with you. Plus, she'll be here every afternoon after school until the essay exam on Friday."

"But I was going to go for a run!" protests Sanjay, dismayed. "And track tryouts are after school this week! I don't want to miss them!"

"It'll be worth it when you go to Paris. Now come on, change out of your running clothes and grab some breakfast—and not that sugary cereal you always eat, something with protein."

Sanjay weakly protests again, but his father replies, "Son, I'm *telling* you, not *asking* you." "Oh, and by the way," he adds, "since you're interested in international business, I scheduled you a tour of the university's foreign studies program. If I were betting, I'd say you have a future in France!" Dad turns and leaves the room.

Sanjay grumbles but knows from experience it's useless to fight. Besides, his dad also got him a great job as a lifeguard at the pool, an A in language arts even though he slept through the final and a puppy when he was ten even though his mom had a firm no dogs rule.

Sure enough, thanks to all the extra tutoring, Sanjay wins the essay competition, and in a few months is on his way to Paris. Somehow, with his dad watching out for him, things just happen to work out.

Just like real life, right? No doubt Sanjay does have a loving and supportive dad. One who's used to juggling work, family, home and other activities, too. He's probably achieved a lot himself and wants the very best for his son. Don't we all?

But when we know just what our kids need, and provide, urge, wheedle and negotiate them into whatever we think is for their own good, we also take away their ability to think for themselves. Sure, Sanjay might get into the foreign studies program of his dreams—but will his dad move in with him to ensure he's spending enough time studying, eating enough protein, arriving at class on time and taking advantage of every opportunity? Even if his dad could do all that, clearly it's a ridiculous idea.

And talk about entitlement! With his dad paving the way, Sanjay will grow to expect the red-carpet treatment in all of his pursuits. Not only that, he'll expect to always succeed and flounder when he doesn't. His dad's well-meaning attempts to launch Sanjay into the perfect adulthood will set the teenager up to feel entitled to it, having not really earned it himself.

Sooner or later, we all have to hand over the reins. This chapter is all about the expectations we set up for our kids, how to line them up with reality and how to face the inevitable—and beneficial—failures along the way. Let's start by exploring the reasons we all develop a tendency to micromanage our offspring.

Holding on for Dear Life

For a long time in our kids' lives, Mommy and Daddy really do know best. When they're babies, we know to not let them chew on plastic grocery bags. As toddlers, we make sure they wash their hands after using the bathroom. As they grow, we get them to brush their teeth, wear snow boots, say thank you and endless other little things. Sometimes it seems that our lives revolve around making our kids do stuff they don't want to but is for their own good. And then one magical moment, they say please on their own or *don't* forget to wash their hands, and we're on cloud nine—we're *awesome* parents! Our kids totally rocked Hand-Washing 101, thanks to our constant reminders!

When our kids are too little to know the difference, it's our job to make sure that the right decisions are getting made. And as long as our kids are under our roof, we still get to call the shots that affect our whole household—that doesn't change. What's more, kids of every age need plenty of guidance ("Can we talk about your new boyfriend?" "How do *you* feel about your math grade?"), and they sometimes simply need to be told what to do without having much of a say in the matter ("It's time for your medicine," "You're going to be sharing a room with your brother"). We get so used to calling the shots that it becomes a habit, until we're telling our teenager exactly what to have for breakfast, or dressing our kindergartener every morning simply because we always have.

While we expect the best for our kids, we don't always know how to help them achieve it in a positive way. We *know* it's important for them to make their own decisions—but it's easy to lose sight of this fact when Courtney is one A away from getting into the college she wants to go to, Anna wants to quit clarinet just when she's getting good at it, Liam is ignoring his Key Club project, or Nolan is in the middle of a drawn-out disagreement with his former best friend about whose superpowers are cooler. A million times a day, we feel like we know what's best for our kids—and just as many times we're tempted to snowplow or helicopter away their obstacles or poor decisions. Who wouldn't? They're our offspring and we love them and we want the best for them. What's more, we know how to get it, and they clearly don't.

Ideally, we want to be the parent who finds the magical balance of encouraging and guiding our kids, but in moments of desperation, or simply out of habit, we overstep our bounds. But sometimes our dreams for our children—whether we're hoping they can make friends on the first day at a new school, learn to swim, make it through the day without an accident or get into Yale—cause us to control, manipulate, nag, bulldoze and resort to a host of other actions that will smooth their way. Sometimes we're willing to do *anything* to help them make the grade, get on the team, win the scholarship or other high-stakes prizes. After all, this is *real life* we're talking about. The competition is fierce, and we're worried our kids will get swallowed up by mediocre—or worse—lives. We want them to be successful.

I hear you! And it's certainly a good thing that parents are involved in their kids' lives, standing behind them and cheering louder than the crowd. With so much at stake, it's no wonder we hold on to the reins for dear life, never wanting to let go. Unfortunately, this hyperinvolved state of high expectations and wielding control is doing more harm than good in our kids' lives. In trying to chase the ever-elusive vision of success we have for them, we crush their chances of securing their own version of success for themselves. Let's take a closer look at the bigger picture of success and the delicate balance between walking alongside our kids versus clearing the way ahead of them.

Steamrolling the Path to Success

The problem is that our well-meaning attempts to smooth the way to success do anything but. When we do everything in our power to clear the path, point them in the right direction, start them walking, navigate the obstacles for them and generally keep them plodding down the road to a successful life, we rob from them the valuable opportunity to do all those things for themselves. And when we don't allow, encourage and enable them to meet life's challenges in childhood, they will be very ill prepared to meet even greater challenges in adulthood. So unless you plan on driving the steamroller (or your other vehicle of choice—see the sidebar on pages 186–87) through retirement, your child is going to need to learn to go it alone. And trust me—she'd prefer it that way.

What's more, when we steamroll for our kids, we also rob them of feelings of pride in accomplishment, the chance to work hard to meet a goal and a host of other significance-boosting opportunities. Worse, we teach them that *they cannot succeed on their own.* When we're negotiating a grade for our twelve-year-old, we're telling them, "You can't earn your own grade, so I need to do it for you." This quickly leads to twofold entitlement. First our kids feel like they *deserve* a good grade. Then they feel entitled to have someone do the work of earning the good grade for them. They're discouraged from even trying to make it on their own, because they couldn't possibly be successful without help, anyway. When it comes to future jobs, relationships and daily life, kids who are used to a steamroll-smooth path will expect all of their ways to be smooth *and* that someone else will do the smoothing *for* them. Double whammy.

In fact, Hire a Steamroller could be another classic tactic from the Entitled Kids Manual.

ENTITLE ME! TOOL: HIRE A STEAMROLLER

Life can be so unfair! Like when you don't get to be the pitcher for the Little League team, or you don't sell the most Girl Scout cookies, or when you get a bad grade even though you worked really hard (well, pretty hard) on your project. What should you do? Take it to your parents and Hire a Steamroller!

> ## Put It to Use
> First, use Whining (from chapter 2) to make sure your parents know how much you wanted to be the pitcher for the Little League team. Then, Play the Victim about how the coach plays favorites with the other kids, how you felt a little sick for tryouts, how the sun was in your eyes and how you just know that you'd be the best pitcher if you were given the chance. Create a Guilt Trip by telling your parents that this has always been your dream, how they've been too busy to play catch with you in the backyard and that you're concerned for your future if you don't get to pitch. This is usually enough to get your parents to jump into action, call the coach and negotiate for you to pitch at least some games.

But don't worry—even if your kids currently feel entitled to a smooth ride to success, they won't after you put your own tools to good use.

Let's look at another example with two outcomes. Celia is nine years old. She really, really wants the small solo part in her tap-dancing class. Her mom also really wants Celia to get the solo part. With the audition a month or two away, Mom starts building a friendly relationship with the dance instructor, always finding a kind word to say after class. The dance school holds a fund-raiser, and Mom not only chairs it but makes one of the biggest contributions. Mom volunteers to do makeup for all the girls for the performance. Mom happens to mention to the instructor, the receptionist and the director of the school how much Celia loves tap dancing and how hard she's been practicing at home (whether she has or not) and how she really hopes she'll get the solo part even though, of course, all the other girls are fabulous dancers, too, and how Celia will probably be taking classes for many more years—which will hopefully be at *this* school, even though there's a different one closer to home. Pretty soon, it's audition time. Celia dances just fine, but so do most of the other students. Mom drops the instructor one last note about how thrilled Celia is with classes this year and how much she's been practicing. And finally, Celia gets the good news. She's earned the solo part she wanted so badly! Congratulations, Celia! Or should we say congratulations, Mom!

Here's another way that could play out: Celia is nine years old. She really, really wants the small solo part in her tap-dancing class. Her mom knows it, so over lunch one day they talk about some ways that Celia can improve her skills, show interest in the class, demonstrate responsibility and practice the other behaviors that make someone a true star. Every week at class, she pays close attention to her instructor, following rules about not chewing gum and not tapping her shoes while the teacher is talking. She always arrives early with her tap bag packed with everything she needs—having double-checked it the night before class. Celia asks the instructor for the exact name of the piece they'll be dancing to in the performance so she can download it and practice at home. A couple of times after class, she asks her teacher to demonstrate again a tricky move. Celia practices daily and even skips a birthday party so that she can make it to class, since she'll have to miss class for a family vacation the next week. When audition time comes, Celia gives it her best. And finally, Celia gets the good news. She's earned the solo part she wanted so badly! Congratulations, Celia!

Most parents aren't quite the steamrollers that Celia's mom was in this case, but can't we all relate? We want—and expect—the very best for our kids. I'm sure you can see the differences in the two scenarios—you can surmise for yourself the various effects Mom's influence would have on Celia's sense of entitlement, pride and confidence as well as her work ethic. With meddling from Mom, Celia gets the part and learns that she couldn't do it on her own—so why try? Even if she does put forth her best effort, she doesn't know whether it's her hard work or Mom's dropped hints that got her the solo.

Without Mom's help, Celia can attribute her success directly to the star behaviors she showed: paying attention, practicing, getting help when she needed it and dedicating herself to the task. She knows she *earned* the solo, and she'll apply the lessons she learned to other areas of life, from her history homework to her first job.

But there are several scenarios I *didn't* include: what would've happened if Celia had put her all into working for the part but another dancer was chosen instead? How devastating! And what if Celia didn't practice particularly hard, and her mom didn't meddle, but she was awarded the part simply because she happened to dance very well that day? These two scenarios are prime examples of real life. Which is what your child will be living in a few short years. Yes, it's frustrating to be overlooked for a part we've poured our heart and soul into. But would we want this to happen for our child's very first time when she's twenty-two and looking for jobs? Talk about crippling! It's much better to get used to the fact that sometimes things don't work out the way we hope early on. We'll discuss this in more detail later when we talk about failure. In the second case—Celia gets a part she hasn't worked hard for—Celia's mom could wisely offer a sincere congratulations, then encourage her daughter to prepare for the solo the very best she can for the show, teaching her she's not off the hook simply because she won the part. No matter what happens, Celia will learn much more without her mom steamrolling a path and be better prepared for the myriad of similar situations she'll encounter when she's on her own.

NAME THAT OVERPARENTING VEHICLE

We've seen all these types at the park, at sporting events and in our neighborhood. But let's admit it: have you ever ridden any of these with your kids? (By the way—I've driven each of these at least once down Main Street, even though I'm not proud of the fact!)

The Steamroller (or Lawn Mower)

Ever feel tempted to charge on ahead of your kids to make sure the path is free of rocks and bumps? The parents who are pros at smoothing the way are the steamrollers of the parenting world.

The Helicopter

This is the parent who's always buzzing around her kids, constantly fretting about monkey bars, mosquitoes and bullies. They hover, they help and they don't know when to pull up a park bench and relax.

The Freight Train (or Snowplow)

Some of us really want things to go well for our kids and we're willing to plow down anything—or anyone—that's preventing our kids' success. Look out, coming through!

The Tugboat

Come . . . on . . . just . . . practice . . . five . . . more . . . minutes. Those of us who fill our kids' summer vacations with endless worksheets, drag them to activities they have no interest in or prod them to join the neighbor kids in a game of street hockey when clearly the child would rather read a good book inside are the tugboats. Let go, literally!

The Race Car

Faster, faster, faster! Sometimes we think that if our kids could just get ahead of the pack, they'd win. But win what? Life's not a competition. Slow down, enjoy the ride!

The Fire Truck

Here's a fire, there's a fire, everywhere's a fire! Fire Truck parents swoop in with their loud sirens and flashing lights to gush helpful solutions on any problems their kids face.

Let's Get Real

You may have noticed a theme in this chapter: preparing our kids for real life. In fact, that should be a major theme of childhood as we help our kids grow up to be *their* very best. That's why it's so important for parents to have realistic views of each child, on an individual basis, as they grow. Without trying to control them, we can keep tabs on our kids' natural bents and abilities, their particular challenges, the goals and dreams they have for themselves at any given moment, and life situations that could help or hurt. And we can use what we learn about our kids to help them in real-life pursuits, while remembering that success can have many different forms. This is our job as parents—not to secure a goal *for* them but to play a solid supporting role, based on our expertise, our knowledge of our children and our love for them.

The ever-changing relationship between parents and their kiddos can be influenced by many things, and one is a parent's expectations for their child. We've all heard about the parents who have dreams of their kids taking over the family business, earning PhDs, becoming professional musicians and other high-reaching goals. And we've heard all the stories about how damaging these high aspirations—many of which aren't held by the children—can be to the family dynamic. It's often a sad story, with the child either wasting away in grad school trying to earn a degree he doesn't want, or the child following her own dreams but losing the love or respect of her parent. Or sometimes kids try their best, wanting to meet their parents' expectations in anything from playing goalie on the junior league hockey team to winning an art competition, but sadly suffer not only failure but also their parents' displeasure at not measuring up. We know we don't want this for our kids.

A lot of times, we resort to seizing our kids' dreams as our own. If James wants to become an emergency room nurse, then we're going to make sure he gets into his top pick for nursing school. If Caroline wants to be a mechanical engineer, we'll pull strings with friends at work to get her an internship. It boils down to this: we expect the very best for our kids. If they might not measure up on their own, we'll do the hard work for them. But is the best always best?

I'm going to suggest something revolutionary when it comes to our kids. What if we simply expected *their* best?

What does this mean? Sometimes, it might mean *lowering* our standards for their lives to be more in line with reality. As much as we want our kids, or our kids want, to become president of their fifth-grade class, solve world hunger as Russia in Model UN, be invited to all the preschool birthday parties or play quarterback on the varsity football team, we might have to accept the fact—and help them accept it—that it might never happen for one reason or another. And that it's okay.

This is what I call having *reasonable* expectations, accepting the fact that we might not have the next Peyton Manning or Sonia Sotomayor on our hands. We might have an amazing preschool teacher, a selfless Peace Corps worker, an upbeat clothing store manager, a dedicated accountant or a hardworking bicycle repair specialist. And whether they're eight or eighteen, we can support them to be their best in whatever activities or roles they have chosen, without overdoing it, to prepare them for real life.

But why shouldn't we dream big for our littles and expect the best for them? After all, we're their parents, and our dreams for them are usually good ones. Aside from the fact that not everyone can be the next person to set foot on the moon, kids are majorly tuned in to the dreams their parents have for them—no matter how hard we try to hide it. They know when we want them to be the first in the family to graduate from college, study abroad just because we wanted to and never did or letter in all our sports. And talk about pressure! It's not easy to let down your parents—no matter how independent your teens act at times. Kids need to feel like they can be themselves and explore a variety of interests without risking their parents' disappointment. When we invest in top-of-the-line cross-country skis, for instance, because the thirteen-year-old has taken a fancy to the sport and we expect great things, we obviously plan for her to stick with it after shelling out all that money. If she fails or loses interest, she's keenly aware that we're upset: "Do you

know how much I *paid* for those skis?" Besides the financial invest-
ment for musical instruments, sports equipment, special classes, private
schools and more, we invest emotionally in other decisions—their social lives, their accomplishments and even their hairstyles. When we
make it known that we expect our little wallflower to cut up the floor at
his first school dance, and can't completely hide our disappointment
when it doesn't happen, we tell him we think he's not good enough.

That's not to say we shouldn't invest ourselves emotionally in our
kids' interests and support the efforts they make toward success in a
particular field. We should always help our kids hold out productive
hope and dream big. Our kids need us to back them! And we can do it
without dominating their goals or their success.

Let's look at some examples. Take eleven-year-old Brendan. He's
really excited about a pottery camp this summer and is dreaming of all
the different creations he'll make. But after his first lopsided vase, he's a
bit discouraged that he can't make his hands do what his mind has
conceived. A parent with expectations that are out of line might do
things like invest in a kid-sized pottery wheel, sign him up for more
classes right away, buy him lots of supplies and books and urge him to
create, create, create! Reasonable expectations, however, would have
you sitting Brendan down for a heart-to-heart about the value of practice, patience and sticking to it, including telling a personal story from
your childhood of when you tried to learn how to knit. You might suggest he use his allowance to buy some clay to experiment with at
home—maybe pitch in half the funding if the cost is steep. If he's still
interested when Christmas rolls around, you might sign him up for
more classes and buy him some supplies. In fact, with your reasonable
support, his interest may hold through college as he minors in ceramic
arts! If he loses interest, you let it go. It's okay to have a passing dream
that comes to nothing—exploration is an important part of childhood.

Then there's Corrine. She has always been well liked, and is on a
fashion kick big-time now that she's a junior in high school. She's very
popular, and rumor has it she stands a good chance of landing a spot on

the homecoming court, a possibility she can't stop talking about. High-expectation parents would be out shopping with her every Saturday, shelling out for expensive and trendy outfits, and letting her host a big (well-chaperoned) party. But what's reasonable? Helping Corrine be her best by encouraging her to explore her interests (fashion design? photography?), be a good friend and use her allowance or clothing budget wisely if she still feels the desire to switch from everyday sneakers to fancy sandals. Make sure she knows you love her quirky sense of humor or that you enjoy seeing all the new ways she does her hair. Then, if Corrine's hopes are dashed at homecoming, she'll have lots of positive things in her life to fall back on. And if she wins? You can offer your sincere congratulations.

And seventeen-year-old Micah. He's digging into a robotics project that could have him competing with a team two states away. Too-high expectations would have parents pressuring him to think nothing but robots every spare minute, micromanaging his activities and discouraging him from going out for tennis so he can focus more on the competition. With reasonable expectations, however, you would express your confidence that he can take charge of his own pursuits—after all, he's done well so far and he's the one potentially taking two days off school for the trip, not you—and then offer to be available to review plans with him, help him prioritize or surprise him with a trip to the science museum's new exhibit on motion one Saturday morning. You'd encourage him to take time for other interests, hold him accountable for his other responsibilities and teach him that no matter what happens, knowledge and teamwork are their own reward. If he chooses not to put in any extra time, you'd let the lost trip (in all likelihood) do the talking and leave it at that. And if he wins? Get together with the other parents to celebrate with a pizza party for the whole team!

Parents with reasonable expectations offer real-life support to their kids. They manage their own expectations to make sure they're realistic with regard to the people their kids are growing up to be. Reasonable expectations allow parents to help their kids in reasonable ways that aren't forced, letting kids take the age-appropriate lead in their decisions and opportunities. This gives youngsters the practice they need for the real world we keep telling them about.

Easier said than done. I know firsthand. Here are a few more pointers for offering real-life support to your kids:

- Make sure your kids understand that the most important thing is that they give it their best and/or have fun. For instance, while English literature might not always be fun, it's still important to do their best. On the other hand, if they sign up for a class on flower arranging just for fun, there's no need to make it any more than that as long as they're respectfully participating in the class.
- It's okay to make suggestions, but let your child take the lead in her ambitions. If she wants to become an editor of the school yearbook, encourage her to develop a plan. Talk her ideas through with her and make a few suggestions if you feel the need, but avoid an overhaul. Remember that with reasonable expectations for our kids, it's okay if the plan doesn't work out.
- If you find yourself going out of your way very often to make something work out for your child, your expectations are probably out of line. If you have to force it, it's not reasonable.
- Only in rare situations should you be the one to talk to a coach, teacher, scout leader or other grown-up on behalf of your child. (It might be a good idea, though, to role-play a respectful discussion with the teacher or coach and for younger kids, be there in person.)
- Keep the focus *off* achievement as much as possible. Encourage enthusiasm, courage, perseverance, kindness and other positive traits (see Encouragement tool, chapter 7).
- Watch your attitude about others. If you scoff at a construction laborer and hold in high regard only people with college degrees, your kids will get the idea that only a certain level of achievement is acceptable.
- If your child shows a genuine interest in an academic subject or

activity and wants reasonable help doing more (visiting a museum, attending a big game, seeing a concert, taking a class, volunteering, job shadowing, lining up a visit with a university professor, etc.), by all means, go for it! Just make sure you're taking a backseat to your child's lead.

- If your child starts to lose interest in an activity or other pursuit, hold him to any commitment to a class or team for the duration or until a logical break point (usually a semester or the end of the sports season). In the meantime, you can try to get to the bottom of the loss of interest—it could be that the reason is unrelated to the actual activity and fixable with some problem solving. If your child still wants to quit, let it go.

Maybe you're reading this and thinking—and I'm sure many are—all this talk about high aspirations? My child's only dream is to play video games all day! You know your child best, and maybe she'd make an awesome video game programmer someday. On the other hand, it could be that with some gentle encouragement and reasonable limits from you and other family members, she'll start to explore some new interests, work toward new goals and find a dream to pursue that doesn't have anything to do with getting to the next level.

While it's a good thing not to push our kids too hard, sometimes they need the nudge. If you feel as though your expectations might be too *low* for your kids, and they're not living up to their potential, you have the go-ahead to gently step it up. For instance, if they balk at any mention of helping out around the house, use Take Time for Training, Family Contributions and When-Then Routines to hold them accountable for one responsibility at a time. If their interests are only as varied as your DVD library, let them choose a new class or activity to try, then set media limits so they have plenty of time for their new pursuit and any other they might come up with. If their grades are mediocre at best—and you know that with a little effort they could do better—help them practice the skills they need (including homework skills) to bring them up.

And it's our job to help kids adjust *their own* expectations. The line between dreaming big and just getting by can be a terribly thin one, but we can help our kids walk it by teaching them how to keep their eyes open for opportunities while staying grounded in reality with a backup plan. So even if their Olympics gymnastics dreams have some real potential, we also want to encourage them to focus on their schoolwork, just in case they're not one of the lucky (hardworking, persevering) few.

Likewise, it's a big leap from winning the pinewood derby to becoming a real race car driver. We certainly don't want to crush dreams, but by putting equal emphasis on related or unrelated backup plans (anything from aerodynamics engineering to car repair to sportscasting), we can help our kids keep one foot on the ground while they shoot for the moon.

As you adjust your expectations and ground your kids in real life, keep in mind that you're not giving up on your offspring. It's okay if they want to quit the school choir even though they are amazing vocalists, if they can't seem to break out of their shyness or if it seems as though they will never get anything more than a C in geometry despite biweekly tutoring. Here's the key: whatever our kids do, it's our job to help them get the most out of it. Impossibly high expectations only discourage kids, and low expectations risk not letting them live up to their potential. With a little tweaking, you'll be able to walk the balance between high and low expectations and help each of your kids be their best—and happy, too.

> Setting the bar too high and too early undercuts a child's potential. Children who grow up embracing our vision of them as a lawyer, doctor or scientist develop an inordinate sense of themselves as inadequate. When the bar is set so high, how can a child feel anything but dwarfed?
>
> —Shefali Tsabary, PhD, *The Conscious Parent*

High, Low or Realistic?

Expecting too much? Too little? Just right? Sometimes it's hard to know exactly how much to ask from our kids. Take this quiz to help you gauge whether you need to back off, ramp it up or keep on truckin'.

Question 1: My fourteen-year-old has a big science project and paper due in three days and has barely started. I:

a. Read over the material myself, drive him to the library to help him find some extra resources, then spend two full evenings working on a minimodel of the solar system with him and helping him with his paper outline.

b. Ask him his plan, then offer to be available to answer questions and proofread his paper before he turns it in.

c. Help him find ways to get the work done as quickly as possible so he doesn't miss his deadline.

Question 2: My seven-year-old wants to try out for a part in a community theater production. I:

a. Sign her up for private acting lessons to get her ready, and buy her a new outfit for the audition that just happens to fit the character.

b. Check out the book or script she'll need from the library and read it with her.

c. Convince her to join soccer instead—she'll definitely be on the team and avoid the disappointment of not getting a part.

Question 3: My fifteen-year-old is headed to his first high-school dance. I:

a. Buy him a new suit, a haircut, music downloads (so he can practice his moves) and a fancy corsage for his date and book him reservations at the most expensive restaurant in town (which I also fork over the cash for).

b. Help him decide which shirt to wear (if he'd like my opinion), ask him if he needs help with planning, spot him $25 toward his meal and snap a couple of pictures.

c. Don't overthink it—just drop him off at the dance.

Question 4: My rising first grader isn't reading yet, but most of her friends are. I:

a. Sign her up for summer school, bring home extra workbooks and offer a trip to the local amusement park as a reward for when she can read *Goodnight Moon* all by herself.

b. Ask her teacher if there's anything I need to be helping with, then sign her up for the library's summer reading program.

c. Eh, she's only six. She'll learn when she's ready.

Question 5: My nine-year-old wants to do more recycling, beyond curbside pickup. I:

a. Organize a neighborhood recycling event with him and schedule a tour of the recycling center for his Boy Scouts troop.

b. Buy some bins so he can sort plastics to his heart's content, then drive him to the recycling center once a month for drop-offs.

c. Tell him the family already recycles and if he wants to save the planet he can start by turning off lights when he leaves the room.

Question 6: My fifteen-year-old would like to start a dog-sitting business. I:

a. Have business cards made for her and pass them out to all my friends and colleagues, then drive her to any job she gets.

b. Encourage her to make a sign to post around the neighborhood and e-mail to the neighborhood directory, then have a good chat with her about safety.

c. Let her do a couple of extra chores if she wants to make more money.

Question 7: My eleven-year-old wants to learn how to play golf. I:

a. Talk to my own golf instructor about lessons for him, then buy him his own set of clubs.

b. Find a summer golf camp and borrow clubs from his cousin.

c. Give him one of my old clubs and a couple of whiffle balls to whack around in the backyard.

Question 8: My nearly sixteen-year-old wants to have a boy-girl sweet sixteen birthday party. I:

a. Hire a DJ and a caterer, then find reasons to make friendly calls or drop e-mails to all the moms to make sure their kids show up.

b. Set a budget, then let her invite her best friends over to help plan and prep the party themselves. Offer to help with a couple of things on their list.

c. Order some pizzas, put up some streamers and put in earplugs for the evening. Kids don't need much to have a good time!

Question 9: My eight-year-old would always rather play alone than with the neighborhood kids. I:

a. Invite all the kids to come play in our yard so that he *has* to play with them, then bring out Popsicles.

b. Ask him if there's anyone he'd like to have over to play one-on-one with his Jenga game.

c. Leave him alone—if he wants to play with them, he will.

Question 10: My fifteen-year-old wants to play quarterback for junior varsity football. I:

a. Call the coach with a random question and mention how excited my son would be to be the quarterback. Later I volunteer to serve the first pregame spaghetti dinner and work the concession stand.

b. Ask him if he'd like help working on his passing, and if he has any other ideas for proving to the coach he's up to the responsibility.

    c. Tell him how proud I'd be if that were to happen and mention there's a twenty for him if it does.

ANALYZE THE RESULTS

Mostly As: Back Off! Watch out, coming through! That's right—you trend toward steamrolling (or tugboating or helicoptering) a smooth path for your kids. It's time to back off. Ramp down your response to your kids' initiatives and let them take on more of the control. Worried about what happens if they fail? Read on to learn why failure can be a good thing.

Mostly Bs: Keep on Truckin'. Your parenting style is well-balanced— you offer a healthy amount of support, while keeping the ball in your kids' court. Keep up the good work as you help your kids become *their* very best.

Mostly Cs: Ramp It Up! While sometimes a hands-off approach can help kids solve their own problems, they also need to feel supported and encouraged. Next time your kids are working on a project or a personal goal, challenge yourself to think of one way to bolster their efforts without taking control. They'll thank you for it as you help them reach new heights.

Fail-Proofing Our Kids

So you've adjusted your expectations to be in step with reality and you've cautioned yourself against steamrolling a clear path (or helicoptering or whatever your tendency) for your kids. Which means that the only thing left is to actually let your kids fly. On their own. Yikes.

    Why the yikes? Because you know one thing is true: they will not get it right all the time. They *will* fail. And like most parents, you're not entirely comfortable with the idea of your kids floundering as they navigate their miniworld. Who would be? We'd all much rather finish the algebra assignment for them than watch them get a D on it. We hated to see them skin their knees as two-year-olds, and that doesn't change when they're ten or twenty. Wouldn't we all prefer that they make the best decisions every time? Unfortunately, that doesn't happen—which is why in this section, we'll learn to prepare our kids for the worst.

Speaking of skinned knees, do you remember the first few times your child got one? While some kids get back to their feet and continue to trot in circles around the driveway like a pony, I think it's safe to say that most are stopped in their tracks. They feel the pain, see the blood and, often, hear the panic in our voices even as we try to calm them down and patch them up. They may be pretty upset despite our reassurances and might hobble around for a while as they decide whether a skinned knee is a big deal. They might show it off for the next week until it (almost sadly!) heals over. But what about the sixty-fourth time she skins her knee? While she still thinks the injury is a little bit cool ("I think I can see bone!"), she has the cleanup-bandage routine down pat. It might hurt, but it barely slows her down. She's had skinned knees before—she knows it's no big deal. It'll heal.

The same is true of failure. If kids never feel it while they're young, they'll be just as tripped up by it when they're adults as a one-year-old with a newly scraped knee. We know that setbacks are going to happen despite our best efforts to protect our kids. But here's the thing—sometimes it's better if we, as parents, *don't* give our best efforts over to helping them avoid disappointments and minidisasters. Children who aren't rescued, aren't hovered over and aren't cleared a path develop all kinds of great qualities that will work toward failure proofing their aspirations later in life. Here's the rundown:

RESILIENCE

The ability to get back on the horse (or bike or cheerleading formation or Youth and Government committee) will serve your kids well in life, no matter their pursuits. Kids who aren't used to facing failure also won't be used to recovering from it. They'll feel entitled to smooth sailing all the time. On the other hand, if they're used to trying out for choir solos year after year in hopes of someday winning one, contesting a particularly bad social studies grade, or showing up for debate club even though they sorely embarrassed themselves the very first meeting, then getting laid off from their first job won't set them back much at all. They'll have learned in smaller ways (yet no less significant at the time) how to pick themselves up, dust themselves off and try again.

PROBLEM SOLVING

Some people see failure as an end point. But prepared kids will see it as a challenge. Let's say the tree fort your twin ten-year-olds were building isn't sturdy enough to actually step on (you know this because you required them to have you inspect it before they tried). What can they try differently? Different materials? A new way to attach it? There's gotta be a way. If you'd done the job right for your kids all along or even after the first failure, they'd never learn for themselves how to evaluate, reevaluate, tweak, look at it from a different angle, seek alternate solutions, ask an expert, try it a new way and finally, get the success they're looking for. What's more, they'd be much less likely to try it themselves with their next project, instead feeling entitled to their parents' version of perfection.

CONSEQUENCES

If at age four you spilled an entire pitcher of juice on the floor because you had no idea it'd be so heavy, at age eight you forgot to complete half of your project on seahorses and had to do extra credit to help make it up, at age thirteen stayed up until 3:00 a.m. at a friend's slumber party only to miss basketball tryouts the next morning, and at age seventeen got a speeding ticket, in addition to all the other things life dishes out, you know that actions have consequences. We've already been through a chapter about this topic, so now just know that letting your kids fail is actually a positive way to create a consequential environment and un-entitle them from escaping the results of their actions.

PERSEVERANCE

Even if kids hear "If at first you don't succeed, try, try again" all the time, they don't internalize it unless given the opportunity. If you've never failed, tried again and found success, you'll be much more likely to give up at the first sign of failure. Kids who fail know how to stick to it until they've exhausted all options.

REAL-WORLD SKILLS AND EXPERIENCE

Failure teaches us lessons about what *doesn't* work, encouraging us to figure out what *does*. By doing so, we gain a wealth of expertise in a host of different areas. If we're nagged and reminded about the right way to accomplish a task or meet a challenge every time, we lose out on the experimentation with different methods that grow real-world skills.

THE ABILITY TO THINK CRITICALLY

When you're a child, you think all your decisions are good ones. If you're allowed to learn from your failed decisions (such as attempting to pull a wagon behind a bike), you'll soon learn to consider all your options carefully and then think through the one you're planning to choose, leading to greater success down the road.

> Do not judge me by my successes, judge me by how
> many times I fell down and got back up again.
> —Nelson Mandela

While you certainly wouldn't let your kids face the failure that comes from trying to fly using a bedsheet and an upstairs window, you'll probably find plenty of instances that your kids would be better off facing without a steamroller or a snowplow. Let them. Then be there to talk it through if they'd like to and let them go make a better decision next time.

Now that we've seen how failure paves a better path to success than a steamroller, it's time to help your kids face the fact that the road of life has many bumps—and no one is going to smooth it for them. How do you prepare your kids to *fail*? And, more important, to be better off for it?

First, make sure they know your expectations for them are reasonable. This doesn't happen in one overarching conversation but rather in hundreds of little ways throughout their childhood. Get your expectations in line so you don't constantly find yourself trying to mask your disappointment in the fact that they flunked the driving test *again*.

Then reinforce the fact as often as it comes up that you only expect your kids to try their hardest and participate respectfully. Take the focus off achievement and tell them "I know history isn't your favorite subject, but I know you'll give it one hundred percent, just like you do your other subjects. That means studying the material, completing your homework and respectfully participating in class. If you're trying your very best, your grades will take care of themselves." Along with this, let your kids know (usually by showing them rather than telling them) that your love for them is unconditional—and certainly not dependent on whether they're able to come up with a winning science-fair project.

When your kids do fail, be there to talk it through (if they'd like to) and offer your assistance in a reasonable way without entirely rescuing them. They might appreciate some help working through solutions, finding the silver lining or coming up with a backup plan, or they might simply need your empathy. Don't make a huge deal out of the setback if they don't, but make sure they know it's okay to express their feelings. For a really big disappointment (not making a team they made last year, not getting into the college they'd had their heart set on since middle school, etc.), check in every few days or weeks to see how they're doing to help them process the failure over a period of time.

Demonstrate an it's-not-the-end-of-the-world attitude in your own life and for theirs. While you should certainly empathize with your son's failed attempt to run a half marathon—after all, feelings of disappointment are just as strong in childhood as in adulthood (if not more so)—gently help him see that life does, indeed, go on. What's more, as you face disappointment, model a healthy grieving or letting-go process. Even if you're simply upset that the color you painted the kitchen turned out more lemon and less buttercup than you were hoping, let your kids see you express your disappointment and then move on, either by repainting when you can or buying matching dishtowels and learning to like the new color.

Be sure to show confidence in your kids, even if they've failed in a similar situation before. If your daughter is trying her hand at gardening, and last year's attempt produced three moldy carrots and a small green tomato, but she wants to give it another go this year, don't hold her past against her. You can guide her to learn from her prior failure ("Are you going to do anything different this year? I'd be happy to go to the garden store with you this weekend if you want to do a little research!"), but kids, especially, need plenty of room to make mistakes when they're trying something new. A "Last year's garden only grew weeds; I don't know why you're trying it again!" will just discourage her from taking risks in the future.

And as for your expectations? Knowing that your kids *will* fail and that it will be okay will help you live through the times when your child gets rejected from the cheerleading squad, struggles with math even though you teach the subject at a university level or majorly fumbles through the essay she's been chosen to read at a fire-safety-awareness event because she didn't practice it the night before. Each failure can be a lesson to your kids that they're not entitled to the best of life, whether they try hard or not—but that they are entitled to your love and support no matter what.

Tools: Applying What We Know

You've already learned a lot of great tools for helping your kids navigate real life successfully. We'll take another look at a couple with an eye to realistic expectations for the real world, as well as how to wield them to teach children to accept inevitable failure.

TAKE TIME FOR TRAINING

The goal of this tool, as you know, is to train our kids in new responsibilities and behaviors (everything from phone manners to safely changing a lightbulb). But if you're not careful, you can unintentionally use it to exert too much control over your child (for instance, insisting on a full prewash when clearly the dishwasher can handle the mess by itself). Be sure to allow your kids to fulfill responsibilities on their own terms (within your limits) or exhibit new positive behaviors in their own quirky style without expecting them to be mini mes. What's more, expect them to goof it up from time to time, especially while they're still practicing the new skill. Keep in mind:

- There might be several (or many) right ways to complete a task, as long as it gets done to reasonable expectations. If the dishes aren't prewashed, one or two might need to get sent around again—but it's not the end of the world. If the whole load ends up that way, a prewash might be in order.
- It's okay if your child fails in a task even after being trained. Use the occasion as an opportunity to help your child problem solve.
- Hold your child accountable to reasonable expectations. If you (reasonably) expect nice shirts to be hung in the closet rather than stuffed in a drawer on laundry day, make an accountability plan (for instance, if the laundry isn't put away correctly, your child will face the consequence of having to take care of her own laundry from now on).

- Not everything needs extensive training. If your child has been enjoying soccer, for instance, that doesn't mean you have to book private lessons with a goalie coach, unless your child specifically expresses interest in improving his skills. When we frequently jump in with private lessons or the equivalent, we send our kids the message that:
    1. You're not good enough as you are. You clearly need extra help.
    2. If you want to pursue an interest in the future, you'd better not try it unless you have special instruction, tutoring or a class.

NO RESCUE POLICY

We've seen all the positive lessons that failure can teach: now it's time to allow life to do the teaching. When you quit rescuing your kids from their repeated forgetfulness, dawdling, procrastinating and the rest, you'll allow them to undergo the process of failing, problem solving, learning and finally, succeeding. These lessons, while they can be painful to watch, help your child far more than running a forgotten lunch to school ever will. Here are some things to keep in mind:

- While you don't want to set your child up to fail, the nature of this tool is to work *with* failure. In fact, it won't really do its job unless you allow the mishap to take place. Recognizing this will help you steel your resolve to follow through.
- You're not completely abandoning your kids even though you're not rescuing them. Be readily available to talk through solutions, but let your kids take the lead in finding ways to make sure the error doesn't happen again. If possible, help them implement their suggestions rather than put forth solutions of your own unless they're completely stuck. Remember that if the goal was to make absolutely certain your child always returned her library books on time, you'd do it for her. But that's not the goal: in real life, she'll

need to remember her books herself, and it's your job to help her set up her own system to do so in childhood and beyond, even if she pays a few fines out of her birthday money on occasion.

- This isn't the *Never* Rescue Policy. While you're working with your child to take responsibility in a certain area—for instance, remembering ballet shoes for ballet class—you won't be rescuing your child. But you can have their back for first offenses, as long as the missteps don't become a habit. After all, we all need a little help once in a while.

WHAT IS YOUR PLAN?

This tool squarely puts the burden on your kids' shoulders when it comes to completing assignments and following through on responsibilities. By asking things like "What is your plan for finishing up your physics project by Friday?" you can get your child thinking about how to get the job done, rather than fighting you every step of the way. One thing I like about this tool is that it's a great way for the parent to take a backseat, putting the child behind the wheel. While a helicopter parent might hover, nudge and nag or a steamroller might do all the groundwork so that the child does a minimal amount of actual work, a reasonable-expectations parent plays a supporting role, letting the child know that he's expected to put in the effort, and that although you're available for questions and occasional help, you won't be doing the work for him.

When using What Is Your Plan? to set up reasonable expectations for yourself and your child, follow these guidelines:

- Be sure that whatever you're asking about is either your child's idea or his responsibility for school or other commitments.
- Ask the question once. This tool is not meant to replace the nagging we all normally do. Having reasonable expectations means we allow our kids to drop the ball with the assurance that they'll learn from the experience.

- If the plan your child develops doesn't seem like it will get the job done ("My plan for my end-of-the-year presentation on the causes of the Civil War is to start it after dinner the night before it's due!"), it's okay to ask a leading question or two ("Do you think that's enough time?" "How long does your presentation have to be and what goes into it?"). The younger the child, the more guidance you should give. By late high school, however, kids should be able to develop a reasonable plan or face the consequences if they underestimate the complexities of a major war and a major presentation.
- Keep in mind that with reasonable expectations, you expect your child to try hard, work hard—and still occasionally miss the boat. While missing a big deadline or handing in poor work due to poor planning is a tough lesson, it's an important one.

7

The Praise Problem

Kayla is truly a remarkable child. She's multitalented and extremely skilled in everything she does, having accomplished an astonishing number of bests in her short life. At age three, in fact, she managed to sit through an entire trip to the grocery store without crying or yelling. Of course, she got to pick out a new toy for that amazing behavior. She also earned prizes for getting dressed every day, saying please and staying in bed at night. After all, incredible behavior like that deserves a reward.

Just before entering kindergarten she drew the best picture of a tree, ever, in the history of the world. The very next year, her parents gave her the titles of world's fastest runner, best singer in the school choir, best shooter on her basketball team, and most dramatic mouse in her school's production of *Cinderella*.

When Kayla joined a soccer team, she was given a shiny gold trophy for best at always arriving in uniform. She added a few ribbons to her collection over the next couple of years for a photography contest she entered in the state fair, for helping a six-year-old practice reading as part of a school program, for participating in a summer camp and for attending her school's field day event every year.

As Kayla grew, she became a really great helper. At age eight, her parents paid her a quarter every day to get ready for school before the bus arrived. When Kayla started to bring home Cs in high school, her parents decided to pay her for good grades, too, and soon she became the smartest person in her class even though she eventually reverted back to C work.

And throughout her childhood, Kayla was met with "Good job!" "You're the best!" and "I'm so proud of you!" whether she was washing her hands before lunch or winning an essay contest.

Kayla is also the cutest, funniest, most athletic, prettiest and all-around-best kid her parents have ever seen. How could they be so lucky? And Kayla knows it. What's more, she wants to make sure everyone knows it. So when she accepts her first job, her top priority will be to make sure her boss and colleagues fully understand how great she is. With any luck, she'll get another trophy.

Can't you just see the headlines? Five-year-old draws best picture of tree—EVER! But I know what you're thinking: What could possibly be wrong with praising and rewarding good behavior and telling our kids we think they're great? After all, we're their parents! If they don't hear it from us, when will they hear it? They need to know they're on the right track. Right?

It's not that we can't show our kids that we're proud of them, that we have confidence in them, that we appreciate their behavior or that we enjoy their company. We just have to be careful *how* we tell them those things. And, just as important, we need to use these opportunities to foster internal motivation and drive that will serve them better than any words from us.

If we dish out empty praise and lavish rewards for the type of behavior that should be expected (such as not pitching a fit because we won't buy them a new action figure or not making rude noises in a restaurant) we're writing a recipe for an entitled child, one who thinks he takes "special" to a whole new level. Since he's been told his whole life how wonderful he is, why can't he expect the very best when it comes to accolades, raises, advancement and more?

This chapter is all about praise, rewards and the pitfalls of both.

We'll look at how rewarding and praising good behavior actually *de-creases* the likelihood we'll see it again, at how shallow praise does kids no good and, in the Un-Entitler Toolbox, how we can use Encouragement to bring out the best in our kids.

Two Types of Motivation

Before we dive into the praise and reward problem facing our kids, we need to learn one key thing about getting good behavior from them—whether they're helping an elderly neighbor shovel his driveway or studying for the history quiz instead of watching TV. It's all about motivation.

I'm sure you've seen this play out many times before. You need Levi to get out of the bathtub and into his pajamas—but he doesn't want to. He's having fun, so what's his motivation? Same goes for getting Ruby to put in extra practice for her piano recital. Why should she?

Kids of all ages—and most adults—think "Why should I?" with every decision they make. This can be a good thing—it's what keeps us from spending our entire paycheck on a new Jacuzzi tub we don't need simply because the guy selling them asked so nicely or from volunteering our next eight weekends to head up three different PTA efforts.

Motivation helps us accomplish goals even when the process of doing so is miserable at times (think of training for a marathon or putting in extra time at work for a special project that could earn a promotion). When it comes to our kids, the motivation of a bedtime story might help them hop out of the tub in good time and the motivation of gaining confidence to face an expectant crowd might be enough for Ruby to practice a few extra scales.

Two different types of motivation push us along to accomplish various goals in life: *extrinsic* motivation and *intrinsic* motivation. Extrinsic motivation is something outside ourselves. We work for a paycheck, we study for a grade, we learn to use the potty for M&M's. Extrinsic motivation is in play when we give our kids a sucker to keep them quiet while we're on the phone or pay them for every A they bring home. Intrinsic motivation, on the other hand, comes from within—and because it does, it's the stronger of the two. This type of motivation is what propels us to volunteer at the hospital (it makes us feel happy to help others), clean our room (we like how it looks), or put in extra time on a science project (we think the study of genetics is fascinating).

Both types of motivation can be valuable. But when parents unknowingly favor extrinsic motivation over intrinsic, the balance swings to our kids' detriment. It's easy to slip into the habit of using rewards or bribes—two types of extrinsic motivation—to get our kids to do what we want them to. After all, offering rewards works in the short term. The problem is that with this kind of system, kids expect this type of treatment and feel entitled to candy for cleaning their plate at dinner or song downloads for making an appearance at their younger cousin's birthday party. That's worth a deeper look, so let's dig in.

Why Rewards Are No Treat

Welcome to the me generation, in which kids are awarded points simply for writing their name on the test paper and ribbons for showing up to swim lessons without regard to whether they have made any progress beyond simply blowing bubbles. The self-esteem movement has made its seemingly permanent mark in that we're more concerned about our kids' feelings than the fact that they're headed to a friend's pool party thinking they're a champion swimmer when they actually freak out if their head goes underwater. Yes, it's great that we want our kids to feel okay about themselves. We're doing them no favors, however, by sending them out into the world unprepared because we are constantly telling them they're the best. We are entitling them rather than empowering them, and in so doing, we're setting them up to fail.

When we hand out rewards at every opportunity, we create a whole rash of entitlement issues. Kids who are used to getting treats, stickers, prizes and TV time for good behavior will continue to think that meeting the very minimum of requirements, like behaving in the store, completing family jobs and not talking back are grounds for lavish rewards. After all, if they were rewarded before, why shouldn't they get the same treatment in the future? They are unlikely to behave, pitch in or do anything beyond the very minimum without the promise of payback.

And while rewards may work at first, they soon lose their luster. So even if the promise of a Giant Pixy Stix gets your child to put away her toys for the first seven days, by the eighth, she'll start negotiating for extra candy, a cupcake and ice cream with a cherry on top. You'll be forced to either endlessly up the ante or resort to the nagging and yelling you were trying to avoid in the first place when you instituted the reward.

Kids quickly get used to thinking, "What's in it for *me*?" whenever they're asked to do anything they don't want to. They quickly learn that they can milk "Will you help me unload the groceries?" for fifteen extra minutes on your iPad—and they won't do it for anything less. Pretty soon you're negotiating in your driveway over the number of bags your child will consent to bring into the house. We've all been there, haven't we? This entitled attitude spills over to every area of life, until you have a child who won't do anything for anyone unless she reaps the rewards. Here's another excerpt from the Entitled Kids Manual:

ENTITLE ME! TOOL: WHAT'S IN IT FOR ME?

This tool will help you make sure you never do anything for free. Whether you're asked to help assemble a salad for supper, go to your little brother's T-ball game or run around doing boring errands with your mom, there's no reason you should have to do it without getting something in return.

Put It to Use

Next time your parents want you to pitch in or show up, avoid giving them a simple yes. But you'll need to act quickly to make the best of the request. First think of something you want, following the three Rs of payback. It should be:

Related: If your parents ask for help with dinner, request extra dessert. Have to go to Aunt Irene and Uncle Steven's boring anniversary dinner, wearing a tie, no less? You should get a couple of extra song downloads so you're not bored while you're there. It's not always possible to make a perfect match, but come as close as you can, and your parents will be more likely to comply.

Reasonable: Let's face it: you're not going to get a new pony for putting away your laundry. You might, however, get to have a friend over even though your mom said no before.

Rare: Your payback shouldn't be something you're probably going to get anyway. Be creative! It might help to make a list of potential rewards so you can always think of something you want.

Once you've determined your ideal compensation, simply say "Sure I'll give the dog a bath. If you'll let me watch extra TV tonight."

If your parents push back, start Whining (see page 33). Make them see it from your point of view: you hate bathing the dog, your big sister never has to, you've already walked the dog today so why should you have to bathe her, too? It won't take much before they give in to your reasonable request.

When kids expect payback, they soon develop a very entitled mindset as they learn to never give a simple yes as an answer. Research shows that kids raised on a rewards-based system often are self-centered and materialistic as adults. They constantly think "What's in it for me?" rather than "How can I help?" They feel entitled to receive without putting in the effort and are less likely to step up to challenges unless they can clearly see they'll be well rewarded. As you can imagine, this stunts both their personal and professional growth.

Kids raised on a diet of rewards lack the ability to function successfully while facing the sometimes cruel realities of life. Realities like only getting a C on a paper or spending most of the game on the bench can trip kids up if they're used to people singing their praises and rewarding them lavishly for putting in the minimum effort. They'll feel helpless to fix the situation and resentful of their teacher or coach for dishing out the injustice. If, however, kids grow up with a more realistic view of positive actions (namely, that positive results aren't simply handed out on a silver platter), they'll see that spending more time studying could've pulled the C up to a B or that extra practice time could've earned them more game time.

And what about the workplace? The over-entitled generation expects raises, bonuses and promotions simply for staying late once or twice or finishing a project—hardly a reality in today's economy. They demand frequent evaluations but bristle under criticism. Companies are struggling with how to manage a whole generation of workers that thinks it walks on water, and young professionals are floundering because they're used to a diet of constant positive feedback, and in most cases, aren't getting it.

While doling out rewards creates all kinds of entitlement issues in our kids, it also causes another kind of problem. According to Alfie Kohn, author of *Punished by Rewards,* research shows that rewards actually erode a child's interest in a particular positive behavior. Rewards can only produce a temporary interest in a behavior, and the more we use rewards to motivate people, the more they lose interest in what we want them to do. "Rewards turn play into work, and work into drudgery," he writes.

So not only do kids expect payback next time, but they actually are less likely to engage in the behavior again at all. Kohn writes in his book that more than seventy studies have shown this to be true: when people are rewarded for a task, once the reward is removed they are less likely to keep working at the task as compared with people who weren't rewarded. The job simply loses its appeal. So if Brooke is given new fairy wings for reading a whole book all by herself, she's actually *less* likely to want to read more on her own in the near future. This is where extrinsic motivation loses to intrinsic motivation. If Brooke had been able to bask in the feelings of pride and accomplishment (not to mention inherent entertainment) that come from finishing Frog and Toad's latest adventure, she'd be more likely to pick up another book in the series sometime. Instead, her attention was diverted to an external reward, taking all the emphasis off the internal feelings of achievement and decreasing her interest in what Frog and Toad would be up to next time.

According to Kohn, rewards also dampen creativity and risk taking. Research shows that people do inferior work—and especially when the work involves creativity—when they expect a reward for it, compared to people who don't anticipate a reward. They also are less likely to take risks or explore new possibilities. Studies show that when there's a reward at stake, people will choose the easiest job to do—the one that involves the least possible work to get the payoff. When there's no reward involved, we prefer to be challenged. We'll try new approaches, investigate all angles and put more of ourselves into the work.

Kohn writes, "It's not laziness. It's not human nature. It's because of rewards. If the question is 'Do rewards motivate students?' The answer is 'Absolutely. They motivate students to get rewards.' And that's typically at the expense of creativity.'" We've all seen this to be true—chances are your high schooler is well versed in the question "Will this be on the test?" And if the teacher's review doesn't follow the test line-by-line, she's annoyed—what an injustice to study something she didn't have to know.

But surely a reward every so often can't hurt, right? After all, you get bonuses at work for a job well done. The truth is your child *will* get rewards every so often. Doesn't he get a sticker every time he goes to the doctor, prizes at school for good behavior and medals for performing well at sporting events? Not to mention the reward of an A on the French quiz or being on the starting lineup for the lacrosse match. Rewards—hard-earned and not—are a big part of our society, and it's okay to let your kids enjoy them. But because they're so prevalent, our job of nurturing intrinsic motivation in our kids rather than extrinsic

---

*   http://hepg.org/hel-home/issues/10_2/helarticle/the-case-against-rewards-and-praise

becomes all the more important. You'll learn a simple tool for doing so at the end of this chapter, but first, read on to discover how your well-intended attempts to bring out the best in your kids may contribute to the entitlement epidemic.

Praise Never Pays

Rewards can be anything from candy to cash to a new cockapoo. You may be surprised to know that one of the most prevalent kinds, though, is spoken praise. Parents, who have been raised hearing the self-esteem message, dutifully toss around "You're so awesome," "Good job!" and "I'm proud of you!" in an attempt to reinforce good behavior and boost their kids' psyche. The problem is that shallow praise has the same negative effect that other types of rewards do. These phrases are actually *discouraging* to kids, because they detract from the positive effort our kids are putting in.

Think about it: we toss around "Great job!" to our kids simply for putting on socks that will keep their feet warm, and gush "Good boy!" for playing nicely with a little sister—rewarding *expected* behaviors and actually judging our kids rather than appreciating a good behavior we see in them. These judgments can turn sour the next time Miles yanks a toy out of Sophia's hands—is he now a "bad boy?" Or what if he's playing nicely and we don't take notice—will he stop sharing, since he's used to us singing his praises for this kind of behavior? This is confusing for kids as they learn the ins and outs of good behavior.

And what about the fact that kids *know* when their work is good and when it's not? When we tell them "That's the best picture of a dog I've ever seen!" our words lack sincerity. Our kids aren't fools—even if they smile at our words, they would rather hear a sincere response than a mass-manufactured, meaningless one, even if it sounds positive. What if Nathan has practiced his clarinet solo every night for three weeks—only to bomb it at the performance? Our "You're the best wind player in the band!" will do much more harm than good. Likewise, if Nathan skips practicing but performs fabulously, our empty comment will only encourage Nathan to slack off in the future. After all, he got lucky this time—maybe he really is the best musician in his school and has been wasting his time whenever he has practiced.

With these phrases we also unknowingly cultivate a what's-in-it-for-me mentality and give rise to praise junkies. If Gianna is used to being praised for helping out around the house, she isn't likely to pitch in when there's no one to notice. She'll feel put out if she's not properly acclaimed and she'll quickly lose interest if her effort earns only a "Good girl" rather than a feeling of contributing to good of the family, or pride in a job well done.

Another common mistake is putting the focus on what *we* think rather than what the child thinks. By saying "*I* love your flower picture!" or "*I'm* so proud of you," we unknowingly teach our kids to tune into the judgments of other people, rather than their own internal compass. While we want our kids to know how much we love them, we don't want them to get used to turning to other people for approval. If a child has to turn to her parents or teachers to validate her performance, she'll lack the skills to self-assess and make her own decisions down the road. This might not seem to be a big deal in the young years, but as kids grow into teenagers we would much rather they judge for themselves whether it's a good idea to get an eyebrow piercing without parental permission rather than ask their friends' opinions. To turn the tide and help kids be their own biggest fan, we can simply ask "What do *you* like best about your flower picture?" or exclaim, "*You* must be so proud of *yourself*!"

Alfie Kohn also brings up the point that praise is inherently conditional and from it, kids learn that they can get the "Great job!" they're looking for from us by meeting our standards. Sure, this works to get them to use good table manners while we're having our boss over for dinner. But it's at the expense of positive long-term behavior. We want our kids to learn to measure their behavior by their own standards.

Learning to set their own standards and being the judge of their own behavior is what actually builds positive self-esteem—not a shallow "You're the best!" from another person. This habit also protects them from becoming praise junkies and looking for others' approval in everything they do, even as adults. (Don't we all know people like this?)

> Praise may inspire some children to improve their behavior. The
> problem is they become pleasers and approval junkies.
>
> —Jane Nelsen, EdD, *Positive Discipline*

Praise, like rewards, is simply a type of extrinsic motivation, and it will erode intrinsic interest in a task or behavior if left unchecked. I know none of us wants this for the next generation. Here's your guide to stopping the praise and rewards.

Lose the Labels

A big contributor to the praise problem is the labels we give our kids. Don't we all have a *smart one*, *funny one* or *natural athlete*? We often label our kids to help them feel good about their abilities, to encourage them to continue to pursue that particular activity or even to inspire siblings to meet the same level of performance, but in truth, this practice backfires. While it may be true that Jocelyn trips over her own feet while Jenna scores goals every game, the label isn't helpful. Hearing her sister called the star player only makes Jocelyn feel poorly about her own lack of coordination and reduces the likelihood she'll take a chance on trying sports in the future. And since she's already a natural athlete, Jenna loses the motivation to try to improve through hard work. Plus, every goal she misses will leave her questioning her natural athlete abilities and the approval she's gained from you and the coach, rather than leading her to practice at home.

In fact, this happens all the time in youth sports. Here's how it plays out:

Jenna is a natural athlete. She walks early, adores her tiny-tot gymnastics class and starts playing team soccer when she is four years old. Since she develops a bit earlier than her teammates, she is stronger, faster and more coordinated than they are and she quickly becomes a star player. Go Jenna! Her coaches love her, as shown by the exemptions to the team's rules they allow her. For instance, Jenna starts every game, even if she was late to practice, and the coach usually looks the other way if she is a bit of a ball hog—after all, she puts points on the board. By middle school, Jenna is dreaming big about her future in women's soccer, and her parents are envisioning the scholarship money that will surely be hers.

And then the trouble begins. Jenna's natural ability, which comes from the simple fact that she developed earlier than her teammates, starts to level out. As her high school teammates and opponents catch up with her abilities, Jenna finds herself squarely in the middle of the pack—and unable to figure out what happened. Why is she no longer the star? Jenna, used to measuring her success by the scoreboard and feeling entitled to the advantages of being a star player, has to make excuses: "The sun was in my eyes!" "My teammate didn't pass the ball soon enough!"

Jenna's equally entitled parents are just as surprised as she is. They question the coach about why Jenna isn't getting more playing time. Jenna has never had to work hard at soccer and lacks the dedication or desire to do so now. Discouraged, Jenna loses interest in soccer—if she can't be the star player anymore, as she has for the past ten years, she doesn't much want to play at all.

Jenna and her family now have to come to terms with the fact that after ten years of soccer stardom, they have a very average player. While it can always be startling for kids to see their teammates catch up and surpass their natural abilities, it'd be easier to take if star players hadn't been labeled as such in the first place.

This phenomenon isn't limited to athletics—natural abilities can

come and go at any age. That's why it's so important to keep from labeling your kids, lest they lose their identities when circumstances change.
Avoid labels in any form, and your kids will be happier for it.

Kicking the Praise Habit

We all praise our kids from time to time. And tangible rewards are so
prevalent throughout society that we can't escape them entirely. Rest
easy—your kids will be fine with a little praise or a reward here and
there. Think of it like candy: a little won't hurt us, as long as Skittles
don't make up 90 percent of our diet. A "great throw" or a trip to the
treasure box at school won't ruin them, but your kids would be better
served if you cut back on the rewards and praise you hand out at home.
And since you'll be replacing them with Encouragement—this chapter's
tool, and one your kids will love—you'll hardly miss them, and neither
will your offspring. Here's what to do:

First tell your kids that they are growing up and becoming much
more independent. Let them know that they're old enough to show
good behavior and complete responsibilities without receiving rewards.
Pick one area to start with, and explain a little about what that means
for your children: no more fivers for every A they bring home, stickers
for getting themselves ready for preschool every day or candy for cleaning their rooms. Make sure they know that they'll still get special treats
every so often, but not for doing what's expected of them. Remind them
that this transition is a normal part of growing up.

Pay no attention to the grumbling (if you feel like it's going to be
particularly bad, use the tune-it-out tools from chapter 2), and follow
through with making a clean break from rewards.

Here's where the going gets rough: your kids will not like the new
system, and the first few weeks might be difficult as they experience the
disappointment of not receiving the rewards they thought they were
entitled to. But that's precisely the reason you need to make a clean

break. Rest assured, they'll get used to it, especially if you use plenty of positive Encouragement (explained next) to intrinsically motivate good behavior. Match this with other positive tools, and pretty soon your kids will be feeling so empowered that they won't look back (much).

Be sure to bring grandparents and caregivers in on your plan. If your kids continue to get a dollar from Grandpa every time they help weed the garden at his house, your new system will be undermined. If Grandpa insists, however, just do your best to keep Grandpa's rules separate from yours in your kids' minds.

When you do want to treat your kids, go for it! Just don't link it to good behavior. Your kids will respond to a "Who wants to go to the park?" every bit as enthusiastically as "Since you haven't fought with each other all morning, we'll go to the park!" The same goes for getting ice cream after a soccer match—do it to celebrate a fun game, not because your child scored a goal. If the fact that your teenager's chopping all the vegetables for tonight's stew saved you enough time to make cookies for dessert with her, it's okay to let her know how her contribution helped, just watch your wording. Try "Looks like we have some extra time on our hands this afternoon thanks to all your help—how about we make some chocolate chip cookies?"

If you are currently using rewards to introduce a difficult new behavior to your child (potty training, anyone?), consider bringing that to an end and replacing the M&M's with encouragement: "Wow, you made it to the potty all by yourself! You are really growing up!" And try not to assume at the outset that only the promise of a new train set will get your child to stop sucking her thumb, for instance—you might be pleasantly surprised at what she can do on her own, and so will she.

Now that you know the pitfalls of praise and rewards, and how to stop, it's time for the fun stuff: one simple tool to help you bring out your kids' un-entitled best.

Un-Entitler: Encouragement

Without rewards and praise, how do we commend our kids when they're at their best, in hopes that we'll see the behavior again in the future? The answer is to use Encouragement. This tool will ward off entitlement by fostering behavior that's actually the opposite of entitled behavior. It'll help you find the helpful words to say to let your kids know you've noticed their willingness to work hard, dedication, kindness and other positive traits. Focusing on their beneficial efforts and attributes will foster intrinsic motivation and help your kids see the relationship between putting in effort and reaping the natural rewards (for instance, practicing free throws at home and scoring the winning basket on the court). They'll learn that being a star player or a straight-A student are not reasons to quit working hard and coast into adulthood. Instead, they'll notice how their positive behavior has produced the positive outcome, and will be more likely to repeat their actions in the future. This mind-set will serve them better than any new plastic dinosaur ever could.

> More than three decades of research shows that a focus
> on effort—not on intelligence or ability—is key to
> success in school and in life.[*]
>
> —Carol S. Dweck, PhD, author of *Mindset:*
> *The New Psychology of Success*

PUT IT TO USE

Encouragement is a great tool to use whenever you feel the urge to call out a "I'm so proud of you!" or "Good job." It can also easily replace a

---

* http://www.teambath.com/wp-content/uploads/2011/07/Secret-to-Raising-Smart-Kids.pdf

physical reward, since encouraging words are actually sweeter to kids than a lollipop (subconsciously, anyway). Any time you want to point out good behavior to your kids, say it with Encouragement.

When you catch your child in the right, for instance, completing her math homework quickly and correctly, your initial response might be to say something like "You're so smart!" Your first act is to hold your tongue. Then think of a *positive aspect of her behavior* to encourage. Your goal is to point out the specific behavior that you want her to repeat in the future. If you saw her working to block out distractions and stick to her work, try "Your laser focus really helped you get your homework done quickly today!" She'll smile with pride that you noticed, and be more likely to do the same thing tomorrow. If, on the other hand, you'd simply said "You're so smart!" she might feel like she didn't have to work hard the next day, since she's naturally so smart.

In another example, maybe your nine-year-old helped a six-year-old neighbor retrieve a kite from a tree. In this case, you might say, "Ben really looks up to you—I think he really appreciated you going out of your way to help!" Your child will be left feeling much better about his actions than if you had simply offered "Good boy."

Sometimes it can be hard to create Encouragement without accidentally praising instead. Here are a few tips and rules of thumb to help get you started:

- Comment on the behavior that produced a particular outcome, not the child. Instead of saying "Good boy," try "You've really shown dedication by cleaning your pet turtle's cage every week without being asked!"
- Comment on the behavior rather than assigning a label. Instead of saying "You're so smart!" try "Your extra study time earned that A."
- Talk about what you can see. If you've asked your kids to tidy up the playroom and they've done a great job, say "Books are on the shelf, toys are in bins, the floor is clear—mission accomplished!"
- Focus on positive traits like effort, teamwork, kindness, persistence

and improvement. When your son wins his tennis match, don't gush "You're the best!" Switch your response to "Your backhand sure has improved since you've been lifting weights."

- Take the emphasis off yourself. Try "*You* must be so proud of *yourself!*" rather than "I'm so proud of you!" Remember, it's okay for you to be proud of your kids but it's more important that they are proud of themselves, to help them build internal motivation.

- Avoid focusing on the end result—the A test grade, the goal scored, getting the big solo in the spring concert. Instead, link the end result to the behavior that made it happen by saying "Your extra practice earned you the solo!"

- Consider asking a question rather than making a comment. Your child will love explaining her techniques as she answers "How did you manage to fit everything so nicely into your closet?"

- Likewise, if you feel the urge to praise something your child has created—or if he seems to want your approval—instead, ask his opinion: "How do *you* feel about your artwork?" He'll benefit more from expressing his own ideas than listening to yours, and the fact that you're interested will show that you care about his creation.

- Talk specifically about the character trait that was shown. "You're so sweet," is not nearly as helpful as "You really showed generosity when you shared your cookie with your brother after his fell on the ground." Or try "It sure took courage to apologize to Mrs. Hawkins for accidentally hosing down her car."

- A simple "Thank you" can work wonders as Encouragement in helping your child feel a strong sense of significance. Instead of a shallow "Great job!" for emptying the dishwasher unasked, switch to "Thank you so much—that's a big job I can take off my plate."

- "I love you" is very encouraging, and never gets old.

> The long-term value of encouragement is not to be
> confused with the momentary pleasure of praise.
>
> —Kelly Bartlett, author of *Encouraging Words for Kids*

Your kids will feel gratified that you noticed their positive behavior and they'll be much more likely to repeat the behavior next time. This tool will also help them develop internal motivation and the ability to work hard until they know they've given it their best.

And if your kids show natural abilities and really can coast through school or sports without really trying? Help them take their talent to the next level if they're interested by encouraging them to seek out extra challenges, dig deeper or aid others who are struggling. If they frequently ace math tests without cracking the book, simply say "You must really enjoy math!"—then pick up an advanced calculus book at the library and leave it strategically on the breakfast table (or encourage them to join the math team at school, learn chess or tutor younger kids). Also, remind them that natural ability doesn't excuse anyone from working hard. Even if math comes easy, writing might not. You'll want to hold back from gushing about geometry scores that were easily won, and instead focus on effort and improvement in language arts. Remember that a B that was hard earned should receive just as much encouragement—if not more—than an easy A.

Tips and Scripts

- Unlike rewards and praise, you can use Encouragement as often as you want—and watch your kids beam with pride as you notice their efforts.
- Don't feel paralyzed by using Encouragement. It's okay to shout, "You are so awe-soooooome!" when your child scores the winning goal in her hockey game. Just be sure to reinforce her extra practice time with Encouragement in a calm moment after the game.
- You can use Encouragement win or lose—whether your child gets the lead part in the play she wanted or is cast as Villager #36 instead. Simply focus on the positive behaviors she can repeat: "You sure put a lot of emotion into your performance at tryouts. I bet it'll help the whole cast if you bring that energy to the rehearsals!"
- Encouragement can seem awkward to deliver at first. Give yourself

time—consider focusing on one behavior at once. With practice, you'll be able to deliver Encouragement with ease.

· Avoid the word "perfect," as there's no such thing.

YES, BUT . . .

I can never think of what to say.

Read on for more help. And although you might not always be able to think of the perfect encouraging phrase, even if you can make the switch half the time, your kids will benefit. With practice, Encouragement will come more naturally, and pretty soon you won't have to think so hard about it. In a pinch, "Thank you" works wonders for responsibilities your kids take on, and the "You worked really hard on that!" angle, as long as it's true that your child has put in the time, does the trick for accomplishments.

I use Encouragement with my son but I often find that he still doesn't perform to his potential. Will my Encouragement lead him to feel that it's okay not to try his hardest?

It's discouraging for kids when we only recognize well-done jobs or tasks. Our kids perceive us as sitting in judgment and may think they'll never meet our approval if we reserve our Encouragement for the times they fully meet our expectations. After a while, they're likely to stop trying at all. Parenting educator Vivian Brault used this analogy: "It's like telling your prize rosebushes, 'I'm not going to give you any fertilizer until you start producing the kind of blooms I know you're capable of.'" Instead, encourage *any* movement in the right direction and any little bit of improvement. Any Encouragement, no matter how small, will work over time to get your son to put forth his best effort more often.

WARNING TO THE WISE:
WATCH OUT FOR PIGGYBACKING!

Nothing kills a good "Your hard work really paid off!" like "Why can't you work that hard all the time?" This is called Piggybacking, a Positive Discipline term. Piggybacking is a zinger you tag on to the end of a perfectly encouraging comment. It's often done in the name of training; you want to drive home an important point, but beware—it can undo all the positive effects of our Encouragement and then some. As difficult as it may be, once you've delivered your Encouragement, leave it at that. Our children will learn the positive behavior in time, and without our piggybacking comments. What's more, piggybacking will put them on the defensive, distracting them from the positive behavior and making them feel angry, guilty or frustrated. Believe me—I know how hard it can be to keep quiet when you want to drive home your point, but you'll be better served by holding your tongue.

Make the Switch

PRAISE	ENCOURAGEMENT
You're the best big sister ever!	Your little brother just loved it when you shared your toys with him! You were so patient with your sister when you helped her get dressed.
You're the best player on the team!	All those hours practicing your left-footed shots are really paying off! Your passing game sure has improved!
You're so smart!	All that time you spent studying earned you that A! You planned ahead and studied hard for that test and it shows!

PRAISE	ENCOURAGEMENT
Great job!	Thank you for taking the extra time to put everything away where it belongs! I really appreciate your help!
What a great picture!	What do you like best about your picture? You seem to love painting!
I'm so proud of you!	You must be so proud of yourself! You should feel proud of your hard work!
Good girl/boy!	You really showed kindness to the girl in the park who got hurt! I appreciate your helping out without being asked!

Other Encouraging Phrases to Try

- "You put a lot of hard work into cleaning this room! It shows!"
- "Look at your improvement!"
- "I have complete confidence in you!"
- "I love being with you!"
- "That's what I call perseverance/courage/kindness!"
- "Thank you for putting your dishes in the dishwasher. I love the teamwork in this family!"
- "You are really growing up! I remember when I used to have to dress you, and now you do it yourself!"
- "The time you're putting into your homework is really paying off."
- "Thanks for helping set the table—that made a big difference."

- "Can you teach me how to do that?"
- "You gave it one hundred percent effort through the whole game!"
- "You showed true sportsmanship today when you helped the opponent up from his fall."
- "That's just like you to be so kind/considerate/helpful!"
- "You must have been encouraged that . . ."
- "That's a really helpful idea. I'm glad you shared that with me."

8

Money and Sense

Fourteen-year-olds Braydon, Dominic, William and Matthew are good friends, having lived in the same neighborhood for years. One rainy Saturday, instead of trying out some new stunts at the skate park as they'd planned, they decide to go see a movie. Each boy runs home to get some cash.

Braydon finds his dad outside washing the car and starts begging. "Can I plleeaassee have some money to go to the movies? Dominic and Matthew are going!"

Dad isn't sure. "Well, remember last week you needed money to go to the arcade? And what about that new jacket you want?" Braydon, however, reminds Dad that he only spent a couple bucks at the arcade, the jacket could be for his birthday and his little sister always gets more money than he does. After a few minutes, Dad forks over the money— but only enough for the movie and not for popcorn. "Have a good time!" he calls.

Dominic hurries inside and grabs his money bank. Good thing he brought home two As from his earth science and art classes last week— he was paid five dollars for each A. Plus, he practiced trombone every day for his lesson and helped his little brother with his math homework, which he also received payment for. He's a couple bucks short for the movie, popcorn and a soda, so he tries his mom. She agrees to give him the rest of what he needs as long as he promises to be home in time for supper.

William checks his money stash and finds a few ones. Then he remembers his mom owes him money for completing a couple of his weekly chores. He finds her and asks for payment for making his bed every day, emptying the dishwasher twice, putting the trash out at the curb and mowing the lawn. William does his best to ensure he's paid for every job he does for his parents, so he usually has plenty of money. Once his mom pays up, he goes to find his friends.

Matthew digs into his wallet hopefully, but there are only two dollar bills. He spent the allowance money he'd saved on some candy and soda and a couple of song downloads he now regrets, plus a new baseball cap. He goes to his dad to ask for an advance on next week's allowance, but he already knows the answer: "Sorry, Son! You know the rule." His parents allow him to do extra jobs around the house—beyond his usual chores—to earn money, but he won't have time to do extra jobs before the show starts. They've also started to allow him to borrow money, but he doesn't feel like paying the small amount of interest they'd charge him since he's saving up for a new skateboard. Disappointedly, he phones his friends and asks if they want to meet up again after the movie, since he won't be able to come along.

It's hard not to feel bad for Matthew in this story. He's the only one who couldn't manage to come up with the cash to see the film. But before we worry too much about poor Matthew, consider a similar situation in ten years, when the young men are out on their own and making a larger purchase, such as a car. Only Matthew is likely to have the practice he needs to budget, borrow, save and consider his purchase before he buys. And if I were him, I'd much rather experience buyer's remorse on candy and soda than on a sports car that I can afford for only a year and that ruins my credit.

Chances are you saw your family's system reflected in one of the boys (or a combination). In fact, most kids learn about money from a very early age—namely, that it comes from Mom's or Dad's wallet and buys cool stuff! From then on, they're hooked. Many parents fund their kids' desires by simply handing out cash on an as-needed basis (Braydon), using it as a reward (Dominic), paying for chores (William) or providing an allowance (Matthew). Most probably use a combination of these techniques. And most want to teach their kids at least a little something about money—how to earn it, how to spend it wisely and that it doesn't grow on trees (or in wallets).

The problem, though, is that in the hurry and confusion of everyday life, important lessons can easily be bypassed or lost if we're not careful. Money can also become the great entitler if we let it get out of control. We live in a culture of plenty and for the most part, our kids rarely get a taste of what it's like to do without food, warmth, shelter, clothing and more. That's a good thing. But it also means that they can grow up with an unhealthy money-can-buy-happiness, entitled attitude.

Attitudes about money can swing a couple of different ways:

1. Money is something I use to buy the things I need and some things I want.
2. Money solves my troubles and gets me what I want.

When kids see money as readily available and the answer to their problems—whether as a means to acquire the prom dress they absolutely have to have as part of the cool crowd or the glow-in-the-dark robotic alien that promises an end to all boredom—they can easily begin to feel entitled to these things. Who wouldn't? After all, kids are impressionable and advertisers are fierce. Besides, don't we all like to look and feel our best? They begin to put an emphasis on things that money can buy: everything from fancy sneakers to lavish experiences, and lose sight of simpler pleasures. They see money itself as a solution rather than a tool, and all the more so when it's easy to come by. They lose the ability to think creatively and critically (not to mention economically!), and are more likely to fall into traps like overspending and taking on debt.

On the other hand, when kids view money more realistically as a limited tool—albeit a complex one that can, indeed, buy lots of fun things—they lose the sense of entitlement and instead focus on how to put it to the best use.

I don't have to tell you that money can be a terribly confusing topic when it comes to raising kids. Parents ask all kinds of questions: Is it okay to pay for chores? When should you start an allowance? What should your kids be expected to pay for? Can they buy anything they want with their money? When is it okay to fork over a little extra? This is the chapter to sort it all out for you. You'll learn how to ensure money doesn't become a reward, when it's okay to pay your kids for jobs, how to use an allowance as a powerful teaching tool and much more.

First, let's look at the ways families often present money to their kids. No need to worry if your habits are currently unhealthy—most families, including mine, have wrestled with these concerns at one time or another, and the strategies in the chapter and tools at the end of the chapter will help you get on the right track.

System #1: Money as Needed

Kids know money doesn't grow on trees—it comes from Mom's or Dad's wallet! Where they apparently think it must multiply, judging from the enormity of some of their requests ("Dad, can we get a swimming pool? I mean the *real* kind, with a slide and maybe a diving board. Can we?"). Since kids know we've got the goods, they rarely hesitate to ask for it. Some families work entirely on this system, with parents doling out cash when their kids want to go ice-skating with friends, get their hands on the new video game or bring home the latest fairy princess ballerina doll.

There are a few problems with this system. First, it means that kids see no real limit to the amount of money they have access to. Even though you might give a no answer in one instance, there might be money available next time and the time after that. And even if your wallet really is empty, they know you have access to a bank account and magical credit cards that can (they think) buy the happiness they want, especially since after payday the picture changes and their requests might be met more readily. Because of the never-ending cycle of ask-give-ask-give, kids never really get the idea that money is in limited supply and that even their most intense whining (or nicest "Pretty please?") can't produce more. This system is ripe for spoiling, too. Kids quickly find that if Dad says no, Mom might still say yes. Or that breaking out the Entitled Kids' Whining tactic will get them the payout they're seeking.

It also puts parents in the position of judging every purchase. Sure, parents often know best, and can prevent their kids from blowing five dollars on a cheap water gun that's going to break the first time they use it. But since Mom and Dad wield all the control, kids never get to make the decisions and get the practice they need for responsible financial decision making down the road.

What's more, kids who grow up seeing money as something you get if you just ask enough don't have a real sense of budgeting, saving or planning. Since they don't have a clear picture of their own total income, they can't possibly make positive long-term decisions to save up for a new skateboard. And why not blow a few dollars here and there if they can always ask Mom for more? Money becomes something they learn to treat haphazardly—which is exactly what we *don't* want them to do when they leave home. Assuming, of course, that they do leave.

And finally, even if kids are simply supplemented every so often from Dad's wallet, they grow up dependent on someone else to provide rather than relying on their own steady income. Unless you want to be that provider, it might be wise to stay away from this system.

It's not that parents can never chip in for unexpected purchases, though—as with many things, the cause for concern arises when a money-as-needed system becomes the standard operating procedure for kids' finances. There are six valuable tools in this chapter that will help you avoid this scenario and assist your kids in accessing cash in positive ways.

System #2: Money as a Reward

Many marketers have figured out that cash is the ultimate reward—as have many kids. The problem is that even money can lose its luster when it's offered as a reward for grades, good behavior and the like. And, as we saw in chapter 7, kids raised with this kind of system expect a payout every time they step up, pitch in or act appropriately. Most households don't finance their kids solely through rewards, but some children do earn a substantial income through good grades, behaving for the babysitter and not telling their little brother monster stories right before bedtime. They see money as something they're entitled to simply for exhibiting acceptable behavior. And if they do go above and beyond to really work hard to get a good chair placement in the school orchestra or to win the science fair, payment will overshadow the positive feelings they would otherwise get to experience. For these reasons, I can't ever recommend using money as a reward. There are much better ways to show your kids you appreciate their help or good behavior (Encouragement), as well as to teach them about money.

System #3: Money as a Payment

I think every parent reasons, at one time or another, "I get paid for the work I do, why shouldn't my kids?" But I would counter, what about doing the dishes? How about changing lightbulbs, unclogging the drain, cleaning out the refrigerator and scrubbing the shower? Yes, you get paid for a job you are hired to do, but not for the thousands of jobs you do simply because you are alive and responsible for the property you live in. It's not that kids should never get paid for any job, but they certainly shouldn't get paid for all of them—or even most of them.

Many families link chores to payment (or allowance) as a way to motivate their kids to get the work done, as well as to provide them with some spending money. The problem is that in this type of system, money becomes a reward, and they're not likely to pitch in without it. They will always ask "What's in it for me?" when presented with a request.

And when you think about it, jobs like emptying the dishwasher, walking the dog and vacuuming the carpet need to get done whether your kids do them or not. So linking them to money still puts you in the position of nagging your kids to get them finished so that you have plates for dinner and a clean floor. If your kids don't have an immediate need for the cash, there's not much you can actually do to get them to lift a finger *right now*. A When-Then Routine, or a simple When-Then, serves us much better than payment to get the responsibility done at a reasonable time.

Kids who are paid for the work they do around the house lose out on the sense of belonging and significance they'd feel if they worked simply for the good of the household. After all, we all benefit from a sense of contributing to a group that we care about. And when they're out on their own and have to empty the wastebaskets without getting a dollar in return, the work will feel a lot heavier than if they were used to pitching in all along.

It's easy to see how these systems get started in the average family home. But when money isn't handled responsibly, kids can suffer under distorted ideas. For instance, kids who are used to having money handed to them at their every whim aren't going to see a big reason to change their situation post high school. Why not continue to live at home, where all needs are met? We've already seen the detriment of rewards, which leave kids unable to function without accolades or payback. And using money strictly as payment teaches kids a what's-in-it-for-me mind-set, until they learn not to lift a finger unless they'll be paid for their trouble. Why should they?

Fortunately, there's a fourth system, and it's the one I recommend. It's called a No-Strings-Attached Allowance and it'll help you train your kids in financial responsibility. We'll cover this fully as the first tool in this chapter. Let's start by looking at how to create a financially responsible environment for our kids to learn from.

Plenty and Want

We live in a culture of plenty—but that doesn't mean we don't all struggle financially. How do we take our kids along for the ride whether the going is tough or it's easy living? After all, we don't want to unnecessarily deprive them or spoil them. Where's the balance?

There's plenty you can do no matter your financial situation to teach your kids positive lessons about money. While having a high income is traditionally associated with entitled kids, lower-income families are certainly not immune. And likewise, all kids should learn about frugality, resourcefulness and financial responsibility, no matter how rotund the bank account, lest they end up with an extra yacht they don't really need. After all, more than a few big lottery winners and first-round NFL draft picks have ended up bankrupt when all is said and done (too many yachts?), and certainly no happier for all their good fortune.

So much of entitlement comes from having more than we need. There's nothing wrong with living in a nice house and having expensive things, but we'll reap the biggest rewards if we teach our kids how to manage finances on their own and prepare them to make do with less if need be. Chances are our kids won't all want to be doctors and lawyers, so we'll be doing the starving artist in the family a favor if we train her to live within her means.

But those with less certainly aren't immune to entitlement issues. I traveled to the poorest county in West Virginia—the heart of coal-mining country—to help parents and teachers address some of the issues they face. They told me that entitlement runs rampant among the poorest population of kids. Why? Churches and other organizations constantly provide materials (clothing, school supplies, toys) to kids via well-meant programs. When kids frequently receive Christmas presents and other handouts from these programs, they come to expect it. At a recent program through the school, a middle school student asked a teacher, "Is this all I get?" Entitlement isn't limited to the young owners of iPhones and designer sneakers. It can affect anyone used to getting special privileges, big and small.

Whatever your financial situation, the first thing to remember is that kids will model what they see—so money sense begins with you. And every child will benefit from a realistic view of money, wherever they end up in life. As your kids grow, make sure you give them plenty of chances to see you making big and little financial decisions, to the point of letting them know when you mess up: "Oops, I really should have done more research before I bought this vacuum. I don't like it as much as my old one that broke, but it was a big enough purchase that I'm stuck with it!" Make a practice of using positive money habits, such as budgeting, planning, saving, price comparing, paying down debt (or finding ways not to take it on in the first place) and contributing to charitable causes. Then monitor your attitude. If your kids see you making impulse buys every time you set foot in a store, they'll follow suit. If, however, they watch you give up your morning Starbucks for a month to save up for concert tickets, they'll see your sacrifice as a workable option next time they're pining away for a remote control helicopter (maybe they could pack their lunch every day rather than spend their allowance on school lunch). And say you've been given a bonus at work. Do you blow it all on a new TV? Maybe—but consider the long-term benefit of letting your kids see you balance saving, spending and giving in a healthy way.

Ben Bernanke, who served two terms as chairman of the Federal Reserve from 2006 to 2014, stated that financial literacy includes practice in each of the following core financial competencies:

- Earning and income
- Spending
- Saving
- Borrowing
- Investing
- Identity protection

If this sounds like a daunting list, don't worry: simply involve your kids in financial decisions and do training on an age-appropriate basis to help them gain the real-world experience they need. Four-year-olds can help you decide whether to spend the treat money for the week on cookies or ice cream at the grocery store, and an eleven-year-old can be involved in decisions about whether to save up for a big family vacation or take several weekend trips during the year. Let your kids see you (and help you) compare prices, clip coupons and openly deliberate between two similar items (plus the old one you are considering replacing— maybe you should repair it instead?). Take them to the bank to open their own savings accounts, explore online the cost of a typical starter apartment they might live in one day and find the best price on the sports equipment they want (which could involve purchasing it second- hand). Show them your investments and encourage them to pick some stocks to follow. Let them tag along when you sign up for a car loan. Point out identity-theft issues in the news and talk about solutions. By the time your child leaves the house, he will have gained from you a realistic view of the real costs of being a grown-up, like paying for trash pickup, insurance and taxes; and real monetary responsibilities, too, such as paying back a loan on time.

And what if you really are struggling to put food on the table or keep the electricity on? Here are a few situation-specific tips that might help, whether you're living with plenty or finding your bank account wanting.

When times are tough:

- Make sure your kids know you will be there to take care of them and their needs. Try not to let your financial situation create a sense of insecurity, while being honest about what you can and can't afford. ("Since we're trying to create a fund to save money for emergencies, we're going to try really hard to turn on the air con- ditioner only during the hottest parts of the day. But you can run in the sprinkler whenever you want.")
- It's okay to let your kids know in a general, age-appropriate way that you lost your job and will be doing contract work on a re-

duced income or that you're working on paying down credit card debt and won't have as much extra spending money. Talk about ways you'll be trying to save money and ask for their ideas and help. They'll enjoy contributing to the discussion, even though your weekly movie outing might need to become an on-demand movie rental at home instead.

- Let your kids help you meet various wants in creative ways. They'll learn much more resourcefulness from making their own pizza rather than ordering delivery.

- Let your kids see you cutting back, too. If you come home with new jewelry after scaling back their allowances, they'll have more trouble accepting the situation.

- Try to leave a little room in the budget for some fun—even if it's just doing a craft project together, or holding an impromptu dance party.

When times are good:

- Put a personal emphasis on frugality and let it trickle down to your kids. Saturday family fun day doesn't need to involve an amusement park, for instance. Make sure your kids know that hiking in the state park with a picnic lunch can be just as enjoyable, if not more so, as an expensive outing. Homemade gifts are still often more meaningful than store-bought equivalents. And fixing older appliances can be better for the environment (and any budget) than buying new.

- If you decide to bump up the allowances in accordance with your recent pay raise, remember to bump up your kids' financial responsibilities, too. You don't need to charge them rent, but do expect them to age-appropriately cover more of their own expenses, such as clothing, family birthday gifts and gas money.

- Let your kids help decide which charities to make contributions to and what to save for as a family. Even if you can afford to donate and save extravagantly, they'll be learning important lessons about how to monitor money (and there's no need to give them an exact dollar amount—in fact, it's often better not to, especially if you're dealing with large amounts of money).

- Link your earnings to your hard work. You didn't land in a management role at a large company simply by flashing your winning smile—it took studying hard through college, paying your dues with an entry-level job, attending night school, staying at your post even with a boss you couldn't stand, working overtime and persevering through a rigorous interview process. Your kids will see that the fruit doesn't come without the labor.
- Set spending limits even if you don't need to. You may be able to afford lobster, but let your kids see you order a chicken sandwich instead. They'll benefit down the road from not expecting to receive carte blanche every time you set foot in a restaurant (or store).

> One of my all-time favorite stories involves a father who
> came home one day with his entire $10,000 paycheck in $1 bills.
> He put the stacks of bills on the table and then proceeded
> to peel off piles to represent all of the family's
> expenses. Talk about transparency!
> —Ron Lieber, *New York Times* columnist and author of *The Opposite of Spoiled:*
> *Raising Kids Who Are Grounded, Generous, and Smart About Money*

Now let's take a look at a couple of tools that will help families everywhere prepare their kids for life in the real world with real finances. Along with setting up your own good habits, these are surefire ways to train your kids in the use of money.

Un-Entitler: No-Strings-Attached Allowance

When done right, a No-Strings-Attached Allowance is the primary tool you need to teach your kids about fiscal responsibility throughout their

childhood. With it, they'll learn about saving, spending, delayed gratification, giving, borrowing, budgeting and investing. They'll learn to
carefully consider purchases, as well as how to deal with inevitable buy-
ers' remorse. You can even use it to branch into special budgets (holiday
gift giving, back-to-school shopping) and credit cards. With a No-
Strings-Attached Allowance, kids will be met with almost every challenge adults face in the real world, but on a miniature scale. And
wouldn't we much rather they make a bad decision with five dollars of
allowance money than with five thousand dollars ten years later? When
kids begin to see the results of their spending actions—positive and
negative—early on, they'll develop good financial sense that will influence their decisions for decades to come. What a gift!

PUT IT TO USE

Lots of families hand out allowances every week—I know this is nothing new. But to make it the most effective in training good money habits, follow the six standards of No-Strings-Attached Allowances:

1. **Cut the purse strings.** It might seem like tying allowance to
    household jobs will solve all your problems with getting the tow-
    els folded, but keep in mind that method is a temporary fix at
    best. As we saw in chapter 7, giving money is a kind of reward and
    should be avoided lest we foster the what's-in-it-for-me attitude.
    Yes, it's true your child doesn't directly earn his allowance, but
    there are plenty of other ways to teach him about paychecks. A
    No-Strings-Attached Allowance is a tool that teaches kids how to
    responsibly use money, not how to acquire it. The allowance
    should be delivered on time even if behavior is bad and family
    contributions are not done. (Remember, you have other tools to
    address those issues: Decide What *You* Will Do, When-Then, Con-
    sequences, Either-Or, etc.)

2. **Detail the budget.** How much money should kids get for their

allowance? I hear this question all the time! But setting the dollar amount is putting the cart before the horse. First you have to determine what your kids will be responsible for covering with their allowance. Based on your kids' ages, decide what you'd like them to purchase. Do they need to buy some of their own clothes? Birthday presents for family members? Food for their pet gerbil? Music downloads? School lunches? The allowance should be enough to *reasonably* cover these things, plus a little extra so they can save up for some of their wants, but it also shouldn't feel entirely comfortable. Be clear with your kids about what kinds of things you'll cover on an age-appropriate basis (fifteen dollars toward a present for birthday parties, a movie you attend as a family, a new pair of athletic shoes every year—or when they grow out of them—one souvenir on vacation, etc.), and what they need to be prepared to spend.

Allowance Through the Ages

AGE	EXPENSES KIDS CAN COVER WITH THEIR ALLOWANCE	WHAT THEY LEARN
4–5	Toys, treats	Delayed gratification. Parents buy toys at major holidays and birthdays, but for other toy purchases, kids learn to save up for them. At the grocery store, the essentials are covered; treats and extras not on your list are on the kids' dime.
6–10	All of the previous expenses, plus media and nonessentials, including chipping in on cooler versions of essentials (for instance, contributing allowance money to buy nicer sneakers than Mom would deem necessary)	Prioritization. As kids' wants become more expensive and their logical thinking becomes more developed, they learn to prioritize which of their wants are most important.

AGE	EXPENSES KIDS CAN COVER WITH THEIR ALLOWANCE	WHAT THEY LEARN
11–13	All of the previous expenses, plus school lunch, school supplies, movies, music downloads and snacks and meals outside the house.	Budgeting. Kids will get a bigger allowance up front, but they'll be expected to cover necessities like school lunches and supplies. With careful budgeting and planning, kids will have the funds for these necessities and still have enough discretionary income for the fun stuff.
14–18	All of the previous expenses plus toiletries, makeup, grooming services (haircuts, manicures, pedicures), gifts for friends, clothing, gas, car insurance	Real-world finances. During a child's last few years at home, they'll learn to budget a larger income (allowance) to cover more adultlike expenses. Kids can supplement their allowance income with part-time employment to earn extra money.

3. **Put the "allow" in "allowance."** Instituting a No-Strings-Attached Allowance is a great opportunity to talk about budgeting, especially if your twelve-year-old wants help figuring out how long it'll take him to save up for the new tennis racket he's had his eye on, but remember that buyer's remorse might be your child's best teacher. Remember that unless your child's purchase is on your do-not-buy list (see the next point), he'll be best served if you let him make mistakes. That might mean he blows his savings on dollar-bin toys and regrets it later when he wants to try the moon jump at the fair, but the lesson will remain with him. After all, isn't that why you're using a No-Strings-Attached Allowance?

4. **Set up embargoes.** Okay, here's where you'll add just a couple of strings to the No-Strings-Attached Allowance. You'll need to let

your kids know what's *not* okay to buy—but make it a very short list. For instance, you might want to consider restricting R-rated movies, M-rated (mature) video games, revealing clothing and warehouse-sized boxes of junk food.

5. **Bail out on bailing out.** When you set up a No-Strings-Attached Allowance, know in advance that sometimes your kids will come up short. There will be anguish. There will be tears. But this tool only works if you refuse to rescue your kids when they've spent all their money on a rainbow sand jar craft kit last week and now can't afford to go skating with their friends. Yes, it will be embarrassing and disappointing for your child to be the only one of her friends not there, but the experience will teach her about saving like nothing you could ever say.

6. **Add fiscal responsibilities.** As your kids grow, require them to put money into a savings account, contribute a portion of their allowance to the nonprofit of their choice and even set up investments. All of these practices will help them reap the full benefits of their allowance as they get a realistic view of what cash flow can look like as an adult.

If you've already been using an allowance but have tied it to chores, your kids will cheer when you tell them you're making a clean break. Use the tools from previous chapters to get your kids completing their family contributions.

Many parents increase the No-Strings-Attached Allowance on their kids' birthdays, adding extra expense responsibilities at that time as well. For example, you may decide when Stephen turns ten that he can now be responsible for paying for his school lunch in the cafeteria. His allowance will increase accordingly, but now he learns to budget that money throughout the week. He may even decide to pack a lunch three days per week so he can more quickly save up the money he needs for a skateboard. By continuing to increase allowance money and kid-covered expenditures, our kids will be used to frequently paying their own way by the time they graduate from high school.

> You must gain control over your money or the
> lack of it will forever control you."
>
> –Dave Ramsey, author of *Financial Peace*

Tips and Scripts

- When should you begin a No-Strings-Attached Allowance? Parents start at widely different times, but you can begin when your kids start asking for things in the store (around age four). I recommend implementing an allowance by the time your child is in school, because the number of wants often expands at this point.
- Starting even earlier, make a household policy that you only buy new toys for predetermined holidays (Christmas, Hanukkah, birthdays). Setting—and holding to—this limit is an essential part of un-entitling your home.
- Have a plan for when your kids ask for the newest talking train set in the store. Simply say, "Would you like to use your allowance for that or should we add it to your wish list?" Once they get used to this response, they might even quit asking quite so much.
- Require your kids to bring their money to the store if they think they might want to make a purchase. This not only ensures they have the funds, but it also reinforces the direct link between saving and spending. Resist the urge to front them the money at the store because it's easy to forget to settle up when you get home, and the lesson will be lost.
- As your kids grow, increase their No-Strings-Attached Allowance and also the expense items they'll be responsible for covering.
- If your kids constantly want more spending money, use the next tool, Job for Hire, to help them responsibly earn the extra.

THE WISH LIST

What would you do if you had a million bucks (or even a crisp new twenty)? First you'd probably pull out your wish list—whether it's on your smartphone or in your head. Your wish list is your running tally of things you'd like, and it's also a great tool for kids to use to manage and prioritize everything from new Matchbox cars to concerts they'd like to attend. The beauty of a wish list is that it gets your kids thinking critically about financial decisions and deciding in advance how to make use of their funds (or what to drop hints about as their birthday approaches). They get to practice deliberating about how much they really want the robotic dog, puzzle, jewelry-making kit or whatever's caught their eye. What's more, a wish list fosters delayed gratification. If an item is on the list, it's not in their hands—but there's always the hope that it might be someday. And practically speaking, it gives grandparents a starting place for special occasions. Next time your kids are pointing out toys at the store or products online, encourage them to put it on a wish list. (Keep a mini notebook in your purse or a running list on your smartphone for this task.) They'll feel empowered to be able to do something about their want in the moment, and you get to say "Yes, that is cool—do you have enough allowance saved, or would you rather put it on your wish list?" instead of delivering another "No, we're not getting that."

YES, BUT . . .

My kids never have any money left at the end of the week and can't afford the things they're supposed to save up for.

Better they experience coming up short now when all their friends are heading to the amusement park without them than a decade or two down the road. Your kids will learn resourcefulness from doing without (for instance, asking older cousins for hand-me-downs), and eventually (with a little training from you) they'll get the brilliant idea to set aside some money every week for the items you're expecting them to cover. If their pet turtle will starve without the food they're supposed to be buying, use the next tool, Job for Hire, to enable them to earn enough to cover it in the meantime. And if your kids still don't get the message, try cutting back on No-Strings-Attached Allowance *and* their financial responsibilities until they get the hang of budgeting. Take Time for Training on budgeting and introduce a compartmentalized bank or envelope system to help solidify the idea that not every penny they bring in should be spent on enlarging their minifigure collection. Whatever you do, don't entitle them to irresponsible spending by spotting them the extra. Bailing them out will do them no real favors for the future and it will only put off the valuable lessons they have to learn.

MINI-TOOL: THE BUDGET

What about back-to-school shopping (both clothes and supplies)? Holiday gifts? And other occasions that require greater-than-ordinary expenditures on behalf of your kids? These are excellent opportunities to teach your kids about budgeting. Here's how to take advantage:

1. **Assess the situation.** Budgets work best for kids who already have some practice saving and spending, and have reached a certain maturity. While you should be prepared to let your kids accept the consequences of blowing their entire school-clothing budget on a designer handbag (and thus suffering the perceived shame of wearing last year's style of jeans this year, too), you want to set them up to succeed by giving them plenty of chances to practice (with a No-Strings-Attached Allowance) ahead of time.

2. **Make a shopping list.** Your kids should be clear about what they need to pay for out of their normal allowance and what budget items should be paid for using a predetermined amount of extra funding you provide. A school-supply and/or school-clothing list is a great place to start before branching into other areas. For in-

stance, if your son's casual shoes pinch his toes, he'll need to make those a priority with his school-clothing budget. With older kids, consider including in the budget everything from underwear to pajamas to gym clothes and dress-up clothes, while younger kids should be responsible for only a few things. For holiday gift lists, discuss recipients with your child so he knows exactly who he's purchasing for (Grandma? His friends? Or just immediate family?).

3. **Fork over the cash.** Do a little research to come up with the amount you'd expect your child to reasonably spend on the items you've listed and then hand it over in a lump sum. Make sure your child knows how long it has to last—for instance, will winter clothes be under a separate budget or is this money his budgeted amount for the year? (For younger kids, break the budget categories into smaller chunks—school supplies or school lunches. Older teens might benefit from a yearlong clothing or entertainment budget.)

4. **Price shop before you really shop.** Encourage your kids to compare prices online and at brick-and-mortar stores without feeling pressured to buy the first item they see. Look for coupons and deals, stop in at thrift and consignment stores or visit some garage sales together.

5. **Allow buyer's remorse.** Be available to talk through potential purchases with your child but don't try (too hard) to sway her away from shelling out half her budget for one dress. If she regrets her decision in the middle of winter when she wished she'd saved money for a sweater, she can always learn her lesson (and stay warm) by dipping into her allowance or bartering room cleaning with her sister for one of her sweaters.

6. **Let them pocket what they don't spend.** But make sure that doesn't happen until the set time period for that budget—the semester or sometimes as long as a calendar year—is up. When August rolls around again and a new clothing budget is handed out, anything left over from the previous year is fair game for her discretionary spending. This also means you'll need to require

them to keep track of their budgeted money, even if it just means setting it aside in a separate envelope in their piggy bank.

MINITOOL: THE LOAN

"Can I have my allowance early?" This common question often leaves parents fumbling. And the most common answers are probably the likes of "Um . . ." or "Ask your mom." Is it wise to let kids tap into their next payday if their friends are seeing the newest movie or the magic set they've been coveting is on sale and there's only one left?

My answer? Sure! Loans are a great teaching tool as long as they meet these requirements:

1. **Ages eleven and older.** Kids ages ten and under usually aren't mature enough yet to fully understand what it means to commit to a loan.
2. **A good credit score.** If you've loaned your child money before, was it paid back in full and on time? Has the child demonstrated responsibility in other areas? If so, a loan can be available.
3. **Interest.** That's right—charging interest on borrowed movie money now will get your kids to think twice about their expenditures and prepare them for reality when they insist on an expensive private college. Settle a reasonable yet not entirely comfortable rate ahead of time (use the same rate for every family member and every transaction) and stick to it.
4. **A repayment plan.** The *child* needs to develop a plan to repay the loan. Parents can then decide whether to allow the loan.
5. **No outstanding loans.** Your kids should only have one loan (from you) at a time.

Un-Entitler: Job for Hire

Even with a No-Strings-Attached Allowance, your kids often want more, *more* money. That's no reason to just hand over the cash. Use Job for

Hire to teach your kids the positive lessons of hard work by letting them earn extra cash by completing additional jobs around the house. They'll learn that while they're entitled to neither a free ride nor a blank check, they can change their financial situation for the better if they're willing to work at it.

PUT IT TO USE

Let's say your nine-year-old is saving up for Slime Factory 3000, a particularly juicy game he's had his eye on for months now. He is still a few dollars short, but his best buddy is coming over to spend Saturday with him and he'd love to dedicate a good portion of the day to squishing slime monsters with his friend. Inevitably, your son asks for money—just this once. (Isn't that what happens every time?) No need to lecture about saving money, instead it's time to hire him to complete an extra job around the house—or two or three depending on the amount of money he needs to make up the shortfall. Once the job is fully completed within your time frame, you can pay him the amount you agreed upon.

Here are the ground rules for Job for Hire:

1. Kids are still responsible for their regularly scheduled family contributions. If these aren't completed, enforce them with the consequences you've set up in advance. Let your kids know you'll be willing to discuss a Job for Hire *only after* all the regular family contributions are done.
2. The Job for Hire should be something extra, like a special project. And it should be something age appropriate they can manage to do by themselves. It should not be something your child is already expected to do and it should take a significant load off your back. Younger kids could scrub a kitchen floor, wash baseboards, clean all the bathtubs and sinks or dust all of the dining room furniture, while older ones could bathe the dog, clean the garage, clean out the kitchen cabinets, organize the attic or vacuum the minivan.
3. Payment for the job should be agreed upon in advance. Bigger

jobs should earn more money, while smaller ones earn less—but the most important thing is that both sides agree it's fair.

4. Be clear about your expectations for the job. If the job is to plant the garden, be sure your child knows how to hoe, space seeds, water, clean up afterward and do anything else you'd like done, lest you end up with marigolds in with the onions, and carrots spaced one inch apart. Write it down if you need to and let him know that it's okay to ask questions, but he needs to do the work himself. Also, tell him that if he doesn't finish the job—and do it well—within the time frame, he won't be paid—just like in the real world.

5. Give your child a reasonable time limit to complete the job.

6. If your child leaves the job undone, or doesn't do it to the best of his ability, let him know how to fix it and send him back (if there's time). No need to get upset or lay on the guilt—just be clear about what you'd like to see.

7. When the job is done—and *done well*, pay up promptly. And don't forget a thank-you and a few words of Encouragement for his hard work!

8. If the job doesn't get completed well within the time frame, pay nothing. You warned him in advance, so there's no need to say anything more. He can try again another time.

Tips and Scripts

- When your kids reach their mid- to late teens, they might start asking for bigger things (a new car, anyone?). This is a great time to help them research jobs outside the house. Lawn mowing, snow shoveling, pet sitting, babysitting and a variety of jobs at local businesses are all great ways to help them transition into the real world, plus learn that even a new-to-you car doesn't come easily.

- Your kids shouldn't be earning a second income by taking on extra work around the house. If a particularly enterprising child tries to do so, redirect her efforts toward a lemonade stand, a neighbor who needs some leaves raked or activities that don't require money to enjoy them.

- If you can't think of any jobs when your kids ask, that's okay.
- Avoid jobs that require lots of decision-making skills or special abilities you haven't trained your kids in. Repetitive jobs that simply take time or elbow grease are usually the best for kids younger than high school.

YES, BUT . . .

I can't think of any significant jobs my kids are capable of doing by themselves.

Use Take Time for Training on a variety of tasks to boost their skills. Once they gain confidence from yard work, cleaning duties and other responsibilities, new jobs will come more easily to them. Also, be sure your expectations are in line. Because of the nature of this tool, your child might not have been trained in cleaning windows when you assign her this Job for Hire. Do some quick on-the-spot training, then encourage her to ask questions if she needs to. Keep in mind that this tool works best with jobs that are repetitive and don't require a lot of special skills. If you need all the trim painted or the wheelbarrow fixed, you might want to just do those yourself.

Un-Entitler: State What You'll Spend

One of the toughest challenges facing parents when it comes to money issues with their kids is that kids really do need a lot of stuff. As opposed to simply *thinking* they need it (like that light-up musical Hula-Hoop in aisle 27). I'm talking about new gym shoes, the opportunity to spend social time with peers, an art class, a sweatshirt, a lunch box, a volleyball, an oboe, etc. Then there's the gray category. This is the stuff that we want to give our kids, but it can get too extravagant too quickly. For instance, when we decide that Zoey will get frostbite if she spends another winter in her slightly small and quite worn gloves that were handed down from her big sister, we might mention the idea of new ones next time we're walking the aisles of a discount retailer. She loves the idea—her friend Ellie has fur-lined, waterproof, rhinestone-studded designer gloves that she absolutely adores and was hoping for a pair. You, on the other hand, had been picturing the eight-dollar keep-your-hands-warm-and-dry variety. Should you meet in the middle? Cave since she's suffered through hand-me-downs for so many years? Or refuse to hear any more of her nonsense since, after all, you're not made of money? This tool will bring an easy resolution to these predicaments that everyone can live with.

It also teaches kids how to tell the difference between a basic need and an extra. It's okay to want the best athletic shoes or a brand-new bike instead of the Craigslist special—but that might mean sacrificing in another area. When kids get experience deciding between life's basics and life's extras, they'll be more likely to make better decisions when they're out on their own.

PUT IT TO USE

Next time your child has a need that could quickly become an expensive want, put State What You'll Spend to use. Simply say "I realize you need new winter gloves. I will cover eight dollars [the cost of the keep-your-hands-warm-and-dry variety]—if you want a pair that costs more than that, you'll need to come up with the rest." Then if Zoey must have the faux-fur-lined gloves like Ellie's, she can cover the extra with her allowance, birthday money, babysitting money or Job for Hire money. If she decides it's not worth it to her, she can settle for the discount-store variety.

Tips and Scripts

- If your child hits you up with a request that you think might turn into an issue, it's okay to research pricing before using this tool. Say, "Sure, I can help foot the bill for a bigger bike helmet but I need to research costs first." Then once you've determined what's reasonable, get back to your child. Say "I'll pay up to twenty dollars for any new bike helmet that fits correctly and has been certified as safe. Anything over that is up to you."

- If your kids manage to spend less than what you've stated you'll spend, they can pocket the extra if you've told them in advance that they can.

- It's okay to change your mind about what you'll spend, but *only* if your child or price comparisons have convinced you that you have a legitimate reason to spend more. Make sure your child knows that the spending increase is a result of new information and not whining, negotiating or badgering.

- You might not know what's reasonable until you get to the store—but it's okay to use this tool in the moment. Say "The ten-dollar umbrella will do a perfectly good job of keeping you dry. If you want the more expensive one, the extra cost is up to you."

YES, BUT . . .

I love to shop with my child and I don't mind spending extra for quality or style.

That's perfectly fine. But everyone has limits, right? Make sure your kids know where yours are. And if you do find yourself shelling out for designer jeans every time, it might be time for a reality check. If kids are always used to getting the best, they'll feel entitled to it—which is exactly what we're trying to avoid. Remember that we are often the culprits when it comes to entitling our kids to expensive needs. Even if we can afford designer jeans now, did we always have them as a kid, when we'd be growing out of them within a year? If we want un-entitled kids, sometimes we need to cut the purse strings—literally—and let them cover anything beyond the basics with their own funds. They'll learn to appreciate the luxuries they do have (the UGG boots Grandma surprised them with for Christmas) rather than to expect them because they feel entitled.

9

Keeping up with the Kardashians, Joneses and Facebook

Just a few short months ago, thirteen-year-old Olivia graduated from eighth grade—and from the middle school two blocks away from her house. Now, suntanned and carefree after a summer riding her bike, swimming at the pool and collecting rocks shaped like hearts, she steps onto the bus headed to the local high school. She can hardly wait for her first day.

By the time she reaches the homeward-bound bus that afternoon, she's already learned so much! For instance, that *everyone* is on Facebook and/or Twitter and that her flip-flops are little girl, so she'll need new ones by tomorrow. She signs up for a Facebook account and is soon happily commenting on new and old friends' pictures, then posting some of her own before you can even begin to dream up a list of ground rules.

On Tuesday, wearing sneakers instead of flip-flops, since there's no way you were rushing out to replace perfectly good flip-flops, Olivia starts begging for an iPhone for Christmas. Flip phones, not unlike certain flip-flops, are dumb phones. Never mind that she spent all of last year begging for her flip phone. She triumphantly announces that she's up to fifty Facebook friends already!

On Friday, Olivia has her first quiz in math class, a review of basic geometry. On the way out the door, she mentions how much she hates math. Wasn't it her favorite subject last year?

Clearly, Olivia is already learning so much in high school. You, on the other hand, have never felt quite so helpless!

One of the most entitled phrases we can ever hear from our kids is "But all my friends do it!" Kids (and adults, if we're honest) are under the impression that whatever anyone else does is fine, good and right. Never mind the inner voice—or the rules—that at times tells us otherwise.

There can be great pain in not measuring up to other kids' ideals or expectations, no matter how trivial or ridiculous—of being the one wearing a tank suit when everyone else is in bikinis, discovering the country music you love is terribly uncool or finding yourself embarrassingly in the dark about various social customs. Wouldn't it be nice if there were a memo sent around about which flip-flops are the right ones or what kind of music, exactly, is cool, lest our kids become fodder for hallway teasing?

But there's no memo—only the harsh judgments of other kids who are still maturing themselves. Some judgments cause bruised egos and that's all, but others are physically harmful, pressuring kids toward everything from substance abuse to "I dare you to ride your bike down those stairs." These are the influences that not only *guide* our kids but also at times seem to *entitle* them to bad behavior.

It used to be that kids were subject to their peers' opinions at school, and only to a much lesser extent at home. Now they can hardly *escape* their peers, thanks to the technological advances that require iconic photos to mark as tiny of an occasion as buying a gas-station slushie, and a nearly constant virtual dialogue about anything from what kind of hat they made the family dog wear, to the history teacher's squeaky shoes. Nor can they seem to escape their technology—which makes regular (uninvited) appearances at the dinner table, and in so doing invites all their friends and a handful of celebrities. All this interconnectedness, while it has its benefits, can also cause problems of epic proportions, fueling the entitlement epidemic already present in our homes.

This chapter is all about technology, peers and their influences. These are no longer separate topics—Facebook, Twitter, Instagram and the rest have reshaped the ways our kids relate socially and judge themselves internally, and social media is not going away anytime soon. The good news is that we don't have to lose our kids to their devices (or their peers), and we can help them make the best use of their connectivity while skirting the negative. Let's get started.

Anti-Social Media

First let's get a couple of things straight: the Internet is not to blame for the fact that we never see our kids' eyes anymore. It's not alive and it's not out to get our children. Neither is television or the music industry. We don't have to—and in fact we shouldn't—ban them from our household. At the same time, we need to realize our kids' generation is the first to be raised on digital devices, and these same devices seem to be running amuck with our kids. This is uncharted territory for all of us. So whether your teens can't keep their eyes off their phones or your preschoolers can't quit talking about a Thomas the Train app, you'll be doing things differently than your parents did when you were a kid.

The digital age certainly presents some new challenges, but we all know it also has its wealth of upsides, from alerting us while we're at the grocery store to the approaching thunderstorm that's going to require us to pick up our child early from baseball practice (a decade or two ago he'd be left dripping at a pay phone and leaving a message on our answering machine) to letting us compare prices on new tennis shoes without driving across town. Plus, it's fun! Let's face it—we all love having easy access to our favorite apps and tunes, Pinterest's latest inspiration and the goings-on of our friends and family. The question that haunts us is when does smart technology become, well, a dumb idea? When do we—and more important, our kids—have too much of a good thing?

Let's take a look at some of the troubles technology—and social media in particular—can breed. Yes, kids can pick up plenty of bad ideas and habits from television and video games, but social media can fuel the entitlement fire like never before.

One of the most pervasive problems caused by social media is the it's-all-about-me attitude. Selfies, likes, status updates—the line between keeping in touch with our friends from summer camp and blatant narcissism is a very thin one indeed. We see it in the way our kids share every mundane detail of their lives, check their status updates constantly and proclaim to the cyberworld, "Don't you wish you were me?" (And let's face it—haven't we sometimes been there ourselves?) In their attempt to be their own version of Justin Bieber, Taylor Swift or any other teenage icon, they lose a sense of their *actual* worth, trading it in for their *perceived* worth, which is valued in the number of likes or comments they receive on their latest post.

Beyond this, our kids begin to experience life in terms of how it will look on their Twitter feed. Our kids are so busy capturing and posting the moment that they don't actually *live* the moment. In the end, the fact that they just finished a 5K or painted their toenails ten different colors doesn't matter to them nearly as much as *what other people think* about the fact that they finished a 5K or painted their toenails ten different colors. And there's nothing more it's-all-about-me than becoming your own celebrity with your own personal fan club that loves everything you do. In just a couple of clicks, a child feels fully entitled to be lauded for every small thing.

Then there's the fact that social media promotes bad behavior and bullying. When kids can post a picture of themselves getting their nose pierced without permission and instantly see that dozens of their peers approve of their negative behavior, they're not likely to change that kind of behavior anytime soon. What's more, when their snide remarks about their classmate's new haircut (or worse) get transmitted to hundreds of computers with the click of a button, bullying can reach epic proportions.

Social media also undermines family values. The argument that everyone else is doing it has never had more backing than in the digital age. In fact, our kids are practically hit over the head with this mentality, whether they're viewing pictures of young celebrities wearing clothing as expensive as it is revealing or their friends living it up at a beach party they weren't allowed to attend. With everyone else working against us, it can be a constant struggle to maintain values for our kids, and hold them to any kind of limits or standards.

And when many of a child's friendships are virtual and rely on back-and-forth commentary about the lame shirt the girl in homeroom is wearing, they lose the ability to relate on a human level. This creates a lack of empathy. In fact, in the entitled generation, in which adolescents are given more privileges than ever, empathy with people who are different or who don't have the same material resources is at an all-time low. Entitled children often seek only their own pleasure, and forget about other people's feelings. It doesn't cross these kids' radar that not everyone grows up with Retina Display—except to hurtfully scoff at the idea.

Ironically, social media also decreases our kids' ability to relate to others. They become accustomed to counting heads rather than spending time developing through-thick-and-thin relationships and in so doing, lose out on one of life's greatest treasures—a true friend. But they hardly know what they're missing because they're too busy texting one peer while ignoring another. It's the real-life moments that build friendships—not commenting on each other's posts. When our kids don't build real-life friendships, they lose out on the opportunity to learn what goes into a long-lasting, committed relationship. This will stunt their social and relational growth down the road. And besides, who will be the best man at their wedding, let them cry it out when their dog dies and bike across France with them? People need friends, not numbers—and who more than our kids when they're undergoing some of the biggest changes of their lives?

Social media has given us this idea that we should all
have a posse of friends when in reality, if we have
one or two really good friends, we are lucky.

—Brené Brown

Practically speaking, social media actually brings out antisocial behaviors in our kids rather than the positive social skills we'd like to see.
Sure, we've all seen teens (and adults, for that matter) so absorbed in
checking game scores on their smartphones they can't carry on a conversation with the person next to them (who may be scrolling through
ideas on their own device for redecorating the mudroom). But the antisocial nature of social media goes beyond distraction and impoliteness.
In a digital world, where the majority of communication is done
through a keyboard or a touch screen, many kids no longer understand
the basics of simple conversation—everything from how to shake hands
and introduce yourself to how to find common ground. As social media
connect us to more people virtually, they're also creating a social skills
deficit in our kids. With so much communication happening online or
via text, kids have few opportunities to see manners and good communication in action, and even fewer chances to practice.

All of this makes it seem that social media contributes to everything
we're up *against* as parents working to raise responsible, resilient and
relatable kids. Again, technology and social media are not inherently
harmful, but if not used wisely, they can wreak havoc on family life.
Seeing as our teens' technology habit may very well be detrimental to
their future, it's our job to help them make the best use of their media
and also navigate the virtual social scene, while respecting their growing independence. And although there are certainly things to watch for
when it comes to keeping our kids connected and un-entitled at the
same time, I promise it's possible.

Moderating the Media

While social media certainly aren't the only contributing factors to the entitlement epidemic, they are actually one of the simplest to put the brakes on. And reducing your kids' access to technology will not only help them engage in other activities more varied and valuable than checking and rechecking their favorite sites, but it'll cut back on negative online behaviors and the inherent dangers that come along with them as well. Here are my tried-and-true guidelines for disconnecting and deemphasizing digital media:

1. **Reveal your technology limits in HD.** Be crystal clear that your kids are not *entitled* to technology. Devices of any kind are a privilege that can and will be removed if the rules are abused. (If your kids claim they need a computer for homework, offer to help them with rides to the public library to use the computers there.)

2. **Monitor the monitors.** Let your kids know up front that you *will* be checking their e-mail, social media and text messages periodically. Inappropriate messages (in or out) are grounds for losing technology privileges. Be sure to discuss how you'd like inappropriate incoming texts or e-mails to be handled (for instance, letting you know about them right away). Not every parent is comfortable with checking in on their kids' online behavior. It's been shown, however, that kids are less likely to engage in risky behavior if parents set limits and kids are aware they're being monitored. What's more, it's still ultimately our responsibility to take care of our kids and train them in positive behavior—which means watching out for them even in cyberspace.

3. **Set screen time.** Implement a technology curfew, and require that phones, computers and other devices live in the Technology Station until homework is finished and after the 8:00 p.m. technology curfew. Your kids will whine, but we all know they're not missing out on anything more important than a friend's newest

hair color, which they'll see the next day at school anyway. (And if your ears really are about to fall off from all the protesting, pull out some of the tools from chapter 2.)

4. **Keep it public.** Make the rule that technology may be used in the public spaces only—for instance the kitchen or family room. No phones, computers or tablets allowed in bedrooms, including devices that are being charged. Remember that your kids won't like the rules, but you're protecting them from very real risks.

5. **Shut down shutting down.** If you see your kids engaging in shut-down behavior like switching screens, covering the screen or quickly shutting down the device (you know—what you do so your boss doesn't see you checking in on your favorite blog at work), chances are they're up to no good. Warn them in advance that this kind of behavior means losing technology privileges, then follow through.

6. **Go offline.** Set a good example by following the same family limits for technology you expect to see in your kids. Keep certain times of the day free of phones and computers, and create quiet, technology-free zones in your house.

INFORMATION AGE: WHEN DO THEY GET A PHONE?

My short answer? When they need one. Sure, your eight-year-old has been asking for his own phone for years, but he doesn't need one (and I'm talking about the standard flip phone variety) until he's staying after school for track practice or when he needs lots of rides lots of places—usually in middle school. You'll also want to consider one if your child will be away from you for extended periods of time and you want to be able to check in. Consider a smartphone with Internet access only when they've demonstrated enough maturity with a flip phone and in other areas that you know they won't be using it to send embarrassing photos of classmates all over town. And remember that all technology (beyond what they need for you to check in or know when to pick them up from their wrestling match) is a privilege—not something they're entitled to just because their friends tell them they need it.

PARENT PROTOCOL: HOW TO BE THE FLY ON THE CHATROOM WALL

- Keep your posts, comments and likes to a minimum. You can wish your kids a happy birthday and the like, but you don't want them to feel like they're being watched. Also keep in mind social media platforms are for interaction with their friends, not with parents. You can chat with them in person or send them a quick e-mail.
- Get permission from your kids to friend their friends or tag them in photos.
- Don't friend or connect with your kids' teachers, coaches or other adults in authority positions unless your kids say it's okay. If you need to reach out to these people, do it via e-mail.
- Discuss concerns or issues in person—not online.
- Don't overshare yourself. Your kids will be mortified if you share too many details or post embarrassing photos of yourself. (It's the equivalent of showing up at their school in Velcro rollers.)
- Never shame your kids online as a form of discipline.
- Expect your kids to make mistakes on social media and don't overreact when they happen. Instead, use their blunders and poor choices as training opportunities.

These rules will help us gain control of technology use in our homes, but they shouldn't take the place of conversation. Talking about technology is akin to talking about sex—it's a conversation we should have with our kids early and often. Expect that kids are going to make mistakes and use these as opportunities to help them learn. Engage them in discussions about their friends' online behavior, or social media as a whole. It's all fair game—and all important for creating healthy technology habits your kids can rely on throughout their adult lives. When kids demonstrate maturity and make good decisions, both online and off, it's okay to give them more freedom. Remember that Wi-Fi access is everywhere, so the only way to truly keep kids safe and responsible is to focus on training good habits.

> What sex education used to be, it's now the
> "technology talk" we have to have with our kids.
> —Rebecca Levey, Founder, KidzVuz.com

Take Time for Technology Training

Does all the techie talk, from cloud storage to 4G to Insta-what? have your head spinning? Do your kids navigate with ease—and without limits? In either case, it might be time for a little training for yourself, as well as your kids.

I know what you're thinking: Do I have to? Even if the digital age has you wishing for your grandma's old rotary phone, the answer is yes. You can't monitor what you don't understand, and you can't responsibly let your kids roam around online without keeping an eye on them. When it comes to technology, knowledge is power—and once you learn the ropes, you can help your kids manage their media safely and effectively.

You'll need to know all about your kids' smartphones, the social media platforms your kids use and the most popular apps. Collect account information from your kids, including passwords. Yes, your kids will protest, but let them know it's part of the deal if they want to enjoy technology privileges. You can assure them that while you aren't planning to read every word of every message they send, you reserve the right to check in occasionally and without warning. You'll also want to set up your own accounts so you know what your kids might be up to, and, as a rule of thumb, if your child is using a site or visiting it, you should too every so often. In fact, your kids might enjoy taking you on a tour of their favorite sites or teaching you how to play their favorite online games. Let them be your guide—you'll not only learn how to back up your files to the cloud, but also how your kids use their hour of technology time every day.

As you learn, be sure to Take Time for Training for your kids to make sure they know how to use all their digital devices safely and appropriately. Discuss Internet safety early and often to keep the message fresh, as well as to keep up with changing trends.

One topic you shouldn't skip out on as you're training is sexting: a 2014 study found that 54 percent of college undergraduates reported that they sent or received sexually explicit texts before their eighteenth birthdays.* What most of them didn't know, however, is that these types of texts can legally be considered child pornography—which means that perpetrators could face jail time or sex-offender registration. The study found that simply knowing this fact would've deterred most from sexting. Which means that having the conversation about this tricky topic could spare your child some steep legal and social consequences.

Finally, teach your kids about their digital footprint by having them Google themselves. They might be surprised at the things they dig up— and equally surprised to hear that college admissions offices and employers are increasingly using Web searches and social media profiles to learn about applicants. Clue your kids in to the litmus test for posting online: Would I want my school principal, my girlfriend's parents or Grandma seeing this? If the answer is no, don't post.

Monitoring and limiting technology is one thing, but how do we raise kids to actually communicate and be themselves in a world of emoticons? While social media isn't usually the best way for kids to pick up positive social behaviors, there's plenty you can do in your

* http://drexel.edu/now/news-media/releases/archive/2014/June/Sexting-Study/

kids' offline hours to train them in what they need to know. Read on to learn how.

A Social Life Without Social Media?

Whether they live at our house or not, we've all seen kids who can't make eye contact, stand awkwardly in a corner at any kind of gathering and never remember to say please or thank you. In their defense, this is not entirely their fault. So much of life and business are conducted on-line in the privacy of our own homes that young people have fewer opportunities than ever to actually observe and model manners and social graces. That just means we need to be deliberate about teaching some of the social behaviors kids used to pick up simply through obser-vation, such as everyday manners and face-to-face conversation. In doing so, we'll help our kids succeed by fostering a technologically driven environment that still values interpersonal communication. This is Parenting 2.0, and here are a few ideas to get you started:

Mind Your Manners. Your kids ultimately take their social cues from their parents. They learn to be fully present in the moment if they see us shutting down our devices while at the playground. They pick up please and thank you more from hearing us use it, such as when we're asking them to hang up their coats or ordering in a restaurant, than any lecture we could deliver. When we make eye contact and engage in a good conversation at a basketball game, our kids might do the same with Aunt Katherine at the next family gathering. And the dinner table can offer a wealth of training possibilities, from how to eat spaghetti or soup without slurping (does anyone really know?) to what to do with a napkin to how to politely refuse an offer of seconds.

Teach Small Talk 101. Social grace and etiquette aren't instinctive, and with fewer opportunities to see them modeled and to practice them nowadays, parents need to be deliberate about training on social graces. Use Take Time for Training to prepare your kids for any social situation they may face, whether they're invited to a formal dinner or complimenting a wrinkly new baby. Work on greeting adults, introducing themselves (and others), speaking up when asking or answering questions, graciously accepting compliments, shaking hands and making eye contact. Older kids may need pointers in engaging adults in polite small talk, including coming up with neutral and interesting conversation topics. And don't forget the phone: even though we don't seem to use phones much for talking anymore, kids still need to know how to politely answer and take a message. Online etiquette is also something you can train: kids will benefit from being able to write a professional-sounding e-mail rather than a two-liner that uses numbers in place of words, for instance.

Practice Makes Polite. Give your kids plenty of chances to try out their new skills, and help them be successful by preparing them in advance. Practice a few key phrases Emily can use at neighborhood cookout when asked how school is going. On the way to Grandma's house for a family get-together, come up with a list of small-talk topics, such as Uncle Jack's new pet iguana or Aunt Elizabeth's recent trip to Florida. Take turns practicing introducing each other before you attend Samuel's piano recital and reception. And develop a nonverbal sign so you can remind your kids to use their manners without embarrassing them or repeating "What do you say?" for the umpteenth time.

Expect Etiquette. Once you've modeled, trained and practiced, and your kids can answer "How are you?" without mumbling and staring at their feet, it's time to raise your expectations. Sixteen-year-old Jackson can politely visit with dinner guests while Dad is putting the finishing touches on the meal, for instance, and seven-year-old Lainey can introduce her friends to one another at her birthday party. Hold them to it to let them know manners are not optional and offer plenty of Encouragement when you see their good manners in practice.

Online Is Not Off the Hook. Keep your kids aware of the fact that just because they're typing instead of talking doesn't mean they can escape from good manners. No need to proofread every text they type (don't we all occasionally sneak in "u" instead of "you" from time to time?), but do keep the conversation going about the fact that there's a real person beyond the screen.

PEER-PRESSURE-PROOF YOUR KIDS

It's one thing to limit technology and teach positive social behavior for a generation that isn't likely to pick it up on their own. But peer pressure is a more overarching challenge than either of these. Even with limited technology time, the pressures our kids face are more prevalent than they were a generation ago. In fact, kids face all kinds of pressures all the time—usually without us around. If we prepare them through positive means, they can often avoid or deter the worst of it. If we leave them unprepared, we make them an easy target for whatever their peers can think up—whether that means crossing the river on the old railroad bridge at night or putting live worms in their teacher's coffee cup.

The crowd mentality is strong and only more so when it comes to kids. Media magnifies the problem, taking pressures that kids used to be able to escape from and making them front and center, fueling the belief that everyone's doing it. Here's an example of what we're up against:

During the bus ride home on Tuesday afternoon, fifteen-year-old Abby's new friend, Harper, asks Abby if she wants to bike to the gas station for slushies. Abby gets permission, and the two make the short trip. Harper decides she wants a candy bar, too. For free. Fortunately, Abby doesn't follow suit, but she does consent to stand between the candy and the cashier to make Harper's act easier.

Harper is popular, and Abby, as Harper's friend, becomes a member of the popular group, too. As the girls' friendship continues, it turns out that Harper knows a lot that Abby doesn't. Like which clothes, jewelry and various gadgets are the coolest—and which can be secured, like the candy bar, for free. In fact, their group of friends becomes increasingly well dressed and well liked, as the girls either manage to get their parents to buy them the nicest things, or find other ways to acquire them. All except Abby, whose parents can't, or won't, foot the bill—and who still doesn't feel comfortable with alternate means of getting what she wants.

Soon Abby's Facebook page is covered with photos of herself with her new in-crowd friends—and she starts noticing that she's the least cool of the group. Then others start noticing, too. Why is she wearing shoes that look like she's had them since middle school? Why do her jeans look like they came from the secondhand store? Comments and photos posted on Instagram start to get to her—and she can't escape, because her social media is always in front of her.

Abby doesn't want to steal. But she's getting increasingly desperate—her friends are starting to turn on her. After all, she wasn't even invited to the big party last Friday and she's heard a few of the things people are saying about her behind her back.

Abby's mom would never understand, so she goes to Harper for help. But the only help Harper will give is in the stolen candy bar variety. Abby has never been so conflicted. What will she do now?

While peer pressure might seem like one of the most powerful entitlers ("Everyone else is doing it!"), it doesn't have to be. By developing resilience, resourcefulness, responsibility and more in our kids, we can help them block out many of the damaging effects of this entitled attitude.

Whole books (or blogs) have been written on the topic of peer pressure, and there's also a lot within this book that can help. For one, unentitling your kids from the mind-set of "It's all about me" or "I can have whatever I want whenever I want" will go a long way. After all, these are the messages spouted by banner ads and social media with every page your child views (not to mention TV), and they're not going to quiet down anytime soon—we have to be proactive about countering them. The sooner your kids learn that it's *not* all about them and that the rule stands for them, even if it doesn't for all their friends, the less whining you will ultimately hear about it.

That's why tools such as Mind, Body and Soul Time, Encouragement and Take Time for Training, are so important to build up your child's sense of belonging and significance in positive ways, so she'll feel less of an urge to post questionable photos or chime in with a hurtful comment on someone's status just because all her cyberfriends are doing it (or skip class or pocket gum from a gas station or smoke pot). They'll feel more confident in their own self-worth and won't feel the need to live up to others' expectations. In addition, tools like Consequences will help kids know that there are limits, and that even online behavior is subject. Take a look at a few positive characteristics the tools in our Un-Entitler Toolbox develop and how they'll help your kids deter the powerful peer influences they face, both online and off:

Resourcefulness. When kids are trained in positive behavior and actions, aren't rescued from mistakes, are encouraged to come up with their own plans and solutions and regularly face the consequences of their actions, they develop the ability to think for themselves and draw upon their own know-how and good sense to solve problems. Rather than feeling helpless to control their fate, they know they can make a difference. And when they're not helpless, they're also less at risk for being pushed to deal with challenges in negative ways. For instance, if there's a big test coming up, the child who feels in control will be more likely to study for it and get a good night of sleep beforehand and less likely to get talked into skipping out on studying, and then referring to another student's test paper for the answers rather than his own knowledge base.

Resilience. The ability to get back up again after falling down will help your kids stay strong and be less likely to bend under pressure even if they find themselves in a tricky or embarrassing situation. Developed through training, problem solving and living in a consequential environment, resilience enables your kids to push through without wavering. This comes in handy if, for example, your fifteen-year-old finds that her singing voice isn't quite what she'd hoped when she performs at a peer-judged talent show. Resilience will help her get past the rude comments and continue to work on developing her vocal skills. Without it, her high school singing stint might be over before it starts.

Responsibility. Ultimately, negative peer pressure influences kids toward negative actions. Kids who are used to facing the consequences of their actions will think twice before falling prey to their peers' bad behavior. They'll know that speeding at their friends' urging might get them a ticket (and/or lost driving privileges), breaking curfew will lose them the opportunity to attend the big game next Friday, and biking around the neighborhood without permission could get their bike taken away until they show greater maturity.

This is all fine and good, but we all know that the old saying about sticks and stones isn't entirely true. It *does* hurt when you're targeted by your peers' scoffing, sneering, teasing, taunting and the rest. As much as we'd love to, we can't wrap our kids in virtual bubble wrap when it comes to the negative behavior they'll face from their peers or see online. But we can make sure they have a place they enjoy coming home to, where they're accepted for who they are—after all, they *are* entitled to be themselves and to be loved unconditionally. You can build that kind of environment at your house, by doing things like emphasizing relationships over things, keeping lines of communication open through Mind, Body and Soul Time and setting a good example by respecting them and others. Along these lines, resist the urge to judge their friends. As much as you would love it if your child's poorly behaved bestie moved across the country, don't let on: you'll only put your kids on the defensive. Instead, find ways to talk about the positive qualities good friends exhibit, and be readily available to discuss poor decisions in a nonthreatening way.

Be Worthy of Your Child's Respect: Whether you like it or not, you remain the most powerful role model in their lives. . . . They are watching how you handle your own stress and provocation. They are seeing how you set goals for yourself and what you do to accomplish them. And they are noticing what character and devotion means to you. . . . As a result, if you make adjustments in your behavior, your kids inevitably will too. If you change, they'll change.

—Loni Coombs, author of *"You're Perfect . . ." and Other Lies Parents Tell*

Teaching Assertiveness

Part of peer-pressure-proofing your kids is making sure they know that they can—and should—assert themselves when the situation calls for it. Just as a four-year-old shouldn't stand for it when his playmate grabs a coveted stuffed stegosaurus out of his hands, a fourteen-year-old shouldn't need to take it in stride when her peers try to get her to sneak some jewelry from her mom's jewelry box, even if it's for the big dance and the friends are sure Mom would say yes if she were around.

Assertiveness is something you can train for and practice with your kids. For younger kids, role-play common scenarios, encouraging them to look the other person right in the eyes and use phrases like "No, I'm playing with that" or "Stop it, that hurts!" Help them learn when to walk away or turn to an adult for help, as well as some conflict-resolution strategies so they can work on reaching a solution, if the other child is willing. For some great ideas to help teach assertiveness, navigate to DoingRightByYourKids.org. The site is an excellent resource for strategies to train children in assertiveness and personal-safety skills.

As kids get older, a simple "I don't want to" or "I don't think that's a good idea," might end the discussion about whether to sneak into a movie, vandalize a classmate's locker or borrow Dad's car without permission. Your kids can probably help you come up with some additional phrases they'd feel comfortable using. But the teen years, especially, can be tricky ones to navigate as kids work to establish their identity, learn their place in the world and, sometimes, just survive the day-to-day. Work on helping your kids see that belonging to the in crowd isn't all it's cracked up to be if it compromises who you are.

As you train them in assertiveness, make sure your kids know how much you value and respect them as they are, and that anyone who doesn't do the same isn't a true friend. Respect is something they *are* entitled to in all of their relationships and anyone who pressures them to do something they know is wrong is not respecting them. Encourage them to foster friendships that help them feel good about themselves and others, and recognize that they'll make mistakes, no matter who their friends are.

A little assertiveness training can go a long way toward helping your kids value themselves and say no to all the little temptations their peers may dangle in front of them. The first tool in this chapter, Family Values, will help you solidify these ideas in their minds, and pull you together as a family, too.

With our homes set up to temper technological influences, foster positive social behavior and ward off peer pressure, we'll make great strides in un-entitling our kids from the negative behaviors they see every day. We can't control everything that our kids see or hear, but there's a lot we can do to help them be their best, even when the world around them tries to get them to behave badly. Which means less worrying and more enjoying the good things in life—even if that's a smartphone.

Un-Entitler: Family Values

Sometimes it seems that all we hear about is what's happening at other peoples' houses—whether the Kardashians', the Joneses' next door or one of your son's Instagram friends you've only met once. We've all heard it before: "But Caleb talks that way to *his* parents!" or "Carmen's family goes to Disney *every summer*!" What about what's happening at *our* house? According to Bruce Feiler, author of *The Secrets of Happy Families,* identifying and solidifying your family's core values—what brings you together and keeps you strong—will help your family build on what it does *right*. Which is something most parents spend too little time focusing on in favor of dwelling on their shortcomings, recent research has shown. In his book, Feiler details how and why to create a mission statement for your family, which was the inspiration behind this tool.

Focusing on Family Values will not only get your family priorities down in writing, but also create a jumping-off point when your kids face rough spots in their relationships. For instance, if your son is having trouble playing nicely with the neighborhood kids, you can ask him which of the family's core values might apply to the situation. Thinking about it, he might respond, "We respect each other," and you can take it from there ("What would it look like to show respect to kids who are younger than you are?"). Your Family Values will foster a sense of belonging and significance, as everyone contributes to their creation, and they bind you together as a team. The values you create now will also give your kids a great foundation to build on as they find their own place in the world later on.

PUT IT TO USE

To start, you'll need to call a Family Meeting (chapter 4) to create your Family Values. Have pen and paper handy for everyone. Your goal is to come up with a short and sweet document (a list is fine) that expresses what you stand for as a family.

Defining core values can be tricky, especially if you're eight and you can only think of things like "Our family has pizza every Friday!" To help, Feiler suggests we think about:

What words best describe our family?
What is most important to our family?
What are our strengths as a family?
What sayings best capture our family?

Write down all thoughts and ideas and then try to compile them into overarching statements. So "We share" and "We talk nicely to each other" might both fit under "We respect each other." You want your Family Values to be short enough to remember and refer to regularly—five to ten core values should be plenty.

Display your core values on the refrigerator or create a piece of art with your list so everyone can focus on Family Values each day. If you have young kids, include pictures to make it meaningful for everyone.

Once you've developed your Family Values and everyone is reasonably familiar with them, put your values to work adding insights to disagreements, challenges and decisions. For instance, if you're wondering where to make holiday contributions this year, ask yourselves, "Which of these organizations are most in line with our Family Values?" If your seven-year-old has been ignoring her friend's requests for play-dates, you could ask her how your Family Value of "We treat others the way we would want to be treated" might apply. Then shift the conversation to talk about how even though it's sometimes true that "Ben never wants to play what I want to play," your daughter can help the situation and keep the friendship.

Tips and Scripts

- Keep in mind that you're not creating Mom's and Dad's Family Rules, but rather the values of the entire family. Your kids might outvote you to include "We love to laugh" instead of "We love to have fun" (laughing *is* part of having fun, right?), but let it stand. They'll be more likely to comply if the Family Values feel right to them. Everyone in the family should be able to contribute and agree on the statements.
- It's okay to edit Family Values if everyone agrees, but avoid turning them into a laundry list. If you need to, create a sublist for the likes of "We love pizza!" that might be important to your kids but not quite material for official Family Values.
- Look for inspiration in your family's faith, family legacy or traditions, community affiliations and even in the activities you enjoy together.

YES, BUT . . .

My kids are having trouble agreeing on a few of our statements. What do I do?

Try to keep your Family Values fairly neutral. If one child doesn't think "We take care of the Earth" sounds like a Family

Value, for instance, ask her what *would* be workable along those lines. She might suggest something everyone can agree on, like "We are good citizens of our country and our world" or even "We take care of what we have." With enough tweaking, you can usually reach agreement with even the nit-pickiest of thirteen-year-olds. If your kids can't seem to get on the same page at all, take a break and get back to it at a better time.

As challenging as it can be to define your family in a nutshell, sometimes it's harder to put what you've uncovered into words. Here are some examples from Bruce Feiler and others to get you started.

Family Values Sampler

We believe in God.
We respect each other.
We like to be together.
We help other people.
We work as a team.
We love the outdoors.
We never give up.
We focus on solutions.
We take care of our belongings.
We always have something nice to say.
We welcome everyone.
We don't judge others.
We always do our best.
We love to learn and discover.
We can express our feelings to each other.
We're honest.
We work hard and play hard.
We are responsible citizens.
We keep our bodies healthy.

10

Un-Centering Their Universe

Fifteen-year-old Jermaine rarely forgets to say please and thank you. He doesn't fight with his sister (too often) and can occasionally be seen putting down the video game controller to work on his homework without even being asked. He doesn't grumble too much about taking out the trash or washing the car and he faithfully practices his trumpet—even if sometimes he chooses to do so at ten at night. His grades are reasonably good and he's second-string quarterback on the football team.

It's a lovely Saturday afternoon, and Jermaine is attending a neighborhood cookout with his family. Ms. Hartwell, the neighbor two houses down, asks him about school.

"It's good; so far I have As in everything except math, but that's a B plus. World history is my favorite."

Ms. Hartwell replies, "History was my favorite, too! I always liked studying the Middle Ages. One time . . ."

Jermaine continues, "And my football team is set to win the championship!"

"I'll be cheering for you! I've seen you practicing a lot in your front yard! You know, our church is running a sports camp for low-income kids for two weeks next summer. I'd be happy to connect you with the folks in charge if you would like to help. They could really use volunteers to play with the kids and serve them lunch each day."

"Hmmm . . . I don't know, I'm usually pretty busy in the summer," Jermaine responds.

"Well, let me know if you change your mind. I'm sure it would be a lot of fun," Ms. Hartwell says.

"Oh, and guess what? My painting from art class was picked to be displayed in the downtown art museum," Jermaine adds.

"How wonderful," says Ms. Hartwell. "My mother has always loved that museum. She'd love to see your picture I'm sure, but she's in the hospital right now. She . . ."

"Do you see any brownies around here? I'm ready for dessert," announces Jermaine, looking around.

"I know where they are, let me get one for you." Ms. Hartwell serves Jermaine a large brownie on a paper plate.

"Oh man, I think these have nuts in them!" Jermaine complains. He takes one bite, makes a face and dumps the rest in a trash can.

And with that, Jermaine is done with the conversation. "Well, bye, Ms. Hartwell, I'm going to get another hamburger!"

"See you later, Jermaine."

Everyone agrees that Jermaine is a pretty good kid—Jermaine included. In fact, he's always happy to tell you about all the great stuff he does. The problem is, he's the only one who actually enjoys the conversation.

We can un-entitle kids from tantrums, ruling our houses, rampant technology use, getting everything they want and general bad behavior. But we can still end up with kids who can't see past their own noses if we're not careful. Yes, we want well-behaved kids, but we also want kids who look out for other people, engage in other peoples' lives and can see beyond themselves enough to gain perspective on their own lives. Not only will they be more successful as adults this way, but also happier for it, too.

That's what this chapter is all about. We'll learn to gently dethrone all the monarchs at our house (without a major military coup) and help them learn such positive traits as empathy and gratitude, and in so doing un-entitle them from the idea that the world should revolve around their personal spheres. The strategies in this chapter will put the final nails in the coffin of the entitlement bug that's infected most families in one way or another. Good riddance.

A Little Gratitude Goes a Long Way

The seven-year-old can't stop talking about her birthday wish list—even though the big day is three months away. The eleven-year-old doesn't seem to know anything more about his best friends other than that they like the same games he does, and the fifteen-year-old freezes at the bus stop every morning because she refuses to wear her new coat, as it's recently become ugly for no apparent reason.

As we've all repeatedly pointed out in our own homes, our kids don't know how good they have it. And clearly, they're rarely thankful for what they have. They often lack the ability to look beyond themselves at the world around them—a world full of people without roofs over their heads, let alone smartphones in their pockets. We know something is missing with our kids—a reference point that would help them put their troubles, such as having to sit in the blue camp chair to roast marshmallows instead of the cool orange one their sister nabbed, in perspective. This missing link is a sense of gratitude. Our kids need to trade in the feeling that the world owes them something for the idea that they might actually owe the world something. Or at least stop taking what they have entirely for granted and relentlessly expecting more.

In our culture of plenty, gratitude is something we have to teach our kids and practice with them (on the other hand, if they never knew where our next meal was coming from, they would be grateful for their green beans rather than calling them alien poop). The good news is that we can help them learn to appreciate their first-world circumstances, without constantly lecturing them about the starving kids in third-world countries. And when we do, we'll have already come a long way toward uncentering their universe. Plus, they'll be happier in their new-found attitude of gratitude when they realize how much they really do have to be grateful for. Research repeatedly shows that gratitude-rich people score higher in happiness and optimism and have fewer in-stances of stress and depression.

True gratitude goes far beyond saying thank you. In fact, thank you is easier to teach than the appreciation behind it, but they go hand in hand, and both are within your grasp. If entitled behavior happens when a child expects the world to be handed to him, *grateful* behavior is the opposite. Appreciating what life has given us wipes out an enti-tled attitude, and it really does happen one thank-you at a time.

My mantra for this chapter will be "Show, don't tell," and it directly applies when teaching your kids how to express gratitude. The most im-portant thing you can do is to offer a heartfelt thank-you, in a variety of forms and fashions whenever you get the opportunity and preferably when your kids are within earshot. This includes when your friend does carpool duty for you because you're sick, when you're receiving your usual order at the coffee shop and when your neighbor dubiously com-pliments how much your landscaping has *improved* over last year. Try to go out of your way to display gratitude through random acts of kindness as well as verbal expressions. Be sure to show your appreciation to your kids and spouse, too, with an "I really appreciate how everyone pitched in to help out—I love it when we work together!" or a "You really went out of your way to make my birthday special for me this year—thank you!"

Varying your responses away from a simple thanks will help your kids pick up new phrases and ways to express their appreciation. You can even do some quick training on how to say a meaningful thank-you—or to help them navigate tricky situations like receiving the same birthday present they got last year or something you don't particularly like ("Thank you for thinking of me!" or "I love these colors!"). Coach them to focus on the thoughtfulness every bit as much as the gift itself and set them up for success with some key phrases to use. And most of all, be sure to give them plenty of opportunities to practice—and expect them to rise to the challenge. Remember that *practice makes permanent*.

Your kids will be much more likely to act appreciatively as older teens and adults if they have learned to do so growing up.

Even as you model gratitude, keep from demanding it from your kids or using guilt to solicit their thanks ("I work day and night for you and no one ever says thank you!"). Not only does this teach them bad manners and an entitled attitude, but it'll also just put them on the defensive and far from actually feeling grateful. They'll learn much more from seeing how grateful you are in a variety of situations. And if they do say thanks in a particularly appreciative way, encourage it. "You're very welcome—I'm so glad I could make a difference. It makes me feel good that you noticed!" or "Your sincere thank-you to Grandma really seemed to make her afternoon!"

THE THANK-YOU NOTE

I know we're all asking if they're really necessary. Rest assured, they are in an un-entitled home. These polite letters of appreciation un-entitle your kids from accepting gifts and returning nothing. Here's how to help your kids write a good one:

- Require that a thank-you note be written within one day of receiving a gift.
- As a general guideline, have kids write one sentence per grade in school. So, a first grader should write one sentence ("Thank you for the new scarf, it's so soft!") while a fifth grader can manage five sentences. The preschool crowd can simply draw a picture.
- Tech-savvy teens can create a video thank-you if they're up to the challenge.

Help your kids learn to vary their written phrases, as they do with a heartfelt verbal thank-you, and remind them that it's not always about the stuff. Encourage them to focus on the relationship every bit as much as the ten-dollar bill from Aunt Lynn.

Helping your youngsters learn the art of the thank-you is a big part of the un-entitling process; however, we all know that "thanks" is not always the same as "thankful." How do we get kids to actually be grateful for all they have and are given? Teaching them to express a heartfelt thanks is a start in keeping them from taking the gifts and actions of others for granted and a good way to help them internalize the message of thankfulness. What's more, they'll start to see that every time they demand a free ride, someone else has to pay for it.

And it sounds simplistic, but expressing gratitude will begin opening your kids' eyes to the kinds of things that they should be grateful for. This does take practice—a three-year-old doesn't yet know that he should be grateful to receive a lollipop at the bank, but by the time he's thirteen, he's old enough to know that when his friend's mom buys him ice cream, a sincere thank-you is in order. This gradual shift will only happen if you help it along.

One strategy you can use to help solidify the idea of expressing gratitude is to follow Gratitude Rituals as a family. Here's the tool that will help you do just that.

> Be thankful for what you have; you'll end up having
> more. If you concentrate on what you don't have,
> you will never, ever have enough.
> —Oprah Winfrey

Un-Entitler: Gratitude Rituals

It's one thing to train our kids to say thank you. It's another thing entirely to help them learn to be grateful. This tool will help your kids get into the habit of *looking* for things—even the littlest things—to be grateful for and also help them learn how to express their gratitude. This practice will contribute to the un-entitlement efforts at your house by opening your kids' eyes to the positives in their lives. The more grateful they feel for what they have, the less entitled they'll feel to being handed everything on a silver platter.

PUT IT TO USE

A great deal of freedom comes along with this tool, but the essence remains the same: find regular times to express gratitude with your kids. Keep a consistent format so your kids know what to expect and so it becomes a habit. Here's what to do:

1. **Set the Scene.** Decide on a time or place to be deliberate about expressing gratitude. This could range from sharing positive things about the day at the dinner table every night to stating things you're grateful for (I call them "gratitudes") as part of your nightly prayers to keeping a gratitude journal to listing things your family is grateful for at every major holiday (or all of the above).

2. **Introduce the Idea.** To kick off the ritual, sit down for a short chat with your kids about what it means to be grateful (a Family Meeting is the perfect opportunity). This isn't a "You have a roof over your head and three meals every day and I can't even get a thank you?" lecture, but a chance for you to open up the discussion about the types of things you and your kids appreciate. It's okay to refer to those less fortunate as a way to expand your kids' horizons but not to shame them into gratitude. Wondering what to say? For young kids, pick up a gratitude-centered picture book at the library to read and briefly discuss together (a quick Internet search will turn up tempting titles). Older kids might benefit from talking about real stories—everything from your own childhood when an ice storm caused you to lose electricity for a week to a recent national disaster will get the conversation started. In a nonthreatening way, simply remind your kids that they have a lot to be thankful for and let them know about the new Gratitude Ritual you'll be starting.

3. **Practice the Script.** The more your kids hear *you* express your gratitude, the better they'll be able to do so themselves. Before your first Gratitude Ritual, set the example by saying "I'm grateful that Grandma recovered just fine from her surgery." Outside the ritual, let them hear your gratitude for life events both large and small ("I'm thankful I found a parking space on Black Friday!" "Words can't express how much I appreciate all your help during our big move!"), and more often for people and experiences than for things.

4. **Revisit the Ritual.** Remember that a ritual doesn't become a habit until it's repeated, whether that's once a day, once a week or once a season. Keep it going, and you might be pleasantly surprised to hear how your kids' gratitude develops and matures over the years.

Tips and Scripts

- If you don't have a daily gratitude ritual (for instance, at bedtime), do your best to find opportunities to express gratitude often so your kids get used to hearing gratitude and thinking of things to be grateful for themselves.

- Even if your child can't seem to think beyond her toy box when expressing her gratitude, resist the urge to judge. Negative remarks ("You can't be thankful for marshmallows *every* week!") will only discourage her from participating in the future.

- You can help your kids keep a positive, appreciative outlook on life by soliciting informal gratitudes anywhere and anytime. For instance, ask "What was the best part of your day?" on the drive home from school or "Wow, that was a tough practice today. What was the silver lining?"

YES, BUT . . .

My teens refuse to participate.

Use some of the other strategies in this chapter (especially serving people less fortunate, and modeling gratitude yourself) to help them see that they really do have a lot to be thankful for. Then stick with it. Your sixteen-year-old might not be able to think of anything deeper than "I'm thankful for Monster Mayhem three thousand," but you can bet your efforts are getting through even if he'd never admit it.

Examples of Gratitude Rituals

Make gratitudes part of your dinner conversation at any big family dinner.

Express thanks and gratitude for at least one thing during before-bed prayers.

Start your Family Meetings with gratitudes and appreciations.

Share a positive thought about your day at dinner or bedtime.

Incorporate gratitudes into your holiday traditions (around the dinner table, before opening gifts, etc.).

Write new gratitudes on the mirror every day in a dry-erase marker.

Every time you give or receive a gift, think of something to be grateful for about the giver ("I'm so grateful you're my friend—you always make me laugh!")

Keep a gratitude journal or gratitude jar as a family. Read old gratitudes monthly or yearly.

THANKFULNESS AND THE HOLIDAYS: TOGETHER AGAIN

Sometimes it seems that even though the holiday season calls for an attitude of gratitude, we rarely find it with our kids among the jazzy music and sparkling lights. But while teaching kids to lead a grateful life can't be accomplished in one month of the year, the holiday season is ripe with opportunities for giving thanks and giving back. Here are some strategies to encourage a truly festive spirit:

- **Give less.** Talk to your kids about their wish lists and let them know (gently) that there will be a limit. See if you can convince your extended family to stick to one gift per child.
- **Lighten the list.** If your kids' lists are longer than Santa's beard, set them to work ranking their favorites. Or do like many families and set up these categories:
  - Something I want
  - Something I need
  - Something to wear
  - Something to read
- **Rekindle the meaning.** Put the focus on why you celebrate the holiday—what it means for your family or your faith. Then talk about why you give gifts in the first place.
- **Shift getting to giving.** When you walk the aisle of your favorite store, talk about what you'd like to give rather than get and encourage your kids to do the same. At home, consider gifts that aren't things, such as a coupon for a backrub, a weekend of yard work or a kid-commissioned work of art. Encourage homemade presents that will truly be meaningful to the recipient.
- **Give outside your home.** Help your kids remember those less fortunate. Once the gifts are unwrapped, sort through gently used belongings to see if anything can be donated. Or sign up to serve a hot meal on a cold winter's night.

- **Give without receiving.** An anonymous gift of money to a family in need or wrapped presents on their front porch will put the emphasis completely on giving, since there's no way for your family to receive so much as a thanks.
- **Practice thanks.** Brush up on gratitude basics by helping your kids practice what to say when they receive a gift.

Once kids learn to express gratitude, they'll naturally start to put the pieces together and begin to realize that there's a lot to life that they can be thankful for even when things don't go according to plan. I was reminded of this a few years ago as I was preparing for an appearance on the *Today* show and I've tried to view life's setbacks differently ever since. Getting ready for my segment, I'd chosen a pair of totally impractical high-heeled shoes that I had no business wearing. As I came out of the bathroom into my postage-stamp-sized hotel room, I tripped over my own feet and crashed—hard—to the floor. Both of my knees were bruised with a rug burn and my wrists and palms ached from the forceful impact. I can't claim that this happens all the time, but somehow in that moment my first thought was "Lord, thank You so much for letting me fall right here." I was so grateful to have fallen on my hotel room floor rather than into a corner of a table or out on the sidewalk in front of Rockefeller Plaza, where I would have done considerably more damage to myself (not to mention my ego).

This reminded me that although things don't always go the way we want or expect them to, we can turn our unexpected setbacks into gratitudes. Whether we're faced with falling down in a hotel room or getting chicken pox right before the class trip, there is always something to be thankful for. This is an attitude you can foster in your kids, and I've turned it into a minitool you can give them to help them throughout their lives.

MINI-TOOL: THE SILVER LINING

We've all said these words—"find the silver lining"—at one time or another, often in an attempt to get our kids to stop whining so much. But there's actually a lot of truth to the expression, and looking on the bright side of an unpleasant situation by finding *something* to be thankful for can help our kids live more grateful lives. When the Silver Lining is used correctly to address life's little setbacks, it can help kids turn their grumbles into gratitude.

Start by finding your own Silver Linings when you face setbacks, and verbalize your thoughts so your kids can hear your shift in perspective. For instance, without sounding preachy, next time you're stuck in traffic, say "This is quite the traffic jam. I'm just glad we have an air-conditioned car to wait in." Or if you have to stay home from a weekend beach trip so you can finish a big assignment for work, say "I'm grateful my boss is letting me show what I can do by assigning this important project to me" or "I'm grateful this big project didn't happen while Grandma and Grandpa were visiting for the week!" Note that this isn't a chance to remind your kids to just be grateful for what they have in the vein of "At least we have food on the table!" As I'm sure we all remember, this gets tuned out—fast.

Then teach your kids what it means to find their own Silver Linings in tough situations. When your nine-year-old's pet gerbil gets loose, ask "What's the silver lining here?" At first you'll probably have to help your kids think of things to be grateful for ("I'm grateful it's summer, so at least if he escapes the house, he'll be okay" or "I'm glad we don't own a cat"), but soon they'll be coming up with their own. Let them know that feeling disappointed, hurt or angry is okay, but virtually every setback has some kind of Silver Lining—and finding it can help them get through the tough times more positively.

You can help your kids see that even when they face difficulties, they still have it pretty good. You can help open their eyes to that fact by calling their attention to what it's like to have less or do without. Here are a few ways to do just that:

- **Institute a One-In-One-Out Policy.** Every time your child brings home a new toy or article of clothing, encourage her to donate another. Make it personal by starting a conversation: "Who do you think might appreciate the jeans you outgrew?" "What do you think another child will like about your old train set?" Not only will you reinforce the sense of gratitude for the new item, you'll help your child learn to feel good about giving to others.

- **Do Without.** Let's face it: we all have it pretty good. But sometimes the best way to appreciate how good we have it is to do without. Commit as a family to using fans instead of air-conditioning for a week or forgoing restaurant meals for a month. Your whole family will feel a renewed sense of gratitude for air-conditioning and takeout when you know firsthand what it's like not to have them.

- **Make It Real.** One of the most effective ways to develop a sense of gratitude in your kids is to let them see for themselves what it's like for real people who overcome challenges or make do with less. For instance, what if they had to sleep in a shelter because you couldn't afford rent? What if they had to wait in line if they wanted a meal or if the only meal they had that day was the one served at school? What if they couldn't see because an illness had permanently damaged their vision? It may take stepping out of your comfort zone—and most assuredly your kids'—but you can help your children appreciate what they have *and* develop a servant's heart by actively looking for ways to help the less fortunate.

A strong sense of gratitude is completely within your kids' grasps— but a friend of mine traveled across the world with her family to give them a gratitude boost and help others at the same time. She took her whole family to India on a mission trip, where they served the children from local orphanages by providing medical care, teaching them to play sports and running a Bible camp. After a few days, her son, thirteen at the time, remarked, "Mom, these people don't have *anything*, and yet they're so happy and content. That's the way we should live our lives." What a transformational experience for this young man and his family!

Most of us can't cross the globe to gain this type of insight, but by putting to use some of the strategies in this chapter, we can develop in our kids a similar outlook on life. And what a gift when their need to receive is replaced by a desire to serve.

SERVING INSTEAD OF BEING SERVED

As our kids begin to recognize that they're not the center of the universe thanks to a burgeoning sense of gratitude, we can also start to foster the idea that they can have a positive impact on the world around them. Not only is this idea un-entitling as kids realize that they are not on earth simply for their own pleasure and enjoyment, but it's very empowering as well, especially when they can actually see firsthand the difference they can make.

> Life's most persistent and urgent question is:
> What are you doing for others?
> —Martin Luther King Jr.

What's more, your kids need to *see* how lucky they are—not simply be told. Our minilectures about "You don't know how good you have it," whether it's the fact that we always had to wait *six weeks* for our new mail-order toy to arrive rather than two days or that many kids would happily eat the broccoli left on our kids' plates, simply make their eyes roll. And let's face it—did the "I had to walk two miles uphill both ways to school" lecture ever work on us when we were kids?

The best way for children to see all the advantages they have is to get a good look at the alternatives by serving the disadvantaged. Doing so will help build their sense of gratitude and also show them concrete ways they can make a difference. Over time they'll develop a servant's heart and the willingness to help people rather than walk all over them—a stark contrast to the entitled attitudes we see all around us.

Developing a servant's heart in our kids can be a challenge within our egocentric society, especially since it might take some shifts and changes within the priorities of the whole family. According to reports from Blue Star Families and the US Department of Labor, 66 percent of military families volunteered in 2013 compared to 25.4 percent of the national population.* The group that sacrifices so much already continues to serve others.

It's not easy to rearrange schedules to wedge in some soup kitchen time, but it can be done, as military families prove—and our own families will reap the benefits in addition to those we serve. When kids give back to society, it reminds them that "it's not all about me." It puts their blessings in perspective and allows them to find joy from things that are not material or self-seeking.

With the myriad of needs all around us, you won't have trouble finding an opportunity for your kids to give back to their community. Check with any place of worship, Girl Scouts or Boy Scouts troops, well-known organizations such as Habitat for Humanity, animal shelters or hospitals or nursing homes for ways to serve. Or look closer to home, especially with young kids: has a neighbor recently broken her leg? Consider preparing some meals with your child or weeding her garden. The particular activity doesn't matter as much as the fact that your kids are doing *something* to serve the greater good.

Your kids might require a nudge to get started, but the more they volunteer and help out, whether walking dogs or playing Monopoly with an elderly gentleman, the more joy they'll find in it and the more likely serving will become part of their adult lives.

MINI-TOOL: RANDOM ACTS OF KINDNESS

We've all heard about Random Acts of Kindness—and may have been the target of one ourselves. If so, we know how powerful they can be.

---

* https://www.bluestarfam.org/sites/default/files/media/stuff/bsf_report_comprehensive_reportfinal _single_pages.pdf (page 24); http://webiva-downton.s3.amazonaws.com/617/0b/0/1584/Comprehen- sive_Report2013.pdf (page 43)

When we perform a Random Act of Kindness, very often the person we helped will pay it forward. One act is multiplied, and several people have their day made (including yourself). In fact, in December 2013, the Tim Hortons doughnut shop in Winnipeg, Manitoba, experienced a three-hour pay-it-forward chain in which 228 drivers paid for the person behind them. But how do we use these selfless good deeds to teach our kids about serving others? Three key actions will help them get the point that kindness is its own reward:

1. **Let them see it.** It's one thing to pay for the person behind us in the tollbooth line and then tell our kids about it later. It's another thing entirely when they're sitting in the backseat. While Random Acts of Kindness are a wonderful addition to your day, they pack the greatest punch when your kids witness them.

2. **Expect nothing in return.** If your kids see that you anticipate or expect recognition, the message is lost. If you'd like them to learn that kindness is its own reward, don't anticipate payback—even a thank-you—for your random act.

3. **Make it a regular and frequent event.** Commit to one selfless act per week and do it when your kids are with you, so random kindness becomes a regular part of family life. Encourage them to do the same. Over time, being intentional about kindness will become part of the way your kids operate.

I know what you're thinking: I have to pay for someone else's tank of gas every week? Not with today's prices! Random Acts of Kindness certainly don't have to cost money. Mow your neighbor's yard, deliver a batch of brownies, or bring in groceries for an elderly person. Your goal is to do something to put a smile on someone's face and let them know another person cares.

As your kids serve others, through organized efforts or random acts, they'll naturally see a whole lot of life they wouldn't normally tune in to. For instance, they'll pick up the fact that when you can't afford new clothes, it's hard to get a job, or when you can't hear very well, you tend to get lonely. These observations will build another key ingredient to the un-entitlement process called empathy—the ability to put yourself in another person's shoes.

Empathy, the Entitlement Exterminator

When kids have a well-developed sense of empathy, an entitled attitude with others quickly dissolves. Just as gratitude un-entitles kids from feeling like the world owes them something, empathy un-entitles them from being able to trample on others to get their own way. Before we discuss how to develop this trait in our kids, let's make sure we're on the same page about what empathy actually is.

For one, it's not sympathy. Sympathy is a way of pitying another person, but through the lens of our own experiences or conditions. So if Alena sympathizes with a friend who was sick and couldn't attend a birthday party, she might say, in sympathy, "That happened to me once. I had chicken pox and had to miss a party. I was so mad." While it's a positive thing for kids to find common ground and be able to relate experiences, notice how it's all about Alena, and not actually about the friend.

Empathy, on the other hand, is the ability to understand and share another person's experiences and emotions. It requires us to look beyond ourselves and see things from another's point of view, even if we have no similar experience to draw on. The focus is on the other person, not on ourselves, as we try to enter their world so we can relate on their level. Empathy is more difficult to develop in kids than sympathy, but it's the better of the two when it comes to understanding others and squashing entitlement. So let's get to work.

You might be able to guess what I'm going to suggest first: show, don't tell. Your kids really are watching and taking to heart the attitudes and opinions they glean from what you do and say. In 2014, the Harvard School of Education surveyed more than ten thousand teens and tweens spanning a wide variety of races, cultures and classes, and found that a large majority value personal success, defined by achievement and happiness, over caring for others.* Students responded that their parents' top priority was achievement and were three times more likely to agree than disagree with this statement: "My parents are prouder if I get good grades in my classes than if I'm a caring community member in class and school."†

Clearly, we have some work to do in shifting our kids' perceptions and priorities—and it needs to begin with us. Actively model empathy by noticing the lives of others, including your own offspring. In so doing, you'll teach them to make a habit of paying attention to other people. Say "I noticed Uncle Ray was looking a bit down and I asked him what was wrong. It turns out his dog is sick. I bet he feels really worried about her." When one child has a fight with her friend, take the time to empathize: "I can tell this is really on your mind and that you're feeling pretty down about the rift with Jada. Would you like to talk it through?" As you talk about empathy, include your failed attempts to empathize with others so your kids know that it's not only an important trait but also a work in progress for everyone.

As you model empathy for your kids (and brush up on its nuances yourself), start the conversation about other peoples' feelings. Train your kids to tune in to others' emotions by noticing peoples' demeanor at the park or other public places. Say in a hushed voice, so it's not overheard, "Do you see the woman over there? She keeps looking around and at her watch, and her face looks like she's upset or annoyed. I wonder if she's waiting for someone who's late." You can make it even more personal by helping your kids look for the emotions their friends and family members might be experiencing. Say "Molly was really chipper today—maybe we could find out what's put her in such a great mood" or "Aunt Becky looks a little down. Maybe a hug will help. I'll give her

---

* http://isites.harvard.edu/fs/docs/icb.topic1430903.files//MCC%20Report%20The%20Children%20We%20Mean%20to%20Raise.pdf
† Ibid.

one." Continue to point out facial expressions, posture and mannerisms and link them to circumstances, and give your kids plenty of practice in paying attention to and picking up on the emotional states of those around them.

Then help your kids imagine how people might feel or respond in hypothetical situations. For instance, if your child shoveled the neighbor's sidewalk on a snowy day, say "Imagine you're Great Uncle Robert, and you open the door to see your snow already shoveled. What do you think your first thought would be?" You can also do this for hypothetical situations like "Suppose you're at a party and don't know anyone. How would you feel?"

As your kids become more in tune with reading and predicting emotions, introduce the idea that *everyone has a story.*

MINI-TOOL: EVERYONE HAS A STORY

This tool helps explain some of the bad behavior we all witness, whether coming from kids or adults. The point is to help your kids see that there's usually more to a person's behavior than meets the eye. For instance, if your child is having difficulties with a peer who treats her unkindly, remind her that Everyone Has a Story and hold back on judgment and criticism. Instead, ask "I wonder what Daphne's story is." Consider that Daphne's dad may have lost his job, she might be coming down with a cold or the mean girls at school may be making her feel like an outcast. It should be clear to your kids that while there's no *excuse* for bad behavior, there are often *reasons* behind it. Thinking about the possible reasons for Daphne's change in behavior can help your child begin to imagine what it's like to walk in another person's shoes. This practice will foster empathy and empower your kids to handle problems in a mature—and effective—manner.

Standing in someone else's shoes will help your kids step out of the little kingdom they've created for themselves and see that the planet is populated by other thinking, feeling people with stories, too. In fact, part of the joy of living in this world is discovering other people and their stories—something kids aren't able to do when they're so solidly invested in only themselves. Teaching kids to look beyond themselves and engage in the lives of others is not only an un-entitlement strategy, but also its own reward.

> Empathy is seeing with the eyes of another, listening with the
> ears of another and feeling with the heart of another.
>
> —Alfred Adler, MD

EMPATHY BOOSTERS

Looking for more ways to teach empathy? Try these techniques:

- Turn on the TV, then turn off the volume and try to guess what each character is thinking or talking about. This works best with dramas and not so well with action movies, as there's not much thinking or talking going on during a high-speed helicopter-boat chase. (David F. Swink, *Psychology Today*)
- Use current events to jump-start empathy-boosting conversations. After watching news reports about devastating wildfires in the west, ask: What do you think those families are worried about? What do you think they'll miss most about their homes? What do you think they might be grateful for in the midst of this tragedy?
- Encourage older children to become tutors or mentors. Even if they're already pros at geometry, they'll quickly learn that in order to effectively teach the subject, they need to understand how the student feels about the subject, as well as his or her specific challenges.
- Use Making It Right (a tool in chapter 5) to eliminate unhelpful

forced apologies and replace them with true empathy. Be sure to connect the dots that feelings give rise to actions that have an impact on someone else.

- Ask open-ended questions to help encourage empathy. By asking "How can we help Dylan feel better about his broken spaceship?" children can brainstorm meaningful ways to show kindness.

Engaging with Others

When kids involve themselves in the lives of others (in a good way, of course) they not only ward off the entitlement epidemic, but they also reap the benefits of real relationships. Like many important traits, however, communication skills don't form themselves. Some kids are natural talkers or good listeners, some can light up a room and some truly have a passion for caring about others. But the rest of us (the bulk of the population) need a little help. And even good listeners might need encouragement to go ahead and open up and vice versa with chatterboxes. You'll do your kids a favor by encouraging any natural communication drives, and then helping them gain confidence in roles they're less comfortable in.

One of the first things you'll need to work on with your kids, if you haven't already, is active listening. When you actively listen to another person, you demonstrate that you're paying attention to what they're saying, often by repeating back important points, making eye contact, facing the speaker and not interrupting. This type of listening is a mark of respect for the speaker, and also a way to get the most out of a conversation. Without active listening, a friend's summer vacation to Mexico might seem rather humdrum—but active listening will pull out the juicy details ("You saw *what* kind of fish when you went snorkeling?") and make the conversation and the relationship more memorable. Teach your kids it's really a win-win situation.

I've learned that people will forget what you said,
people will forget what you did, but people will
never forget how you made them feel.

—Maya Angelou

MINI-TOOL: LEARNING TO LISTEN

How do we teach active listening? You guessed it: show, don't tell. Let your kids see that you are interested in the lives of others. For starters, tune in to your kids' riveting accounts of what happened in biology class with the same type of active listening you expect to see from them. That includes putting down your iPad, tearing your eyes from the TV and putting your grocery list on hold. If you can't make that commitment and will have to resort to uh-huh and hmmm with your responses (you really do need to finish the list so you can get to the store so you can be home to make dinner before bedtime), it's okay to respectfully ask your child to push the pause button: "I can't wait to hear what happened, but I can't give you my full attention right now. Could you save it for when we're in the car on the way to the store?" Also practice active listening in front of your kids in the way you talk to your spouse and others, so they can watch plenty of real conversations unfold.

Then teach active listening to your kids by playing a simple game. First assign roles: you'll need a talker and a listener (you can also assign a watcher if you're working on this skill as a family). The talker's job is to tell a story about something she cares about—maybe something funny her pet did or what she's been learning on her diving team. The listener's job is to listen carefully, paying attention to the key points in the story. After the talker as finished, the listener will repeat what he heard and what he thought was most important. Meanwhile, the watcher pays attention to both the talker and the listener. He gives the talker constructive feedback on her ability to tell the story in an interesting and clear manner, and the listener feedback on how well he *showed* he was actively listening, as well as on how accurately he remembered the story.

Switch roles and play again. Help your kids hone their listening skills by periodically playing this game during your Family Meetings.

CARRYING THE CONVERSATION

Listening is, of course, only half a conversation and most kids need a little help learning how to carry on a conversation with their peers and especially with adults. Faye de Muyshondt, author of *Socialsklz :-) for Success: How to Give Children the Tools to Thrive in the Modern World*, plays a game of catch with her students to teach them how to converse back and forth, using the following rules:

1. Ahead of time, each student comes up with three what, how or do questions they can ask anyone. Examples include: "What brings you here?" "How is your day going?" "Do you have any weekend plans?"
2. Also ahead of time, each comes up with three topics they like to talk about (hobbies, school, sports, etc.).
3. During the game, one child tosses the ball to another while asking a question. ("What is your favorite football team?") The recipient answers the question while holding the ball, and then passes the ball—along with a new question—to someone else. ("My favorite team is the Steelers because my parents grew up in Pittsburgh. What is your favorite sport to play in school?")
4. During the game (and ideally in most conversations) you can never give a one-word response.
5. Share as much information as feels appropriate—the whole purpose of a conversation.
6. You can't hold the ball for more than thirty seconds (when you're first meeting someone).

As kids take turns talking only while holding the ball and asking a question to pass it, they get a feel for the flow of a friendly discussion. They'll also learn to demonstrate active listening and get practice asking pertinent questions that show they're paying attention. What's more, they'll find that relationships are more enjoyable when they actually take an interest in sharing about themselves as well as hearing what others have to share.

Engaging with others encompasses much more than active listening and holding a conversation, however. As kids grow, they should be learning the complexities of relationships—the give and take of "He always wants to play restaurant, but I want to play outside," how to handle disagreements, how to respect and be respected and differences in types of relationships ("I'm not sure Grandma will want to talk about alien poop. Maybe you could tell her about the rocket you made in art class instead."). Many of these things develop naturally, but many take some work. The key is to offer your kids plenty of examples ("Uncle Jason always wants to go fishing, but I prefer golf. So we've decided to take turns picking the activity when we see each other.") and plenty of opportunities to practice their skills. Keep the conversation going by talking over new situations as they arise. You don't have to be an etiquette or communication expert to help your kids develop their relational abilities, but you do have to be available.

Before we end this chapter, let's revisit Jermaine, our friend from the beginning of the chapter. Over the course of his fifteenth year, his parents have put the tools and strategies in this chapter to work, and Jermaine's worldview has increased from his immediate periphery to include other people and experiences as well. Here's a snapshot of next year's neighborhood cookout:

Sixteen-year-old Jermaine earns good grades, plays varsity football and buses dishes at a nearby restaurant on the weekends to save money for college or a new car—whichever comes first. But he's known for much more than his accomplishments nowadays. For instance, he voluntarily tutors his little brother's best friend in math and language arts, plus helps him perfect his passes for his tag football team. Jermaine helped out at a camp for kids with disabilities during spring break and performed trumpet at the nursing home down the street a couple of times in the past year. He's valued as a close friend for being such a good listener. And even when things don't go well, his positive attitude keeps him going.

It's a lovely Saturday afternoon, and Jermaine is attending a neighborhood cookout with his family. Ms. Hartwell, the neighbor two houses down, asks him about school.

"It's good, I'm taking German, and I might get to be an exchange student next semester."

Ms. Hartwell replies, "How wonderful—I've always wanted to go to Germany, but so far I've never left this continent."

"What's your favorite place you've been?" Jermaine asks.

"One time I went on a cruise in Alaska, and it was beautiful! We saw so much wildlife—even a killer whale! I would love to go back!" replies Ms. Hartwell. "By the way, I hear you made the varsity football team this year—congratulations!"

"Thanks! It's going to be a great season. And next summer our whole team is going to help with the Special Olympics!"

"That's fantastic!" exclaims Ms. Hartwell. "My sister was in the Special Olympics one year in tennis."

"Cool! How'd she do?" asks Jermaine.

"She actually got injured and had to leave the competition early. And her injury was bad enough she wasn't able to play much after that," Ms. Hartwell responds.

"Oh no, she must have been really upset after all that work. Did she find another sport or a hobby?"

"She did! She enjoys karate almost as much as she loved tennis. Now, are you taking art again this year? I'm so sorry your painting didn't place at the state fair—but I liked it."

"Thank you. Yeah, I was really upset and I almost stopped painting. But then I realized that I love to paint and I don't need a ribbon."

"I'm so glad, Jermaine," replies Ms. Hartwell. "Oh, and thank you for the nice note—I'm thrilled you're getting some use out of the oil pastels. I tried them once but never really used them much."

"I've had fun trying them out, thanks again!"

"Well, Jermaine, have a great afternoon—I'm going to go see how Mr. Weber is doing."

"Thanks, Ms. Hartwell, it was great talking to you!"

Everyone agrees that Jermaine is a pretty good kid. He'll make a wonderful adult, too.

With the ability to feel a sense of gratitude, make a difference in the world, empathize and engage with others, our kids will feel much less entitled to watching the world revolve around them. Even better, they'll be better prepared to take their place in the world as they grow—and to fully appreciate and enjoy the balanced, un-entitled, happy people they've become.

11

It's Okay Not to Be Special

You didn't think you'd get teary-eyed as eighteen-year-old Victoria crossed the stage at graduation, but here you are, digging for a Kleenex. And there she is. You hear her name called and then watch as she delivers a confident handshake to her principal and beams all the way back to her seat.

You couldn't be prouder. You know how much hard work the diploma represents, and you've been sure to tell Victoria along the way. Her efforts have paid off, earning her the choice of two colleges: the state school with an excellent academic reputation and a well-known private college one state over. She chose the state school after deliberating everything from finances to study-abroad opportunities to distance from home. Notably, remembering how she struggled to pay back a loan (plus interest) you gave her so she could buy an eight-year-old car, she balked at the idea of taking on nearly six figures of debt over the course of four years at the private school. Of course, academics haven't always come naturally to your daughter, as you both know. But the routines you helped her set up—as well as the times you let her make poor decisions about putting off assignments until the last minute and consequently facing poor grades—honed her study skills and motivated her to keep at it.

But she's recently informed you she won't be starting college in the fall. Of her own accord, she got permission from the admissions office to defer her enrollment. She plans to go on a three-month mission trip building houses in Mexico in the fall, and hopes to line up an apprenticeship at a vet clinic in the spring. She's thinking about pursuing either architecture or veterinary medicine, but wants to get some real-world experience before she makes her decision. Plus she's excited about the opportunity to serve an underprivileged community. You can't help but be a bit nervous about her plan—after all, what if she gets distracted and decides against going to college at all—but you can trust her to make the most of her opportunities, after seeing the positive choices she's been making for years. Besides, you've gotten used to the idea that she needs to live *her* life, not yours.

You watch your daughter's peers cross the stage, one by one, and you can't help but tune in to the little details about your own graduate. Victoria's clothes and gown are neat, not wrinkly. You remember when Victoria learned how to do her own laundry and ironing—two tasks she tried to fight for weeks until she realized no one was paying any attention, and meanwhile her laundry pile wasn't going to start smelling better on its own. Sure, you helped her iron her graduation gown (it takes special training to avoid putting a giant scorch mark on that satiny fabric), but she's learned everything from changing a tire to cleaning the oven, and you know she'll do just fine on her own.

Come to think about it, Victoria has always had the drive to fight back (what three-year-old or thirteen-year-old doesn't?), but along the way, you've learned a thing or two about fighting, too. Like how *not* to fuel the fight, or the fact that just because five-year-old Victoria really wants a new sparkly cat purse so much that she is willing to pitch a major fit for it in the store doesn't mean she should have one. And over the years, the two of you have managed to find ways to settle your differences with mutual respect and without a huge fuss (most of the time, anyway). Sure, she pushes against your limits now and again—the time she wanted to attend an unsupervised homecoming party last fall with all her friends comes to mind. She was mad, but she knew you were right to be concerned, and it turned out your worries were fully justified according to what your daughter heard about the party from her friends.

In fact, she later made her own decision to avoid a certain postprom party, not wanting to get mixed up in the activities that might happen there.

Most of all, you think about the precious time you've spent with Victoria during her eighteen years under your roof. You know your relationship will always be strong, thanks to the Mind, Body and Soul Time you've carved out, day after day (barring stomach viruses and that one time both family cars broke down at the same time) to spend quality time together. Now that she's going out on her own, you wouldn't trade that time for the world.

And what a world you're sending her into! You can't help but worry about the shady people, tricky places and tough experiences Victoria might come across. But you hold on to the fact that she's already faced many of these before, and overcome them one way or another, like finally breaking up with the ex-boyfriend who couldn't survive if he didn't talk to her every single night and see her both days on the weekend. Sure, she's made mistakes, and so have you, but you've done your best to make sure she learns from her poor choices (skipping study hall to go to the mall) by facing the consequences rather than your rage.

The ceremony ends and your daughter comes to find you for a picture. You wipe the tears from the corners of your eyes—this is a time to be happy. You've done it! You've raised a daughter. One you can be proud of. One you love no matter what and can send into the world confidently, knowing she can think for herself and enjoy the journey. One who will be happy to return home from time to time to catch up. Congratulations. To yourself and, more important, to Victoria.

If you're like me, you might be wiping a few tears from your eyes yourself. What a huge task we've taken on—parenting. Raising our kids to be un-entitled, responsible and contributing members of society by the time they leave our home after eighteen years. And yet wouldn't we all heartily agree that it's worth it? From long nights to giant fights to great heartaches, we wouldn't want to miss a second. (Well, okay—maybe when they dropped the giant jar of pickles in the grocery store, or when they gave the grouchy neighbor's award-winning poodle a haircut.)

Maybe you're feeling overwhelmed at the work cut out for you. We all at times look at our growing families and wonder if our precious little monsters were switched at birth, and if someone else is raising the little angels who are our natural offspring. We've all seen entitled attitudes that are enough to make our blood boil, and feel at a loss to do anything about it. But whether your over-entitled kids are on the brink of kindergarten or graduation, the good news is you've already done something about it by reading this book. And if you're thinking, "I need help—and *fast!!!*" don't worry—the tools start to work in days. You can effect a big change and start to bring out the best in your kids quickly simply by making some adjustments to your family life. It won't be easy, and your kids won't like it, but it will work—I've seen it happen time and time again with thousands of families worldwide.

And even though our kids won't like the process, they will *love* the result, whether they'll admit it or not. Even better than all the gadgets, trinkets and thrills we can give them is the gift of un-entitlement. When kids don't feel that they *need* gadgets, trinkets and thrills to be happy, they will be happier. When they don't feel as though they are inherently more special or important than the rest of the human race, they will be able to enjoy their world more. Un-entitling our kids will free them from a chronic feeling of discontent, of chasing after the next big thing and of expecting the world to revolve around them. And when our kids are free from the need to post selfies taken from a brand-new convertible they can't afford or at a fashionable party where they don't know anyone, they might actually do a few things they really like.

Take a look at what English teacher David McCullough Jr. had to say to the Wellesley High School graduating class of 2012:

Like accolades ought to be, the fulfilled life is a consequence, a gratifying byproduct. It's what happens when you're thinking about more important things. Climb the mountain not to plant your flag, but to embrace the challenge, enjoy the air and behold the view. Climb it so you can see the world, not so the world can see you. Go to Paris to be in Paris, not to cross it off your list and congratulate yourself for being worldly. Exercise free will and creative, independent thought not for the satisfactions they will bring you, but for the good they will do others, the rest of the 6.8 billion—and those who will follow them. And then you too will discover the great and curious truth of the human experience is that selflessness is the best thing you can do for yourself. The sweetest joys of life, then, come only with the recognition that you're not special.

Sorry, kids, you're not any more special than anyone else on this planet—but that's a good thing. What does it mean not to be special? It means you can be yourself.

To Be Yourself

The whole concept of being oneself is, as we all know, great on paper, and a little more difficult to implement with the teenager who has an acne problem or first grader whose best friend gets to fall asleep to a different movie every night. Try as we might, we can't convince kids that their acne is barely noticeable when, in fact, it forms the Milky Way across their face, or curb jealousy when our kids clearly aren't having as much fun as their peers. For this, and for all the other acne moments in our kids' futures, we need bigger answers, and a changed mind-set. By un-entitling our kids, we will release them from the need for perfection in the form of a supermodel complexion or every-night movie night, and free them up to take the tough stuff in stride, knowing that their worth doesn't come from appearances, things or even experiences, but from being human, just like the other billions of people on the globe. Un-entitling them changes "I am special" to a much more positive "I can make the best of my unique circumstances."

As you're probably very well aware, the idea that "I am special" leaches into every area of our kids' lives, affecting their ability to get along with others, contribute to the household, complete their schoolwork and act with kindness and empathy. It's not that our kids aren't special *to us*—in fact, we love them more than our own lives. But thinking they deserve special treatment is what leads them into the entitled behaviors we're trying to stop.

Sometimes it seems that we spend all of our kids' childhoods trying to train them against this very attitude: I am special. And really, how many adults out there feel the same way about themselves? As we know, everyone can't be special—but everyone can be themselves. In fact, helping kids be themselves is a powerful antidote to entitlement that will create a happier home while ridding it of negative entitled behaviors.

How do we get our kids to be happy with who they are, acne (or two left feet or braces) and all? Many of the tools will help. But they might need a nudge or two to help them shift their mind-set and enable them to develop their own unique personality. Here are a few ways to start:

- Let your kids know, frequently and in a variety of different ways that you love them for who they are, not for what they *do*.
- Use Mind, Body and Soul Time to help your kids discover who they are, exploring their different hobbies and interests alongside them.
- Don't allow comparisons. The words, "Why can't you be more like ____?" should never cross your lips, and avoid comparing your kids with their siblings or friends. If your kids insist on comparing their lives to their friends', don't play along. Without trying to convince them that acne can be cool, help them understand that while everyone experiences a different set of challenges and advantages, it's how we react to these that truly matters.
- Lead them by example in focusing on the positive instead of dwelling on the negative, even when you have an acne moment of your own.
- Validate and support their varied interests and activities, and not just the ones you enjoy.

- Keep the focus off possessions and appearances in your home. Value people and experiences instead.
- Go ahead and help your kids fight their acne (or other personal challenges), because it's true that breakouts can *nearly* ruin lives, although maybe not to the extent that your teen suspects.
- Encourage older kids to keep a personal journal (photo, video, audio or written), art book or other method of creative expression to explore their growing individuality. Urge them to keep it at least semiprivate (i.e., not on Facebook) so that they won't be judged by their peers.
- While you shouldn't critique your kids' friendships, you can ask them on occasion, "How does Lydia make you feel when you're around her?" or "Does Jacob let you be yourself?"
- Make it a standard practice in your family to cheer each other on in your various pursuits.

As your kids come into their own, they might encounter some bumps and roadblocks along the way, whether their newfound hobby is an unpopular one (snake breeding, anyone?) or they tried a new haircut that ended up being an epic fail. We can't protect them from these, but we can un-entitle them from expecting life to be perfect. Which brings me to my final point.

It's Also Okay When Parents Aren't Perfect

I have a final word for parents out there reading this: It's okay if *you're* not special. You don't have to be superparent to make a difference in your kids' lives. In fact, sometimes it's better if you're not, so they can learn from your mistakes as well as their own (assuming you let them). You've just read an entire book full of parenting tools—now pick a couple to start with. Be sure one of those is Mind, Body and Soul Time, the tool that packs the greatest punch. Once you've made some progress with a few tools, pick a couple more. Your kids don't have to (and can't!)

become un-entitled overnight, but in the weeks and months ahead, as you keep implementing new tools, you'll start to see some very real changes for the better. Here's a sneak peek at what's in store:

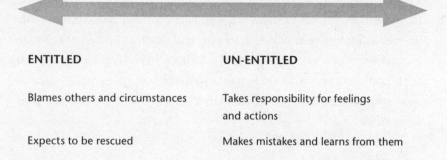

ENTITLED	UN-ENTITLED
Blames others and circumstances	Takes responsibility for feelings and actions
Expects to be rescued	Makes mistakes and learns from them
Can't handle disappointment	Bounces back from adversity stronger than before
Inwardly focused—the "me" mentality	Operates in service to others

Is it worth the work? Absolutely. As you go forward, think about each of your kids crossing that stage at graduation, whether that's a year or a decade away. How would you like them to see themselves? What kind of an impact could they make on the world? What would make them proud of themselves, and confident as they enter the next stage of their lives?

In our kids' world, ego rules—but that doesn't have to be the case in our homes. Whether you are a parent, a grandparent or a community leader, expect more from the young people in your life. Be willing to disappoint your child and hold him accountable. Pack away the parental lawn mower and let him experience difficult consequences and tough times so he can learn important life lessons and develop the resilience he'll need down the road. Set an example of giving back and use Encouragement liberally, but for the things that are worth your words—hard work, perseverance, teamwork and serving others.

Your kids matter. And even more than the new build-your-own-dinosaur set on aisle B9, more than the R-rated movie you won't let them see, and more, even, than Facebook, you matter to your kids. They need the better future you have to offer them, and they need you to be behind them every step of the way. If you do the work, they will reap the benefits as you cheer them on. And when the entitlement epidemic has met its end in your home, your kids will finally be free to thrive, as themselves, every bit as special as the billions of other people who call Earth home. As you un-entitle your children, you will entitle them to the very best that life has to offer: the chance to be the very best that they can be.

Acknowledgments

At the center of my being—and the center of this book—is an incredible sense of *gratitude*. Deep, profound, overflowing gratitude for the opportunity to write this book and for the people who believe in and encourage me.

To Sara Carder and Brianna Yamashita at Penguin Random House, *wow*. I couldn't ask for a better publishing team! Thank you for taking a second leap of faith with me. Your support and encouragement is unwavering and I will be forever grateful to you.

To my wonderful literary agent, Paul Fedorko, a champion for this book and for me—I thank you from the bottom of my heart.

To Rebecca Dube from *Today Parents*, many thanks. I am honored for the opportunity to contribute, and so very grateful for your kindness and encouragement.

A special thank-you to my two favorite Adlerians: Vivian Brault, my first teacher and mentor. I'll never thank you enough for inviting me to volunteer in your classes so many years ago. Your encouragement, faith and wise advice to ignore my doubts and jump feetfirst into parenting education is what put me on my path. And to Jane Nelsen for the kindness you've shown me. Your expertise, leadership and passion in Positive Discipline have inspired parenting educators and parents worldwide. We all owe you a debt of gratitude.

To my faithful friend and rock star publicist, Jill Dykes. You've made this phenomenal journey so much more by being you. Thank you for always having my back, it means the world to me.

To my brilliant editor, Mary Odegaard—a true visionary who doubles as supermom. Thank you for juggling three young children to help me bring these ideas to life in way that will be much more entertaining to read. You are an absolute treasure and I'm more grateful than you'll ever know.

To my loving parents and siblings. Thanks to all of you for continually showing interest in this book project and for encouraging me every step of the way.

To Ryan and Brent, the amazing, funny, faithful, loving young men in my life. I always say being your mom is the best job I've ever had, and I always will. I pray you'll look back and think I've done it reasonably well!

A great big thanks to you, Dave. You are the best friend, husband, father and business partner I could ever imagine. Thank you for always being right where I need you and for cheering me on all the way!

Index

To learn more from Amy McCready

and get free parenting tools, visit:

www.PositiveParentingSolutions.com

www.AmyMcCready.com

If you enjoyed this book, visit

www.tarcherperigee.com

and sign up for TarcherPerigee's e-newsletter to receive special
offers, updates on hot new releases, and articles containing
the information you need to live the life you want.

tarcherperigee

LEARN. CREATE. GROW.

Connect with the TarcherPerigee Community

· · ·

Stay in touch with favorite authors

Enter giveaway promotions

Read exclusive excerpts

Voice your opinions

Follow us

TarcherPerigee

@TarcherPerigee

@TarcherPerigee

If you would like to place a bulk order of this book,
call 1-800-733-3000.

Also by Amy McCready

"A must read! *If I Have to Tell You One More Time* . . . delivers practical, step-by-step tools for well-behaved kids and happy families."

—Dr. Michele Borba, author of *The Big Book of Parenting Solutions* and *Today* show contributor

"I've always said that if parents do their job right, they eventually work themselves out of a job. Finally: the tools we all need to achieve 'parental unemployment.' And best of all, you never have to get mad."

—Wendy L. Walsh, Ph.D., human behavior expert on CNN, cohost of *The Doctors*, and mother of two

"Packed with clear direction—including really practical tips and simple strategies—for how to put an end to whining, tantrums, battles, and all the rest, this book will be a giant relief for parents who want to bring out the best in their kids."   —Dr. Christine Carter, author of *Raising Happiness*

978-0-39916-059-2
$15.95